Western Trout Fly Tying Manual

By Jack H. Dennis, Jr.
Drawings by Author

Photographs and Cover
By Dan Abrams

Color Fly Plates
By Roger LaVake

Cover Design
By Bobbi Dailey and Dominic Crolla

Printing
By Sun Lithographing Company
Salt Lake City, Utah U.S.A.

Snake River Books
Jackson Hole Wyoming

Copyright © 1974 by
Jack Dennis
Snake River Books

Brief quotations may be used in reviews or articles. However, any other reproduction of the book including electronic, mechanical photocopying or any other means, written permission must be obtained either from the author or publisher.

To all fly fishermen
who love fishing the West.

CONTENTS

Forward	vii
By Curt Gowdy	
Preface	x
1. A Word About Western Style Flies	2
2. The Materials and Tools of the Trade	5
Materials and Feathers	5
Vises	7
Scissors	7
Bobbins	8
Hackle Pliers	8
Whip Finishers	9
Bodkin	9
3. Some Special Fly Tying Methods	10
4. Dry Flies	20
Blue Dun	21-23
Adams	24-26
Light Variant	27-29
Carmicheal	30-31
Spruce Fly	32-35
Rio Grande King	36-38
Mosquito	39-41
Renegade	42-43
Fall River Special	45-47
Black Midge	48-50
Black Ant	51-53
Badger Spider	54-55
Bird's Stone Fly	56-60
Sofa Pillow	61-64
Hornberg	65-67
King's River Caddis	68-70
Colorado Captain	71-73
Joe's Hopper	74-77

5. Special Hair Fly Section ... 78
Dry Flies ... 78
- Humpy ... 79-84
- Royal Humpy ... 85-89
- Parachute Humpy ... 90-94
- Adams Irresistible ... 95-102
- Blue Dun Irresistible ... 103-105
- Parachute Irresistible ... 106-108
- H and L Variant ... 109-115
- Royal Wulff ... 116-118
- Grey Wulff ... 119-123
- Deer Hopper ... 124-129
- Bucktail Caddis ... 130-132
- Parachute Royal Coachman ... 133-135
- Parachute Grizzly Wulff ... 137-139
- Paradrake ... 140-144

Streamers ... 145
- Muddler Minnow ... 146-155
  - Dennis Style ... 148
  - Bailey's Style ... 149
  - Dry Style ... 150
- Missoulian Spook ... 156-158
- Maribou Muddler ... 159-161
- Spuddler ... 162-165

6. Nymphs ... 166
- Montana ... 167-169
- Stone Fly Nymph ... 170-175
- May Fly ... 176-178
- March Brown ... 179-181
- Tellico ... 182-184
- Fresh Water Shrimp ... 185-187
- Grande Stone Fly ... 188-190
- Mosquito Larva ... 191-193
- Muskrat Nymph ... 194-196
- Gold Ribbed Hare's Ear ... 197-199
- Fledermaus ... 200-201
- Dark Caddis ... 202-204
- Zug Bug ... 205-207

7. Streamers 208
- Spruce Fly 209-211
- Mylar Mickey Finn 212-214
- Maribou Streamer 215-217
- Buck Royal 218-219
- Little Rainbow 220-222
- Red Ant 223-225
- Silver Hilton 226-228
- Black Ghost 229-230

8. Wet Flies 231
- Wooly Worm 232-234
- Blue Dun 235-236
- Rio Grande King 237-239
- Carey Special 240-242
- Western Coachman 243-244

9. Western Fly Pattern Dictionary 245
- Dry Flies 246
- Wet Flies and Streamers 254
- Nymphs 258

Color Fly Plates
Fly Tying Tool Plate 18
Fly Hook Plate 19

FORWARD
By Curt Gowdy

I owe Jack Dennis this forward to his new book on fly tying. In fact, he could ask me for many more favors, and I would feel obligated to fulfill every one.

You see, I cost Jack the chance of bringing to net a trophy native cutthroat of at least 6 or 7 lbs. I had to grab an airplane out of Jackson, Wyoming to fly somewhere for a major league baseball telecast over NBC. The plane was the last one out that day — if I missed it, I would blow my broadcasting assignment. Time was running out, as we had a half-hour run to the airport and the plane was due to leave in forty minutes.

"I hate to do this to you," I yelled to Jack as he tenderly played a big trout on a spidery 6X tippet. The fish had been hooked for nearly twenty minutes and was still strong and tenacious in the cold of the crystal-clear spring creek we had been fishing.

With a pained and saddened expression, the young guide nodded, then applied the pressure, and the arch of the slender rod suddenly straightened out and the big fish was gone. The fish disappeared with a number 16 Royal Humpy and a wisp of leader trailing from the side of his mammoth jaw.

It was a silent ride for the first ten minutes from streamside to the airport. I had sat on the bank after a morning of marvelous fishing and watched Jack spot the huge trout, and spend about fifteen minutes maneuvering himself for that all-important first cast which would float the tiny dry fly over the trout's feeding station. It had been a superb show, but the climax was eliminated because of a business deadline of mine.

As our station wagon bounced along the country road, I remembered back in 1970 the first time I ever met Jack Dennis. I wanted to produce a segment for the AMERICAN SPORTSMAN T.V. series from Jackson Hole, Wyoming. A float trip down the Snake River sounded like an exciting show. Jack Dennis was highly recommended to me to be the guide for the show.

What a great week we had! Entertainer, Phil Harris, Jack, myself, and our T.V. crew. Dennis was not only a boat man of consummate skill, but quite an entrepreneur. He owned a fly-tackle shop, employed other guides to man his small fleet of rubber rafts, was one of the best fly tyers I had ever met, and had all this going for him while still in his mid twenties.

What really sold me on him though was his enthusiasm for the out of doors — for trout fishing — for conversation — and his love for my native state. His knowledge of the ways of the trout, understanding the hatches, and reading the waters are unmatched in my opinion for a man so young.

We fish together every summer now. On the New Fork, the Snake, the Green, and some delightful small streams to add variety. Aside from the fishing adventures we have, and the companionship, I think I most enjoy Jack's streamside lunches. They are masterpieces!

Muddler Minnow

There is one other favor I owe Jack Dennis: someday I want to reverse our roles, and I want to be the guide. I would like to take him out in my skiff in the bonefish flats of Key Biscayne, Florida and watch his excitement and anticipation of his first cast with a small streamer fly to a tailing bonefish.

Then, Jack, my debt is over for stopping you short of finally beaching or finally netting that monster cutthroat that you would have released after the soul-satisfying challenge of this victory. I can just picture looking down into that cold, clear water and watching that magnificent champion swim away knowing you both were in a class by yourselves.

Curt Gowdy
April 22, 1974

ACKNOWLEDGEMENTS

I would like to express my gratitude to the following persons for their assistance in producing this book:

Sandy, my wife, and my son, Brian, for their love, understanding and patience.

The Wyoming Travel Commission for photos used.

Mr. Curt Gowdy for his friendship and encouragement.

Mr. Fred Terwilliger for sharing his knowledge of Montana flies.

Mr. Sam Melner for his encouragement to me to produce this book.

Mr. Hugh Chatham for sharing his California flies with me.

Mrs. Eliza Mathieu, my secretary, for keeping some semblance of order in the midst of chaos.

PREFACE

Sometimes, in this country the Rocky Mountain West gets left out. In many cases the books of the fly fishing and fly tying world are solely devoted to fishing in other parts of the country to the neglect of the West. Even fewer books devote emphasis to tying western fly patterns. Usually they are confined to a small section of the book or never mentioned at all. I sometimes wonder whether this is because no one thought that Western flies were worth mentioning.

Once I heard this feeling of neglect stated by Curt Gowdy while announcing a football game. He gave the advertisement for an upcoming game: 7:00 p.m., Eastern Standard Time, 6:00 p.m., Central Time, 4:00 p.m. Pacific Coastal Time. He suddenly stopped and mused,

"You know, I have been doing these games for a long time, and I can never understand why they never mention Rocky Mountain time." He continued, "Don't they think anyone lives out there?" He then quickly noted that Westerners are just as important as the rest of the country!

Being from the West himself, he may be just a little prejudiced, but so am I! I was raised in the West, born in Jackson Hole, Wyoming, I fished Idaho, Montana, Colorado, and California as a young boy and as a young man. I feel that the West is an important place, especially for fishing.

People travel from all over the world to fish in the streams of the West where they find probably the finest dry-fly fishing in the whole world.

I have written this book to describe some of the most useful western fly patterns to both the fly fisherman and fly tyer.

Some of the patterns are different, some are standard ones that you have often tied, some are standard ones with a western twist, but there should be something for *every* fisherman in this book. I have tried to present a cross-section of flies from all sections of the Rocky Mountain West, and I believe that these can help you tie others that are not even listed. I wish you good luck as you tie these patterns, and tight lines when you fish them.

I will be most interested to receive reports, comments or criticisms resulting from the use of flies described in this manual. It will be an asset to my future tying as well as a help to fishermen who enjoy the West as much as I do. You can write me in care of Snake River Books, Box 286, Jackson Hole Wyoming 83001. Your response will be appreciated.

Jack H Dennis

Western Trout
Fly Tying Manual

A Word About Western Style Flies

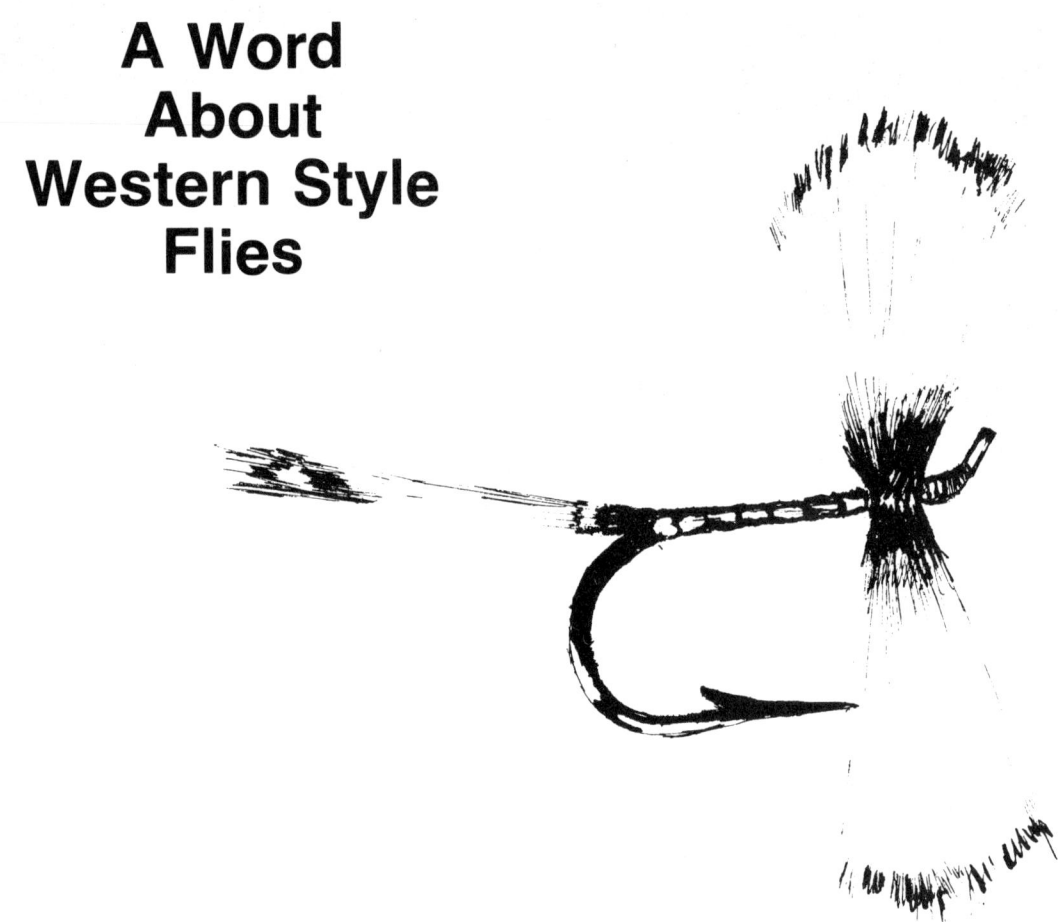

One of the first noticeable differences between eastern and western dry flies is that usually there is more hackle tied on western flies than their eastern counterparts. This is called "over-hackling the fly" to give it more buoyancy. But there are often cases where sparse hackle, especially good stiff neck hackle is superior. In clear springs, creeks and in the calm, quiet holes of other streams, it is often important to have a sparsely hackled fly. Again, I stress that you should tie your flies for the water that you will be fishing. This is one of the most important aspects to be learned from tying your own flies. In fact it is one of the basic principles in fly tying, and one reason for taking it up.

You will find that western wet flies and streamers are often larger and more heavily dressed than eastern styles. One of the most notable examples is the Muddler Minnow which is tied in the West in sizes 2 and 4, while in the East it is usally tied in sizes 6, 8, and 10.

Nymphs, whether eastern or western, are basically the same, and good eastern nymphs usually work fine in the West. The West has some rivers which have large stonefly hatches where larger nymphs often work better than standard-size ones. These are mentioned in the book, and Eastern tyers should not hesitate to tie them in smaller sizes for their waters.

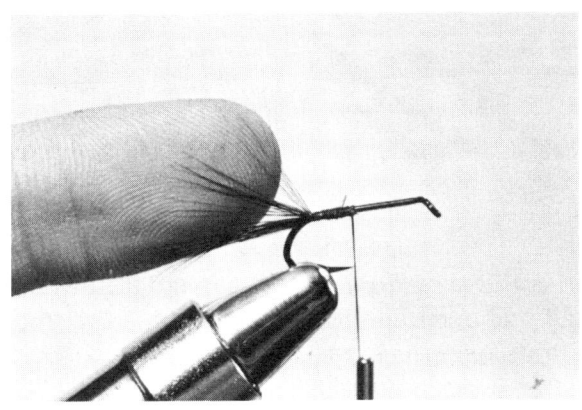

Hackle Fiber Tail

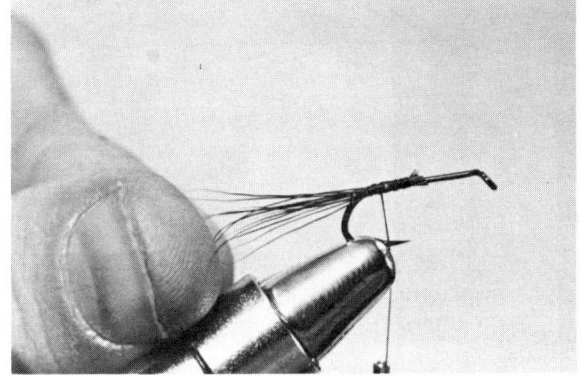

Hair Tail

Another important aspect of western flies is the tail. I have found that the use of stiffer tail material adds to the fly's life as well as its buoyancy. Many times the standard dry fly patterns were first tied with hackle fibers for tails. I have converted many of these patterns into more effective western flies by adding hair fibers for tails rather than hackle fibers. The best hair for this purpose is either moose or elk. Every color of tail can be matched by the variety one finds in the shades and colors of moose and elk hair. I suggest that you experiment with this and see what you can learn. In the photographs is a hackle fiber tail spread apart with the slight pressure from one finger. With the same pressure on a hair tail you can see that it stands up much better.

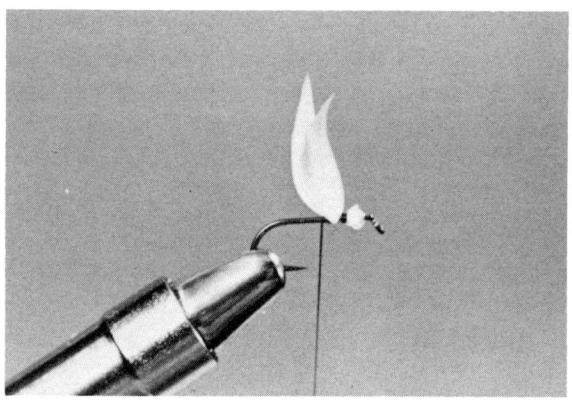 

Another important aspect of western patterns is the departure from the standard divided duck quill wing. A duck quill wing really becomes tattered and unnatural looking after a few trout have hit it. It breaks apart and molds into the hackle, thus losing its form. Quill wings are also more cumbersome and less buoyant than some alternative wing materials.

I prefer hackle tips to quill wings. I feel that they present more natural appearing wings and also offer a greater variety of colors.

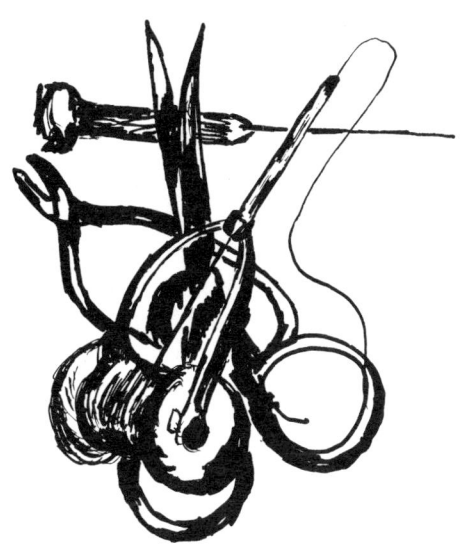

THE MATERIALS AND TOOLS OF THE TRADE

Today, the pleasurable pasttime of fly tying is quickly gaining in popularity. The tyer is constantly confronted by changing methods and new materials for his use. Even the professional fly tyer finds it difficult to keep up with the many changes that take place every year. I have seen a drastic price increase in the feather market with no immediate end in sight. This, of course is raising the cost of commercially tied flies. Some of the materials listed in this manual may be in short supply and will be very expensive. However, I have tried to suggest alternate materials whenever this is the case. One of the most difficult materials to obtain is grizzly hackle (barred plymouth rock). Its price varies each year along with the variations in the quality of this hackle. There are several places today which offer a "super grizzly neck" with a price of $15 to $30. These usually prove to be a more sensible investment than wasting your money on a $9 neck which can yield only six or seven dozen usable hackles.

Grizzly Hackle

Another neck that is becoming scarce is white. So many companies are seeking light cream to use for dying that the limited supply quickly disappears from the market. Several alternates for dyed blue dun have been developed in the past several years. Eric Leiser has created a new method called photo-dying which takes light brown and other necks that are in less demand and transforms them into blue dun neck hackles. I highly recommend his book, FLY TYING MATERIALS, as good background information for all fly tyers. I recommend that you dye many of the materials yourself. This is a fine way to learn how to find the best materials to match the natural insects you wish to imitate.

Indian Cock Neck   Korean Cock Neck

Also, today's market offers two types of game cock necks: one comes from India, which is a smaller neck and has mainly hackles from sizes 22 to size 12. These necks are about the size of the palm of your hand. The other neck is the Korean or Philippine type from a larger fighting cock. These are about twice the size of your palm and are beautiful neck hackles from size 6 through 14 or 16. The Korean type does not include many badger colors, but are mainly brown and ginger with some creams and whites. Almost all good game cock necks are imported because the domestic sort are usually too large for dry flies, but are excellent for streamers.

One of the most revolutionary materials to come along for a while is polypropelene for yarn and dubbing. This amazing material has a specific gravity less than that of water, comes in many different shades, and offers a new dimension to the tyer. I suggest that you obtain some of this material and give it a try when tying some of the patterns in this book. Poly-dubbing a 100% polypropylene dry fly dubbing material in 40 different colors is an easy to work material not in sheets or yarn but ready to dubb on the thread can be obtained from Fly Fisherman's Bookcase and Tackle Service in New York.

I have tried many types of hooks, but I have found that Mustad still makes the best hooks on the market for my tying. In this book I recommend only Mustad Hooks. If you have another hook that is your favorite, of course use it. A hook which I have found to be tough and good for western flies is the Mustad 7957B. It is sometimes difficult to acquire in certain areas, but can be obtained from most reputable fly shops. It is a heavier hook and will stand more abuse than the standard 94840 dry fly hook. In many cases I recommend the standard hooks that are recognized throughout the country as the better style hook, but I suggest that you try the 7957B.

Many of the western streams have rocks at their banks and many flies suffer the casualty of broken hook points which have been clipped by these rocks. So a good hook is essential. Also in many cases trout are larger in western streams, and the water is heavier, so that a stronger hook is desirable. The floating qualities of a fly tied on a slightly heavier hook does not seem impaired (especially when dressed with heavier hackling.) That little extra strength can be important especially in small hook sizes.

As in any trade, tools are one of the most important parts of mastering your task. Fly tying can be more work than fun if you do not have the proper tools. I have found that the tools which I prefer are available to both the amateur and professional tyer. I would like to briefly mention some of my favorite tools and the reasons I have chosen them.

Vises

VISES: Throughout my years of tying I have used the Thompson Model A vise. Many new vises have come onto the market and I tried them all, but I always come back to the old standard of the industry — Thompson A. It is adjustable in height for your convenience and is adjustable for large as well as small flies. I tie flies everyday and have used the same vise for nine years. Occasionally the collets have to be replaced, but with average use, the amateur will have no problems with this.

Another very good vise on the market which I have used is the Crest Model 300 from the Crest Company in San Carlos, California. Either of these vises is adequate for the amateur's needs and should be all he would ever need. It is much better to learn on good equipment than to struggle with inferior products. Both of the companies mentioned have excellent reputations and back their products 100%. I have never known either company to turn down a legitimate claim on any defective merchandise. In this day and age that is a rarity!

Scissors

SCISSORS: Many fly tyers fail to realize the importance of a good pair of scissors. The fly tying market in the last few years has provided few good quality scissors. I think that the best scissors having fine points are made in Solingen, Germany. There are many different brands and they are becoming harder to obtain year after year. I suggest that you go to a reputable fly tying dealer and look over his selection of scissors until you find one that fits your needs. There are several kinds: small fine point ones for dry flies, heavier and more durable ones for hair work. You should make sure that the finger holes are large enough so that your fingers can go through them and that the scissors can remain in your hands. This is much better than picking up your scissors each time you want to trim something. There are also several fine mail-order houses which sell a standard Solingen scissor which I have pictured. One important thing to check often on your scissor is the small screw that holds the blades together. After many hours of work the screw loosens and the blades become loosened. Then the screw eventually shears off. If you check this occasionally you can lengthen the useful life of your scissors. The average life of a pair of scissors for a professional tyer is about three to six months. For an amateur tyer scissors should provide many years of good flies.

Bobbins

BOBBINS: The last several years has brought great changes in bobbins. One of the biggest problems that bobbins first had was that they were too heavy and they cut the thread at the tip of the bobbin. There are several improved bobbins on the market today. It is important to check each bobbin before purchasing it to make sure that it does not cut the thread. Most good tackle shops check each bobbin before selling it to you. I highly recommend the Frank Matarelli stainless steel bobbin. These handmade bobbins are a real work of art and are produced in San Francisco. His are the lightest and most durable as well as the smoothest operating bobbins on the market today. They are sold by most good fly shops. The Orivs company calls this same bobbin the "Orivs Bobbin," but its characteristics are unmistakable, and most professional tyers employ it.

Another excellent bobbin and one that pioneered the clip-type bobbins is the Crest custom bobbin. This is an excellent tool of good serviceability and durability. It is slightly heavier than the Matarelli bobbin, but it is about half the price. Fly tyers that are on a budget or youngsters who are just learning can find this bobbin an excellent buy. Either bobbin will do a good job.

Hackle Pliers

HACKLE PLIERS: It is important to have a good set of hackle pliers, especially when tying small dry flies. There are many hackle pliers on the market today, but the best that I have seen is a brand manufactured by Veniard of Thornton Heath, England. These are available in many tackle shops in the United States. They are easily recognized by the dull, gold-like color of the stainless steel. They are extremely light and have the finest jaws that I have found. But they are hard to find compared to other hackle pliers. One good brand which is available in most places in the United States is the Thompson Duplex hackle pliers. They have rubber on one end and metal on the other and are excellent hackle pliers for learning, when it is important to get the "feel for fly tying" without having trouble struggling with tools these are good ones.

Another good hackle plier is the Crest Sure Grip. These are excellent pliers and are available almost everywhere. They have good points and will hold hackle without breaking it. All three of these hackle pliers will do a good job. There are some midget hackle pliers for tying small flies. For those who enjoy tying small midges it is important to have a good pair of small pliers. There are also several custom pliers on the market available in some shops. I have found several of them quite good. One suggestion is to try a friend's hackle pliers or test the ones in the shop to find out which one you like best. Each person has his own preference.

Whip Finishers

WHIP FINISHERS: There is only one really good whip finisher on the market today in my opinion: That is the Thompson Whip Finisher. Many of the old professionals scoff at the whip finisher tool, and many new tyers tear their hair out trying to learn how to use this gadget and end up tossing it to the bottom of the fly-tying box. I believe that it is a very important tool to put on a smooth even, whip finish. I have used one for a great number of years and would not be without mine. One of the nice things about using a whip finisher is that once you have it mastered, it is easy to tie small dry flies off without catching any of the hackle fibers in the eye. I have included some detailed instructions on using the whip finisher on page 13. I suggest that you do give it a try and if you do have one hidden away down in your box bring it out and try my instructions to see if they will help you.

Bodkin

BODKIN: This is a handy little tool to have around. Whether it is picking up fur or guard hairs out of fur bodies, or applying head cement to thread, or any number of fly tying tasks it is an important tool to have. You can make your own, inserting a large sewing needle in a wooden dowel handle, or you can buy many different types. They usually range around $1 and it is one of the best dollars you can invest.

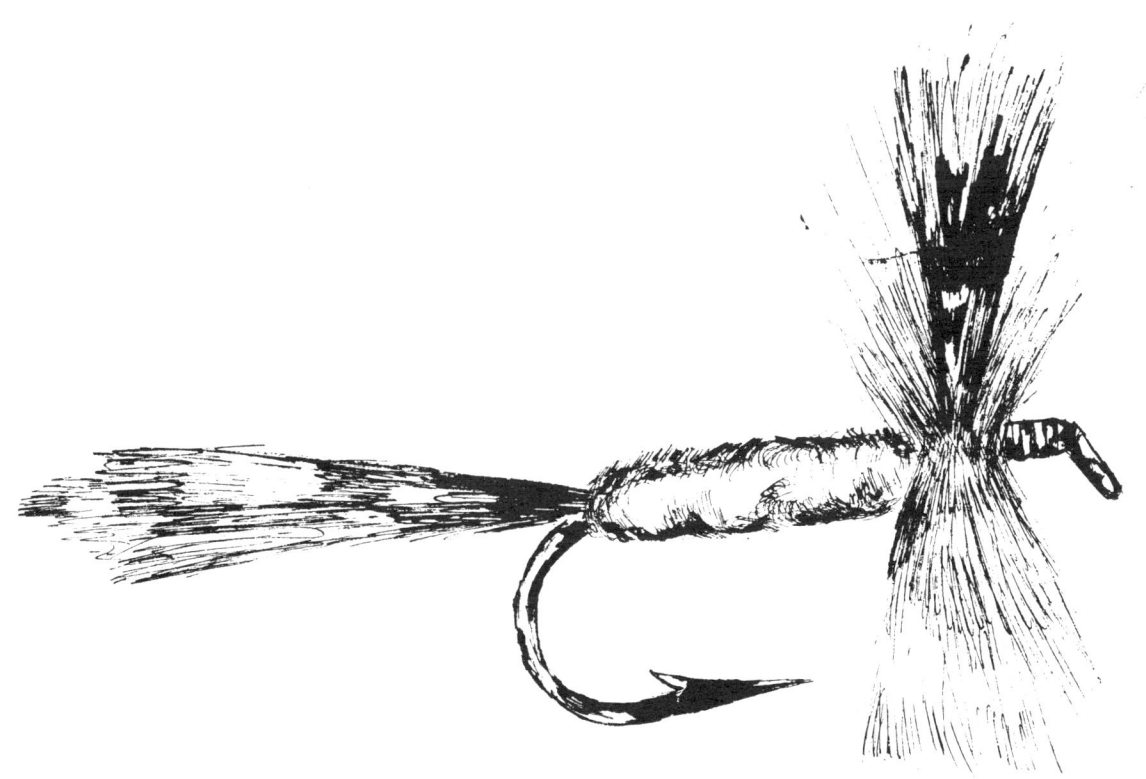

Some Special Fly Tying Methods

Every fly tyer has his own methods of tying flies. Some are unique, some are copies of methods learned from other tyers, some are taken from books. But most important, any new methods learned by the fly tyer will add to his enjoyment off fly tying. In this chapter I will outline some fly tying methods and some helpful hints that may improve your fly tying. Several of the methods are in the upcoming instructions.

Selection of Material

One of the most important things to learn in fly tying is the skill of buying materials. Learn how to purchase good materials because without them your flies will be faulty no matter how well they are tied. Find a good source of materials, whether it be a mail order catalog or a local fly tying store. Some people are blessed with the choice between nearby stores, but usually there is only one place to purchase materials in any area. Of course, the best method of purchasing materials is directly on sight. This enables you to check the quality and get just what you need. Unfortunately, most of these stores do not have everything in stock at the same time. Some materials are hard to find and must be ordered by mail. One of my pet peeves, stemming from my experience of selling fly materials through the mail, is that someone would order materials without specifying what type of flies he was planning to tie. For example, a patch of deer hair comes in many different shades and textures. If the deer hair were to be tied on hair-body flies it must have a soft, thick texture. Whereas other people are interested in hair-wing flies and for them the hair should be silky and smooth. So, I suggest that before you order the materials, find a reputable dealer and be sure to tell him what flies the materials are intended for. The same goes for hackle and all types of hairs and fur. When selecting hackle, specify the size of the majority of the flies you will be tying. Each neck usually has an abundance of one size. It is difficult to find a neck with well distributed sizes.

Dubbing

There are several methods of dubbing. One I particularly like is actually dubbing the fur right onto the tying thread. This can be done one of two ways: The first is to apply a good tacky wax to the tying thread, then dub the fur right onto the tying thread, evenly distributing the fur to the thread and rolling the fur with the thumb and forefinger until it is nice and tight to the thread. When applying this, many people usually apply too much wax; thus light cream or white dubbing becomes darkened in color.

I suggest the second way, which is to use the new waxed threads now on the market. Dubbing can be applied to these threads without applying additional wax. By dubbing the fur directly to the thread rather than onto a separate theard it will be much easier to taper the body. More fur can be added if necessary or taken away by simply unwrapping the thread.

When using pre-waxed thread, be sure to keep the bobbin clear of the wax which tends to build up. A straightened paper clip is small enough to clear the wax from most bobbins.

A Note on Hair Flies

When tying hair it is important to make good use of head cement. A touch of cement will secure the hair to the hook, thread, or other materials as necessary. Do not be afraid to use plenty of laquer. For example, when tying hair bodies it is good to lay a base of thread and then over it drop a touch of laquer. The hair thus becomes cemented to the thread allowing the body to be much more durable. On hair wings it is good to cement the base of the hair after it is tied down by the tying thread. This again cements all the fibers and keeps them from pulling out individually. Again, when buying materials for tying hair, it is important to get materials suited to the type of hair work you plan to do.

Wrapping Hackles

This method for tying two or more hackles is one that I have used for years and it has proved to be a definite advantage when tying flies commercially. Many amateurs have asked me to show them how to tie several hackles at one time. Many of them who have tried it have found that the hackles are too loose and come off. I recognize that many tyers believe that the only way to secure two or more hackles is to tie each one individually. I have found that if the hackles are tied properly they can be tied securely enough to last the entire life of the fly. A good pair of hackle plyers are essential for tying multiple hackles. It is a good idea not to tie four saddle hackles at one time. Just tie two at one time and then go back and pick up the other two. On small dry flies I have tried tying four neck hackles at one time, but it becomes difficult to tie that many. Usually it is best to tie together three of them at most; however, you can find your own capabilities and adjust to them.

Assorted Helpful Hints to Improve Your Fly Tying

1. Do not take more wraps of thread than necessary when tying small dry flies. If four or five wraps are sufficient do not make ten or more. Wrap what will hold the material securely and no more bulk than is necessary.

2. When tying larger flies, large streamers or ocean flies, be sure to adjust your vise for holding a larger hook. If you fail to do this and force the hook in, the pressure applied to hold it can stretch or break your collets.

3. Most people get used to tools and cannot use another's fly tying tools. When tying in a group or in a fly tying class, mark your tools with a small piece of adhesive tape. In most fly tying

classes or groups someone wants to borrow a tool or picks up the wrong one. This will save you a great deal of misery.

4. Buy a pair of scissors with loopholes large enough so that your fingers can go through them. This will save having to pick your scissors up off the desk every time you need to trim something.

5. If you use a lot of laquer, keep from screwing the cap each time by taking the cap of a hook box and poking a wooden tooth pick through the box. This makes a handy applicator while at the same time providing a lid for the bottle that will prevent evaporation of the cement.

6. Plan to tie four or five dozen flies at the same time. Take the time to select all materials in advance. Trim all the hackle, trim all the right amount of floss and lay it all on the desk in front of you. This way you won't have to search for each neck or trim each piece of hackle as you tie the fly. This procedure can make the four dozen go much faster, and you will find yourself more relaxed.

7. If you have a permanent fly tying bench you can attach your floss and tinsels by slipping each spool over a nail. This way you can just pull on the floss and it will self feed any amount you need.

8. Use waxed thread instead of having to add wax when necessary. This especially will help improve your dry flies and it is good for dubbing on fur. When tying dry flies which call for yarn, use polypropelene. It is a material which is lighter than water. It can be purchased many different ways both as dubbing and as a yarn.

9. When weighting all nymphs, strip the coating off the top of a wine bottle which is a flat lead. Trim and wrap it around the shank to add the right amount of lead to weight a small nymph.

10. When tying flies do not trim the hackles to get the proper size. You should use properly sized hackles. Do not trim either wings, tails, or hackle. This interrupts the natural ending of the hair and hinders the floating qualities of the fly.

WHIP FINISHER INSTRUCTIONS

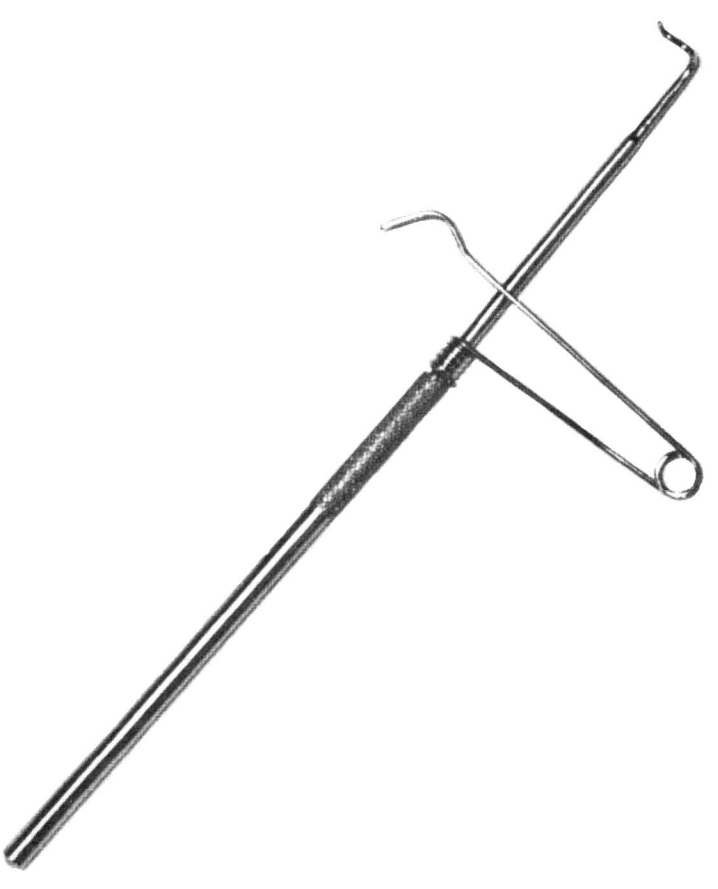

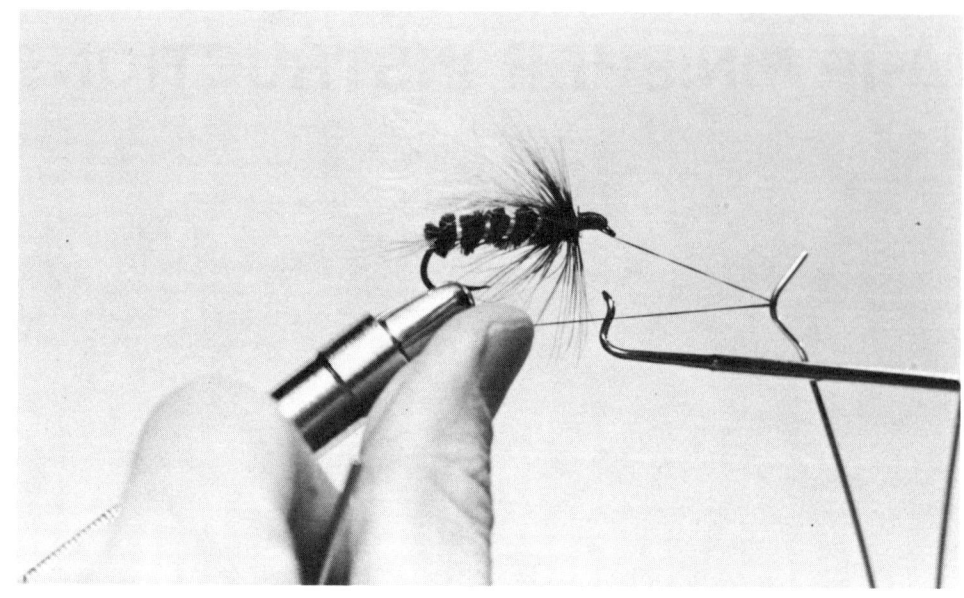

1. With whip finisher in position as shown above, attach thread to the spring and with thumb apply medium tension moving the spring forward toward the hook. The thread should be on the outside of the hook and you should try to exactly match the picture above.

2. With thumb in the same position, tilt whip finisher up and with hook grab thread just under the head. Tension should remain the same.

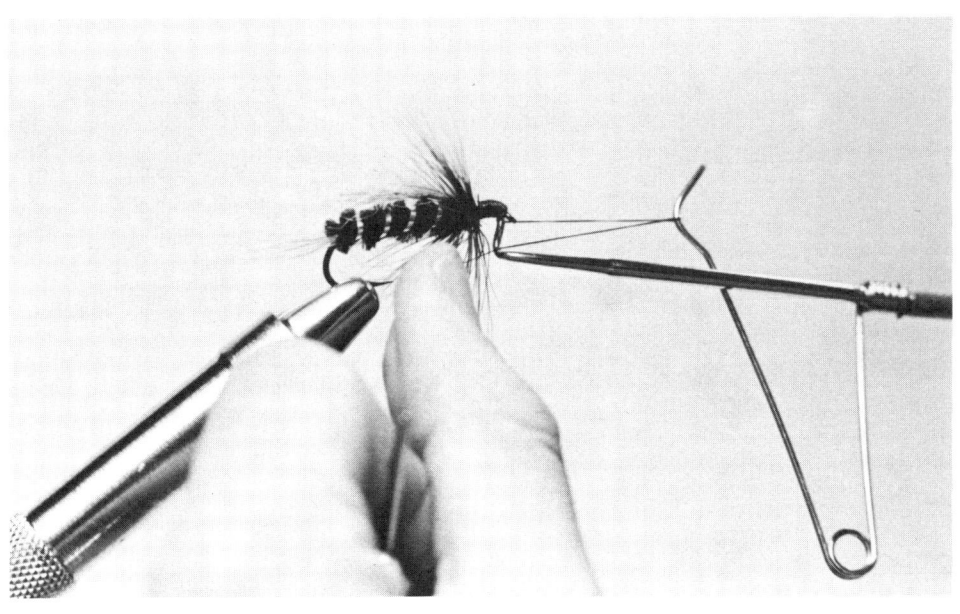

3. With thumb lay thread in the loop on the hook. Whip finish. Main body should be brought to a parallel position.

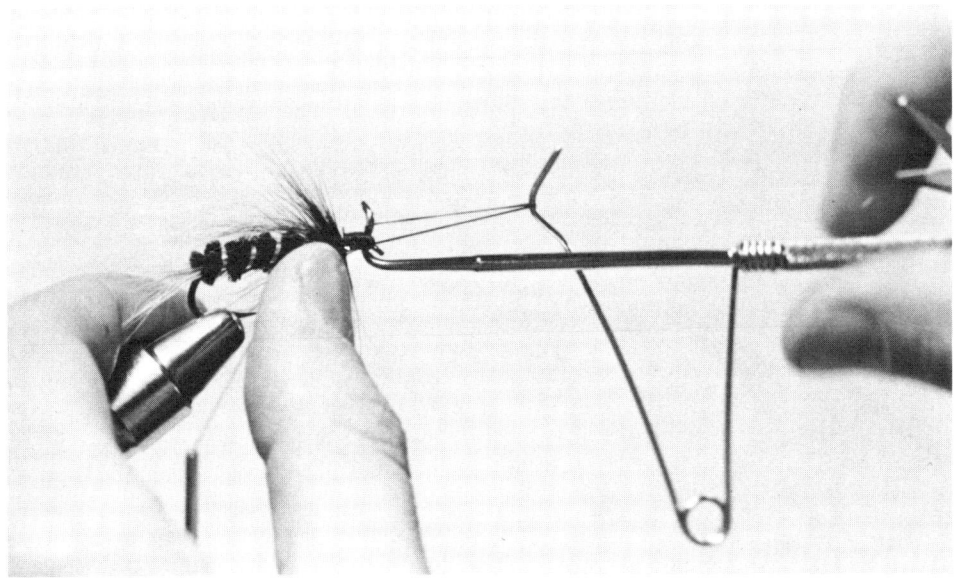

4. Using the thumb and finger of your right hand, start twisting whip finisher in a clockwise fashion. Tension on left hand should remain the same. Lift slightly up on the whip finisher when starting to twist.

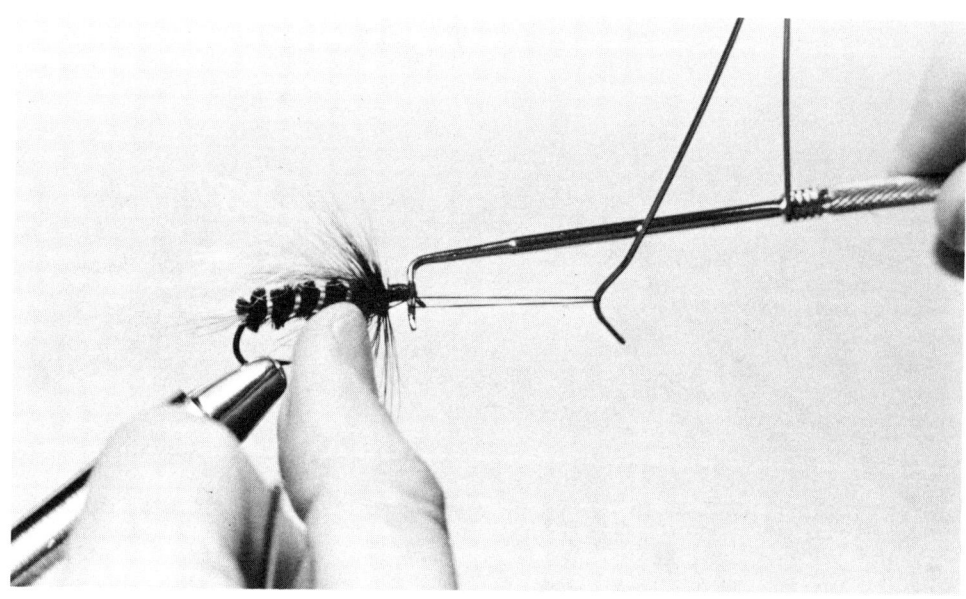

5. Continue to twist keeping whip finisher slightly up at the rear end. This is important to keep the thread from twisting off. Be sure to notice the position of the hands. About five or ten wraps depending on the size of the thread and the size of the fly.

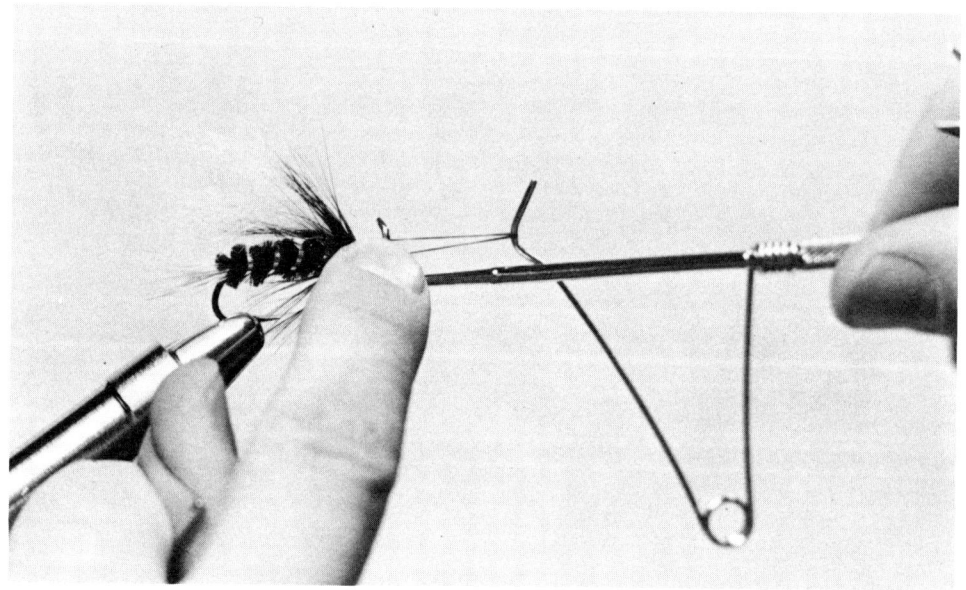

6. After finishing the wraps you are ready to remove the hook from the fly. With forefinger of left hand on thread maintain tight pressure.

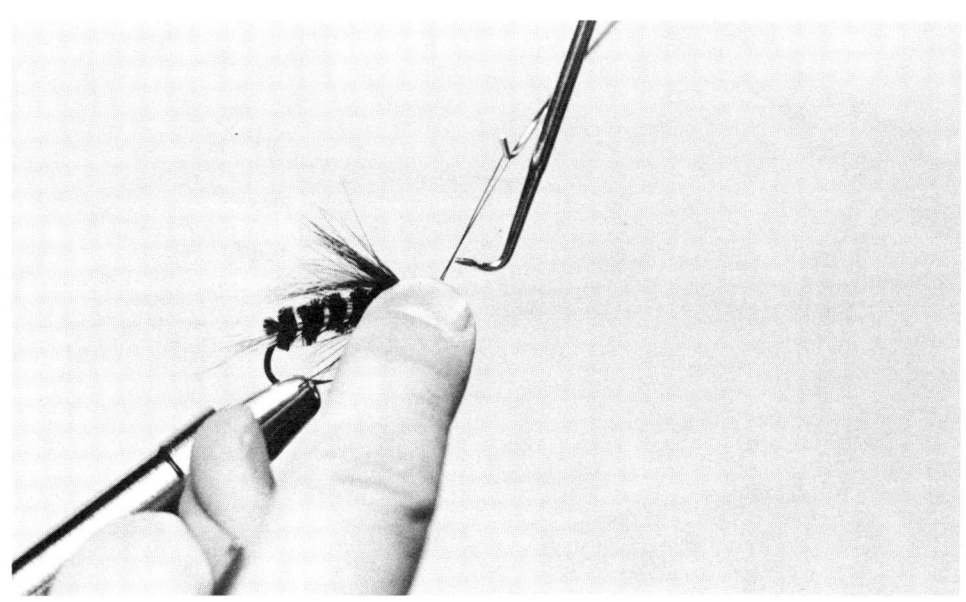

7. Remove hook from thread but thread remains in spring. Finger also holds the thread down on the head keeping it from snapping off when releasing hook.

8. Pull tightly on thread with thumb and finger of left hand and pull thread loop down toward eye. Remove hook, pull tight, and trim thread.

TOOLS OF THE TRADE

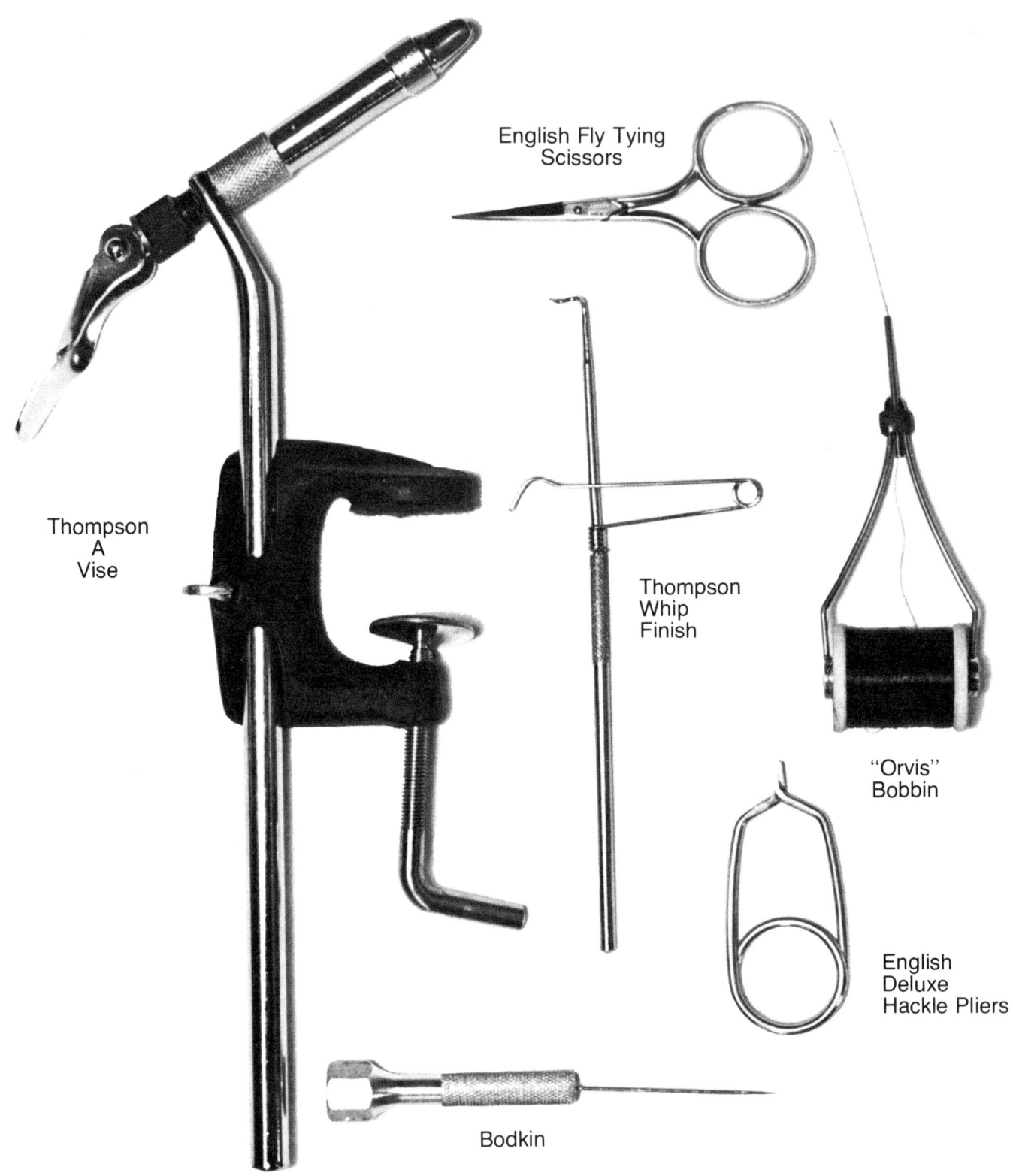

HOOK PLATE

Qual. N. H7957-B MUSTAD-VIKING Hooks
Hollow point, forged, straight, bronzed, turned down tapered eye, long shank.
Size 4, 6, 8, 10, 12, 14, 16, 18, 20

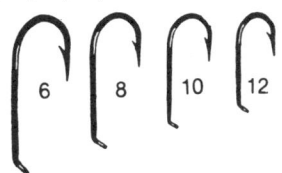

Qual. No. H3906 MUSTAD-SPROAT Hooks
Hollow point, turned down tapered eye, bronzed.
Size 2, 4, 6, 8, 10, 11, 12, 14, 16, 18

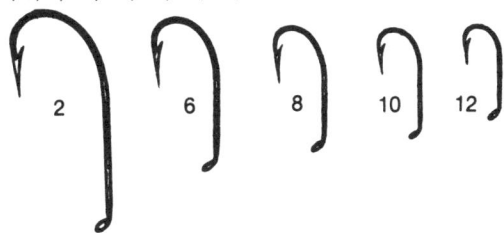

Qual. No. H9671 MUSTAD-VIKING Hooks
Hollow point, forged, straight, turned down tapered eye, bronzed, 2 extra long shank.
Size 1, 2, 4, 6, 8, 10, 12, 14, 16, 18

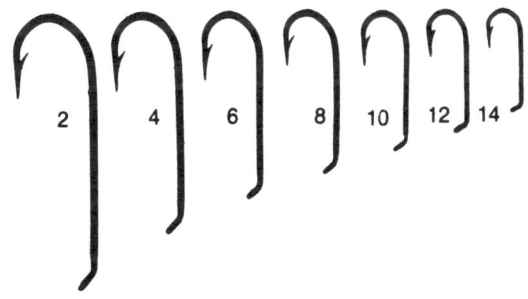

Qual. No. H3665-A MUSTAD-LIMERICK Hooks
Hollow point, turned down tapered eye, bronzed, ½" longer than regular.
Size 1, 2, 4, 6, 8, 10, 12

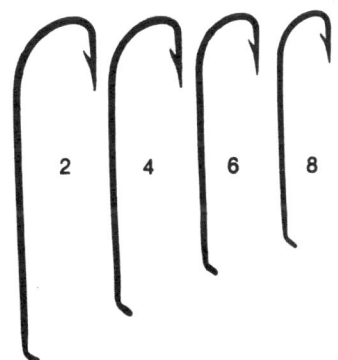

Qual. No. H94840 MUSTAD-VIKING Hooks
Hollow point, forged, straight, turned down tapered eye, bronzed, extra fine wire.
Size 1, 2, 4, 6, 8, 10, 12, 14, 16, 18, 20, 22, 24

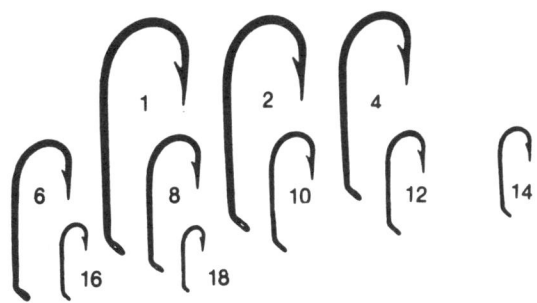

Qual. No. H3906-B MUSTAD-SPROAT Hooks
Hollow point, turned down tapered eye, bronzed, extra long shank.
Size 1, 2, 4, 6, 8, 10, 12, 14, 16, 18, 20

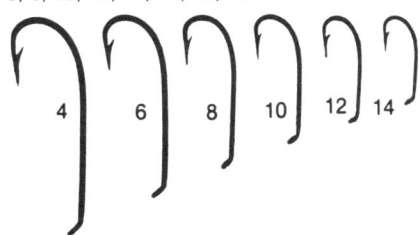

Qual. No. H9672 MUSTAD-VIKING Hooks
Hollow point, forged, straight, turned down tapered eye, bronzed, 3 extra long shank.
Size 1/0, 1, 2, 4, 6, 8, 10, 14, 16, 18

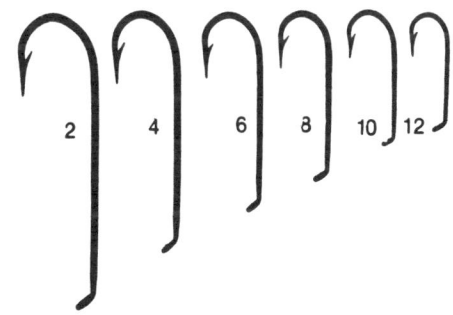

Qual. No. H79580 MUSTAD-VIKING Hooks
Hollow point, forged, straight, turned down tapered eye, bronzed, 4 extra long shank.
Size 1, 2, 4, 6, 8, 10, 12, 14, 16, 18

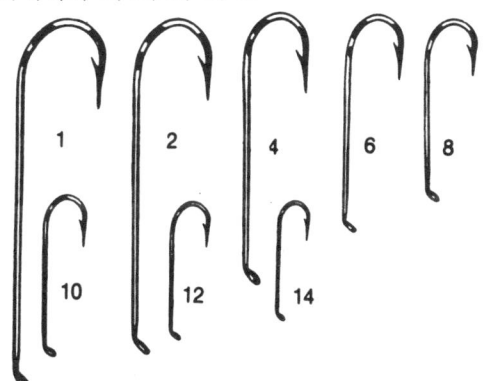

Dry Flies

Step by Step Instructions

BLUE DUN
(DRY)

The Blue Dun dry fly is one of those patterns which have been around for a long time and has proven its worth by taking thousands of trout in both eastern and western waters throughout the years. The neutral blue-gray color of this fly makes it a useful pattern for imitating several types of mayflies.

The standard pattern uses a duck quill wing, but I have found that a blue dun hackle tip wing makes a better fly for western fishing. Not only does the divided hackle tip wing look natural, it is much more durable than a duck quill wing. This is an important consideration in fishing the rough waters of our streams in the West where a dry fly is often pulled under the surface by swirling eddies and white-topped riffles.

I have found this to be an effective fly on some of the mountain lakes. It is also one of the "must" patterns when fishing the great trout streams of Yellowstone Park. In late July and August, a small Blue Dun tied on a #16 or #18 hook is just the ticket for sly brown trout in the Upper Madison.

The serious fly fisherman should have a good selection of Blue Dun from large #12's down through #20 Midge-sized ties.

MATERIALS:	Blue Dun
THREAD:	Pre-waxed gray Herb Howard.
HOOK:	94840 or 7957B.
SIZES:	8 to 24.
TAIL:	Dark moose hair fibers.
BODY:	Dubbed grey muskrat fur.
WING:	Medium blue dun hackle tips.
HACKLE:	Medium blue dun saddle or neck hackle.

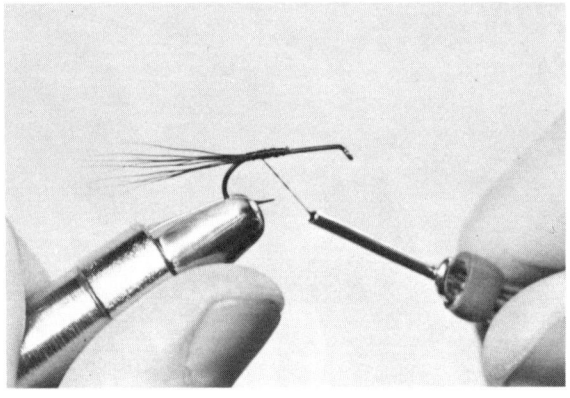

1. Tie on four to eight strands of dark moose hair. Tail should be the length of hook.

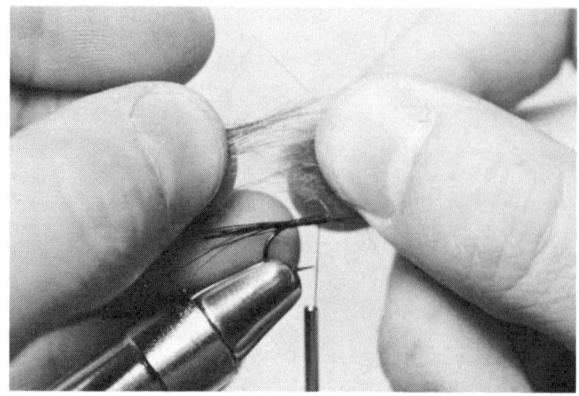

2. Separate guard hairs from gray muskrat fur.

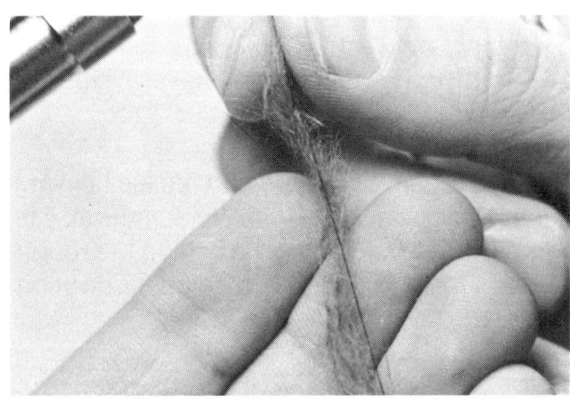

3. Attach muskrat fur to Herb Howard tying thread using thumb and forefinger to roll on.

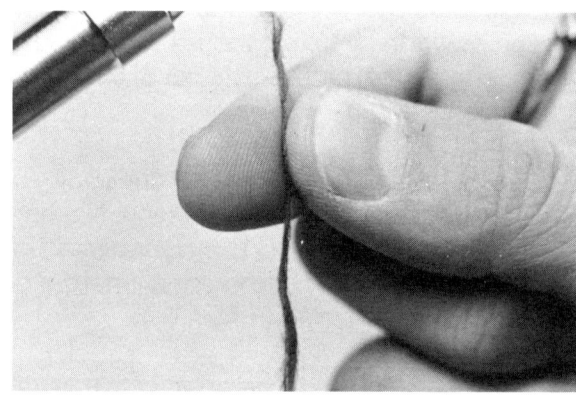

4. Using thumb and finger roll back and forth rolling fur on the thread.

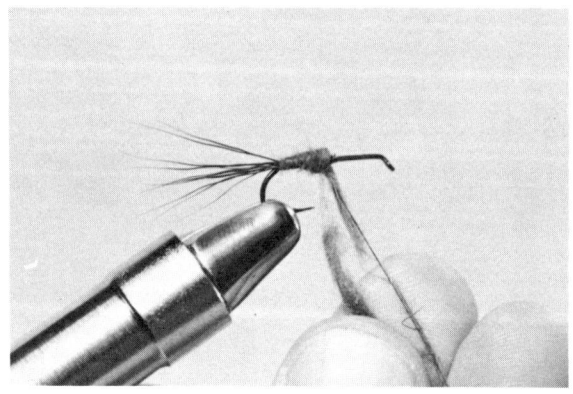

5. Wrap fur forward tapering adding extra fur when necessary to complete body. Notice taper.

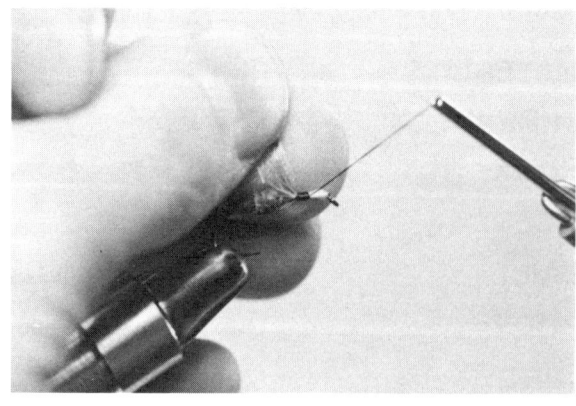

6. Select two blue dun either medium or rusty blue dun hackle tips. Measure, tie on.

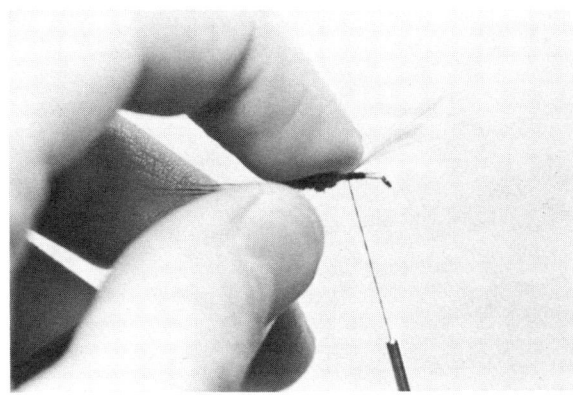

7. Use finger to straighten hackle tips and cock them forward.

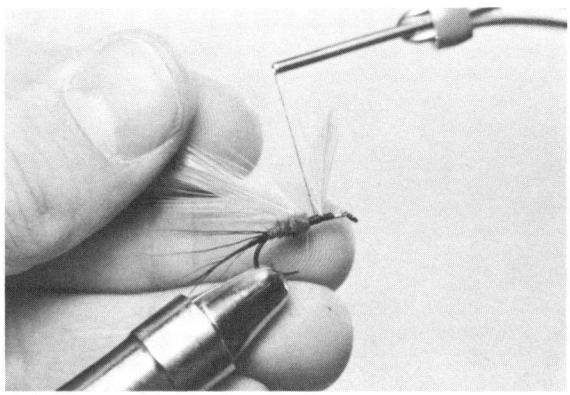

8. Tie on two medium or rusty blue dun hackles.

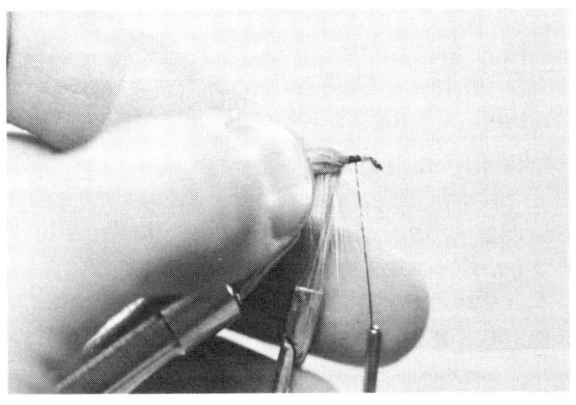

9. After wrapping hackle to wing, pull back on hackle including wing and wrap forward as shown above. Tie off thread to form head, whip finish, laquer.

10. Use finger to straighten out hackle tip wings.

Finished Fly

23

ADAMS

One of the most popular patterns in the United States, the Adams is one fly that everybody should have when fishing the west. This fly (and its variations) has led to the demise of more fish than any other I know. It can be tied with different tails, and different body materials, but it basically remains the same fly. Its general resemblance to several different natural insects accounts for its popularity. It could be nominated the best all-round dry fly for western fishing.

In recent years the declining quality of grizzly hackle has had its effect on commercially tied Adams flies. My suggestion is to use a high quality brown hackle which gives the fly extra stiffness. If both brown and grizzly are used, often the coloring is good on grizzly but the quality is poor. For Western fishing I would suggest using two brown hackles and one grizzly to make a fly with good, stiff hackle without sacrificing coloration. For the tails of Adams flies, I prefer several strands of moose hair over the standard golden pheasant, or mixed brown and grizzly hackle.

In the West we usually use heavier hooks than the standard Eastern Adams, for two reasons: First, the fish are usually larger and can break off the tip or snap the hook at its bend. Second, most Western rivers have gravel banks with a great deal of brush and rocks behind them. A slip on the back cast can run a hook over a large stick or rock and break or badly dull it. A heavier hook usually eliminates these problems. If the point on the heavier hook is dulled it usually can be quickly sharpened with the use of a hook hone. I recommend heavily hackled Adams for fishing in larger rivers, in sizes 10 and 12, and sizes 14, 16, 18, and 20 for fishing small creeks, ponds, and lakes. These should be tied very sparsely on a good quality hook.

MATERIALS: Adams

THREAD: Herb Howard pre-waxed either black or gray

HOOK: Mustad 94840, 3906, or 7957B

SIZES: 8 to 24

TAIL: Several fibers of dark moose hair or golden pheasant tipped fibers or brown and grizzly hackle fibers mixed.

BODY: Dubbed and tapered gray muskrat fur.

WING: Grizzly barred hackle tips, medium shade.

HACKLE: One brown neck and one grizzly medium shade hackle mixed.

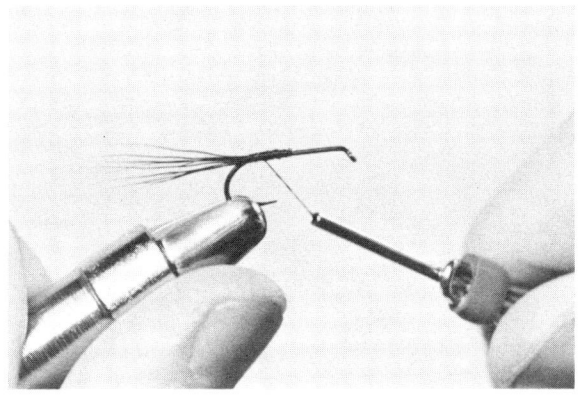

1. Tie on several strands of dark moose hair.

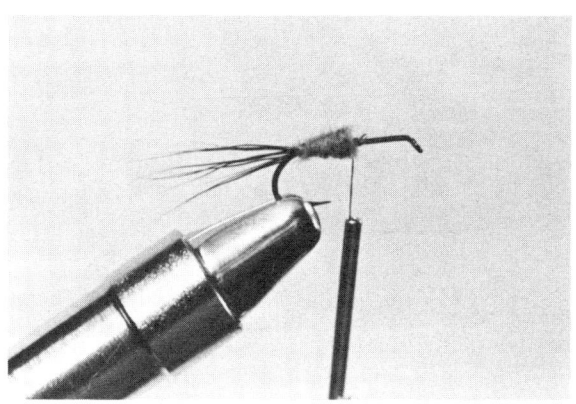

2. Dub as explained previously light to medium muskrat fur. Taper and use proportion as shown above.

3. Tie on two matched grizzly hackle tips.

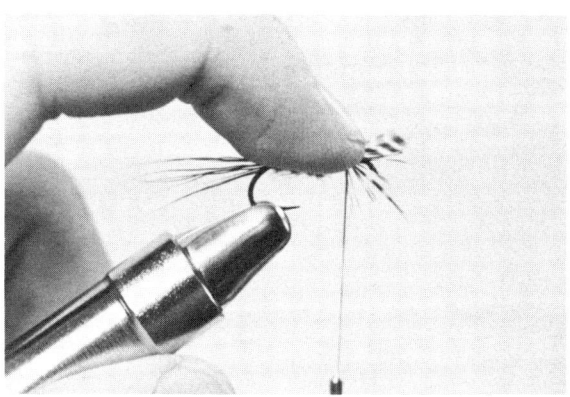

4. Use forefinger to divide hackle tips.

5. Select one brown and one grizzly saddle hackle or neck hackle. Brown should be reddish or deep brown. Grizzly should be well-marked.

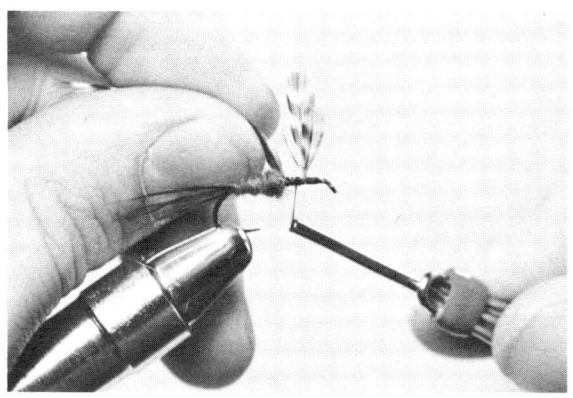

6. Tie in hackle.

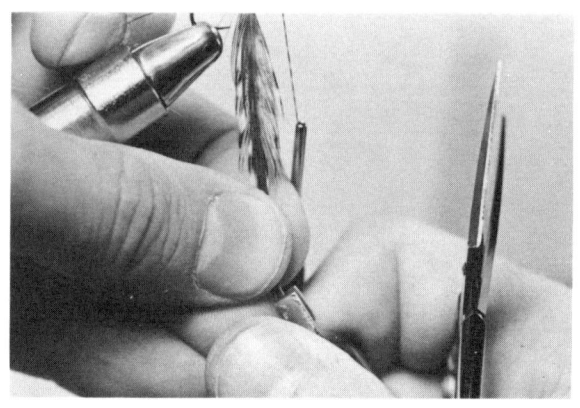
7. Meld both hackles together using thumb and forefinger and attach with hackle pliers.

8. Wrap straight up and down. Again tie behind the wing and in front of wing. Be sure to leave plenty of room for head. Tie off, whip finish and laquer.

Finished Fly

LIGHT VARIANT

The Light Variant is one of my favorite dry fly patterns. It was first developed by Bob Carmichael, the famous Yellowstone and Jackson Hole guide, considered by many to be the greatest fly fisherman ever to fish Yellowstone Park. The man who first tied this fly for Bob was a California fly tier by the name of Roy Donnelly whose steelhead patterns are now considered classics. He and Bob put their heads together and came up with a western version of a Ginger Quill or Light Cahill, which could float better and would resemble the fly hatches that occur in the Yellowstone-Jackson Hole area. Prior to their invention, about the only hackle-tip fly in use was the Adams, one of Bob Carmichael's favorite flies. At that time, it seemed that most dry flies were tied with duck quill wings. Bob concluded that these quill wings were not only unnatural, but also would disintegrate after several fish. The Donnelly Light Variant combined hackle tip wings with a soft fur body and good stiff saddle hackle, making it a fine floater for Jackson Hole waters.

Bob and his fly tying friend, Roy, collaborated in developing several other great western patterns that are fished regularly to this day. Bob's tackle shop in Moose, Wyoming, stocked various eastern patterns adapted to the west tied mostly by Roy Donnelly under Bob's careful supervision. Every fly was designed to give the fisherman a western touch or it was a new pattern, designed strictly for this area. Among these patterns were the Whitcraft, Carmichael's Indispensable, Donnelly Dark Variant, Dry Spruce Fly, a Hackle Tip Blue Dun, Western Black Gnat, and many others.

The thousands of fishermen that have fished the Jackson Hole and Yellowstone area still use these patterns and have taken them to other parts of the country. The Light Variant is one of the most effective light mayfly patterns that I have ever found. You would do well to give it a try in both Eastern and Western waters. It can be tied as a very sparse pattern for use on eastern streams, small springs, or ponds.

MATERIALS: Light Variant
HOOK: Mustad 94840, Sizes 8, 10, 12, 14, 16, and 18.
THREAD: Pre-waxed Herb Howard cream thread.
TAIL: Cream or ginger hackle tips (or several stiff light elk hairs).
BODY: Spun badger underfur; red fox underfur; light otter dubbing (or any light cream body material).
WINGS: Cream or ginger hackle tips.
HACKLE: One cream hackle combined with one ginger hackle. Neck hackles are preferable for small sizes, saddle hackles for larger sizes.

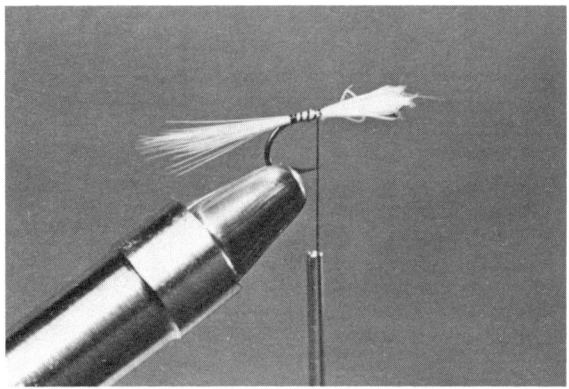

1. Tie on a medium ginger hackle fiber for tail.

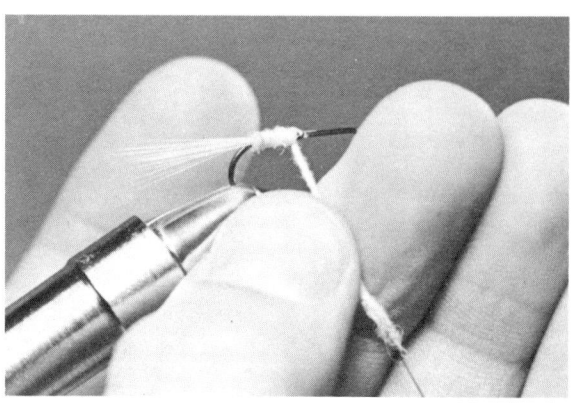

2. Dub on a light cream fur to tying thread and wrap forward. While wrapping fur body you may have to keep twisting fur to keep body tight.

3. Body should look like picture and portions should be as such.

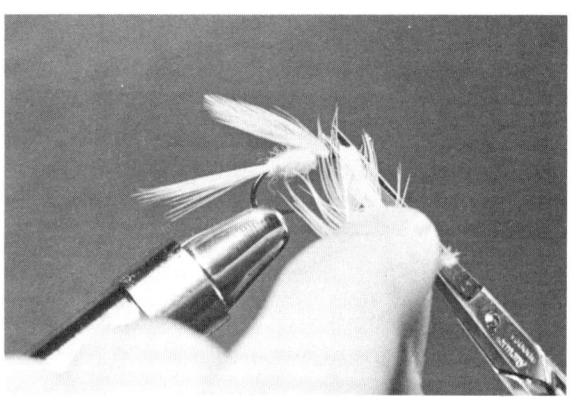

4. Tie on two matched light ginger or cream hackle tips. Trim butt ends.

5. Wrap thread around, cocking feather as shown above using thumb and finger to separate wing.

6. Trim excess hackle fibers.

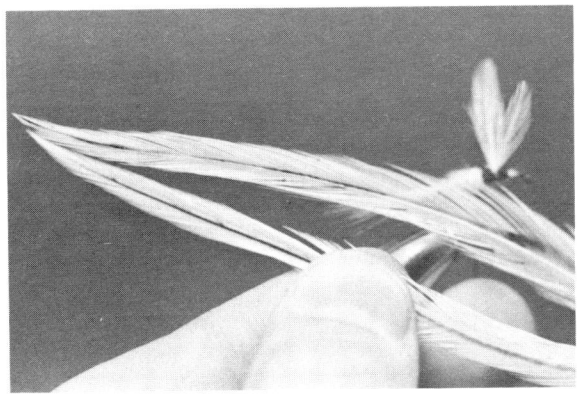

7. Select one dark ginger and one light ginger or cream saddle hackle.

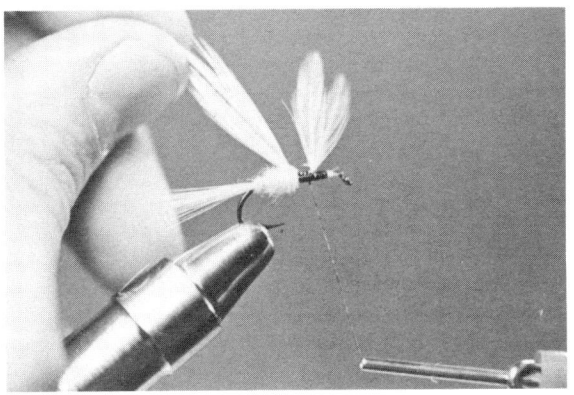

8. Tie hackle in securely. Dry fly style.

9. Wrap hackle behind wing and over wing. Tie and off, and whip finish and head cement.

Finished Fly

CARMICHAEL INDISPENSABLE

This fly is another Bob Carmichael invention. It is basically an Adams pattern with a pink wool egg sac and a smooth yellow body. It is an attractive pattern and is a standard dry fly around Yellowstone and Jackson Hole. When feeding trout swim up to inspect and then refuse a conventional Adams pattern, tying on a Carmichael and floating it over the same trout will often be successful. I suggest that all fishermen who are fond of fishing an Adams dry fly should try a Carmichael too. I have had reports from fishermen in the Colorado-Nevada area which say that for them the Carmichael works better than the standard Adams.

MATERIALS: Carmichael Indispensable
HOOK: Mustad 94840, sizes 8, 10, 12, 14, 16, and 18.
THREAD: Herb Howard pre-waxed black or yellow thread.
TAIL: Several moose body hairs.
BODY: Yellow floss and pink wool.
WING: Two wide grizzly hackle tips.
HACKLE: Brown and grizzly neck hackle.

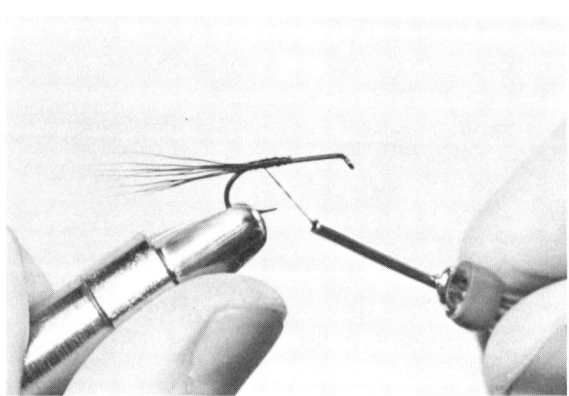

1. Tie in several strands of moose hair.

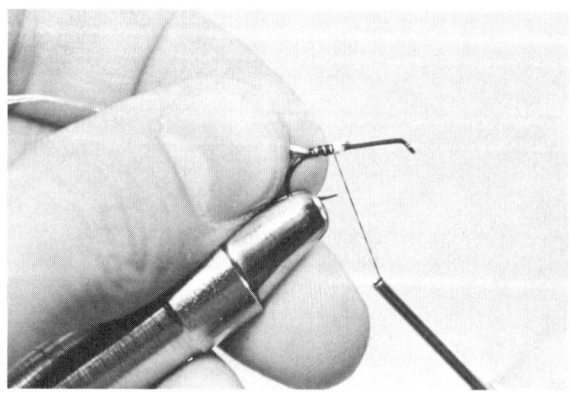

2. Tie on piece of four-strand yellow floss.

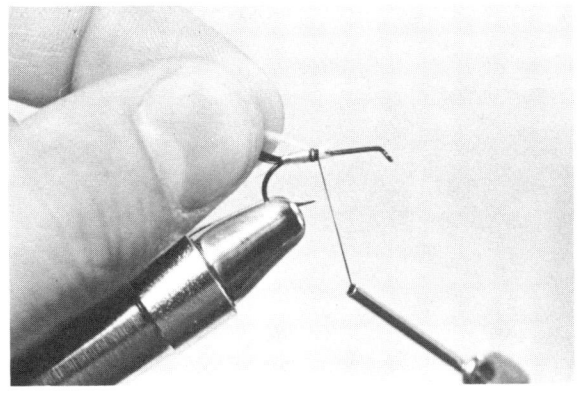

3. Wrap yellow floss forward. Tie off and tie in one strand of pink wool.

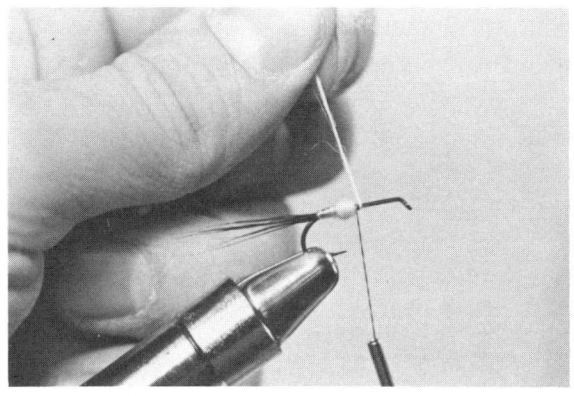

4. Tie wool forming egg sac as shown above.

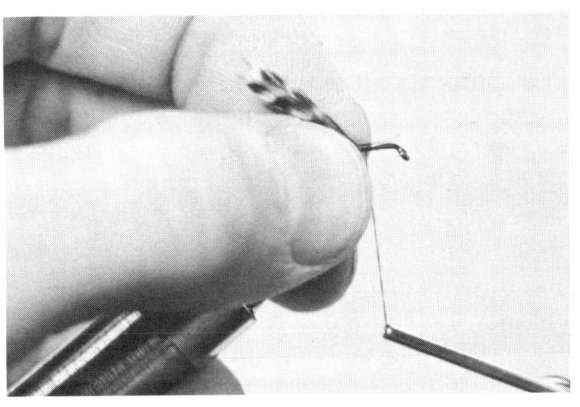

5. Select two matched grizzly hackle tips placing dark sides together forming wing. Tie down as illustrated.

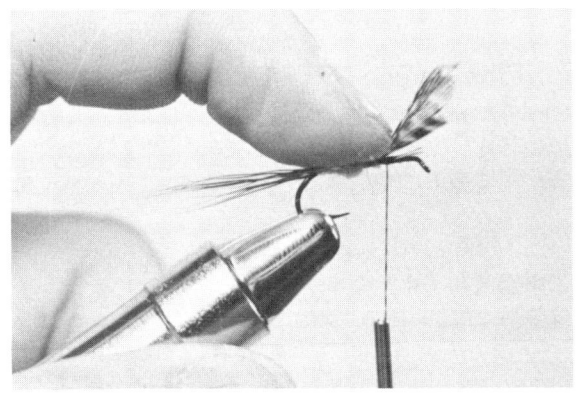

6. Use finger to divide wings.

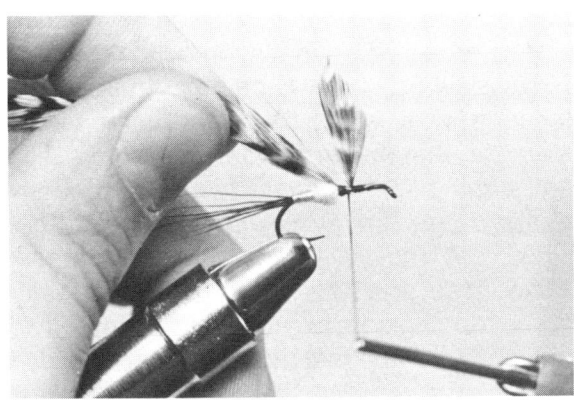

7. Tie one grizzly and one dark brown neck saddle hackle. Be sure hackles are tied in at base.

8. Wrap hackle forward evenly and smoothly forming a thick bushy hackle. Tie off and whip finish and lacquer.

DRY SPRUCE FLY

The Spruce Fly is a well-known wet and streamer pattern, but many people do not realize that it is also a fine dry fly. First popularized in the Pacific Northwest, its acceptance has spread into the Rocky Mountain area. Many large fly shops carry the Dry Spruce Fly in sizes 16, 18, and 20. It is a highly recommended dry fly for spring and pond fishing.

My experience with the Dry Spruce Fly is with brown trout in Yellowstone Park. There I have found it to be a killer! One year during October, when browns usually give their full attention to spawning rather than much surface feeding, I found that the Spruce Fly was deadly during a mid-afternoon hatch. It was a fairly warm October day and the skies were filled with the last of the season's hatch before the oncoming winter snows. I had several 14 and 16 patterns, Blue Dun, Humpy, Adams, and a few other selected flies, but I had no luck casting to the large brown trout. We were working the Lewis River area between Shoshone and Lewis Lakes just above a section called the Aquariam Pool. Many anglers hit this area in September and October. It is usually fished with wet flies such as Wooly Worms, Wet Spruce Flies, and Muddlers, as the days are usually cold and sometimes snowy. But this particular day held the perfect dry fly situation. The browns ran 1½ lbs. to 4 lbs., and in the crystal-clear water it was breath taking to see the fish rise to the surface. I tried a Light Variant, which is a cream-colored pattern that seemed to resemble the hatching insects more than any other fly I had. Several large browns came right up to the surface and nudged the fly, but none were takers. Because I was using a 5X leader I immediately thought that my leader was either floating and casting a shadow, or it was too large. I thus switched to a 6X tippet and a smaller Light Variant, again with the same results. Extremely frustrated my fishing companion and I compared boxes and came up with one Dry Spruce Fly that he had purchased from a fly shop in Spokane, Washington. We quickly tied on the size 14 morsel and drifted the fly in the slow current. It floated about fifteen feet and BANG! We had a nice 1½ lb. brown. After 1½ hours we had released five other browns ranging from two to three pounds, all on the one Dry Spruce Fly. We kept passing the rod back and forth the rest of the day, until finally I set the hook too hard in the mouth of one large brown, and off it went. We tried several other flies, but nothing produced a hit. This ended our fall dry fly fishing day on the Lewis River.

The next day we returned to Moose, Wyoming and walked into the famous Carmichael fly shop. We told Bob Lewis, one of Carmichael's renowned guides, (and who has since retired to Mexico to fly fish and tag marlin for the Mexican government), about our new found discovery. Bob laughed and proceeded to pull out a box of about fifteen dozen beautifully tied Spruce Flies.

"You guys haven't told me anything new," he joked, "we've been using them for years! We just don't tell all the dudes about this one, its our secret fly."

Since that time, I have always kept a few Dry Spruce Flies in my own fishing box and a few in the shop for the special dudes. We can't let out all our secret flies to all the fishermen who walk in the shop — pretty soon there would not be any trout! Seriously, give the Dry Spruce Fly a try, especially if you are in the East, because in small sizes it will surely be effective on eastern waters.

MATERIALS: Dry Spruce Fly

THREAD: Black monocord or herb howard pre-waxed thread.

HOOK: Mustad 7957B or Mustad 3906.

SIZES: 10 to 24.

TAIL: Several strands of dark moose hair or badger hackle fibers.

BODY: Red floss, then three fibers of peacock herl.

WINGS: Badger hackle tips tied upright.

HACKLE: White tipped badger saddles for large sizes, neck hackles for small sizes.

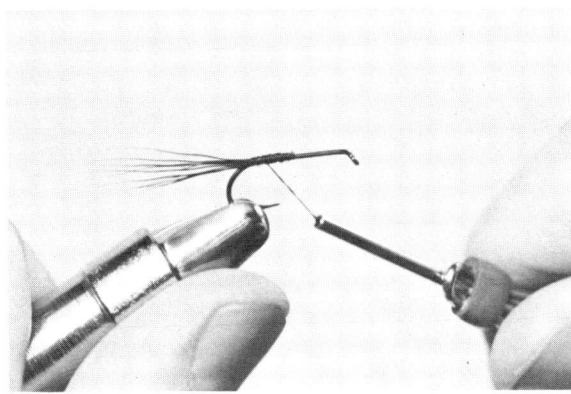

1. Tie on several strands of dark moose hair.

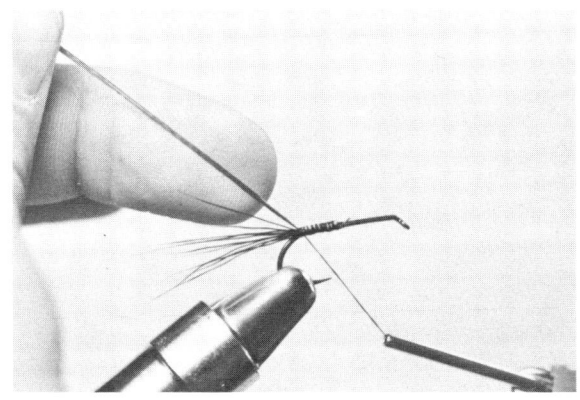

2. Tie on some red flat floss.

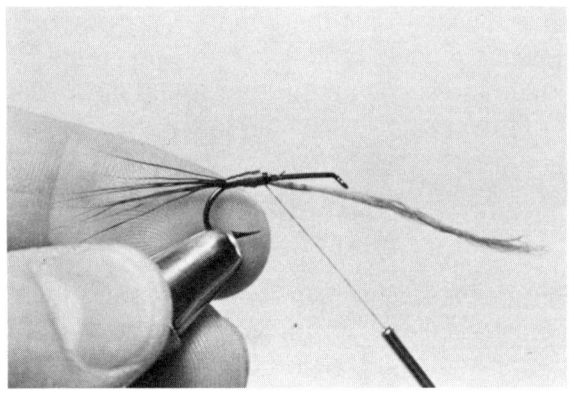

3. Wrap floss forward so it protrudes slightly beyond the point of barb. Tie off and trim.

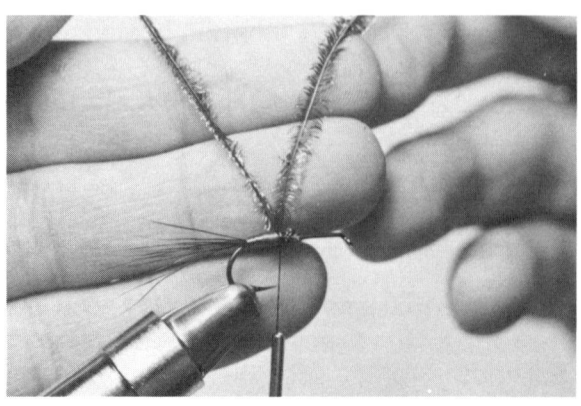

4. Wrap two strands of peacock herl forward forming a small tuft.

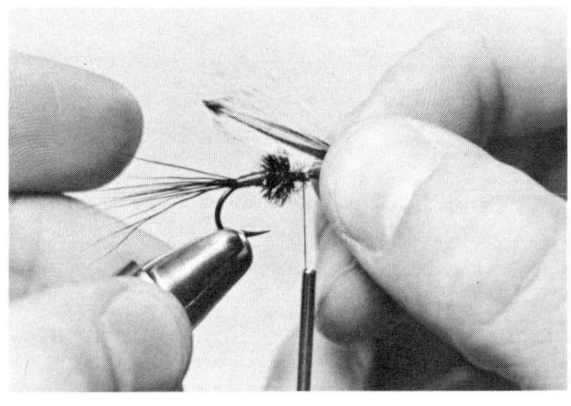

5. Take two matching neck hackle tips. Badger with white or silver tips. Measure for size.

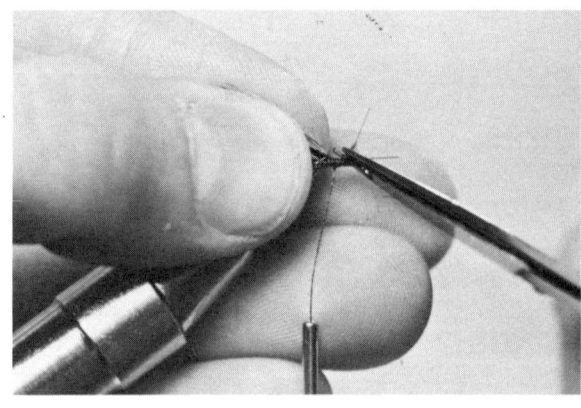

6. Tie down hackle tips and make sure that hackle tips are facing each other or glossy sides are facing eath other. This will give it the proper divided wing effect.

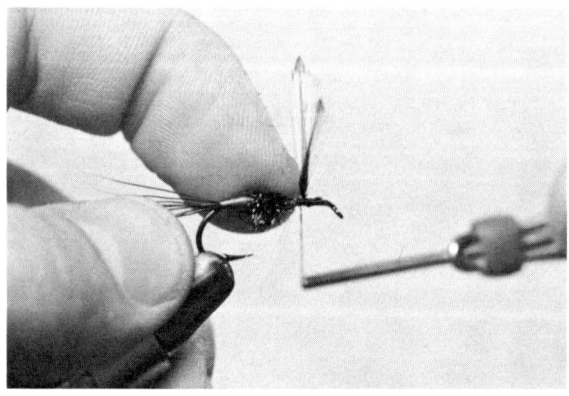

7. Use forefinger of left hand to push forward hackle tips and wrap behind wing.

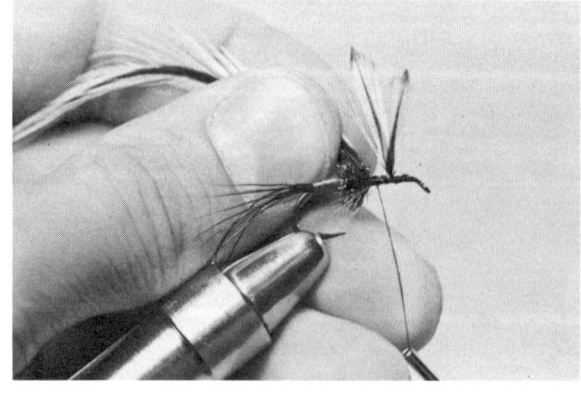

8. Tie in two badger saddles or neck hackles. Should be silver or white tip badger.

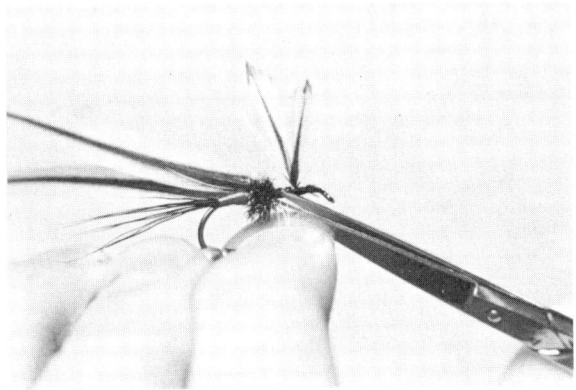

9. Trim out any fibers that might be in the way or tied down.

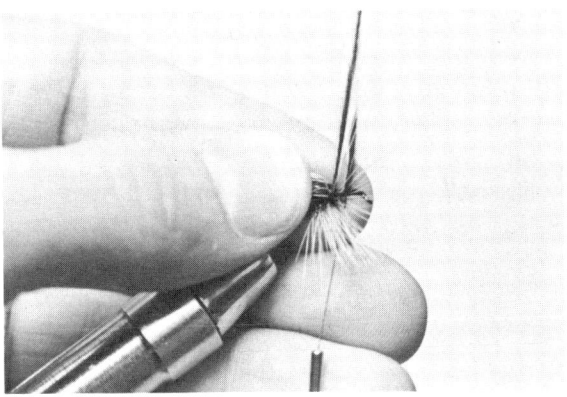

10. Wrap hackle forward. Wing should be in the middle of hackle. It should be equally wrapped in front and back of wing.

Finished Fly

DRY RIO GRANDE KING

If you are ever checked by a game warden in Colorado you may be fined if you do not have a Dry Rio Grande King in your box. It is almost a state tradition in Colorado to fish with one of these. I myself, have never had much faith in this white-winged fly, but I find it hard to argue with its many adherents who have had great success with it. For many people, trust in this fly rivals their faith in the Almighty. There are some fishermen who will not fish with anything else, and they become even hostile when you suggest that it might not work in your area. Throughout Idaho, Montana, Utah, California, Colorado, Washington, Oregon, and Arizona the name Dry Rio Grande King is well known and revered. In almost every tackle shop in these areas there are Dry Rio Grande Kings for sale. The dry fly version is a popular style of this pattern.

My experience with this fly is limited, but its avid followers tell me it is best fished in fast, turbulent water in the same manner as you would fish any dry fly. I have even been asked (by one of its ardent admirers) to tie some of these in sizes 18 to 22. The fly can be tied several ways, but the one here is the standard approved version. I might note that calftail can be used to replace the duck quill wing.

MATERIALS: Dry Rio Grande King

THREAD: Black monocord.

HOOK: Mustad 7957B, 3906, or 3906B.

SIZES: For large streams and lakes: 2 through 8. For small steams 10 through 16.

TAIL: Golden pheasant tippets.

BODY: Black chennile.

WING: White duck quills or white calftail.

HACKLE: Brown neck hackle, medium shade.

HEAD: Black.

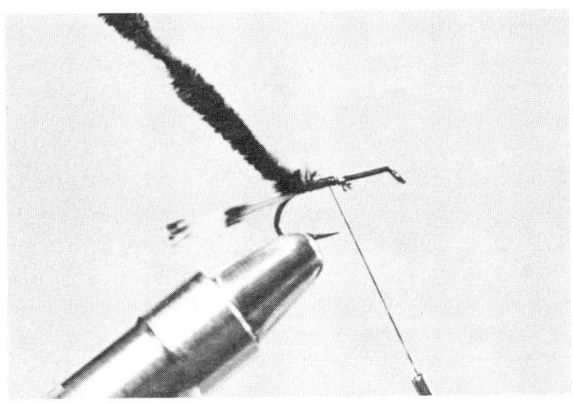

1. Tie on several fibers of golden pheasant tippets. Pheasant tippets should be the length of the shank. Then tie on one medium black strand of chennile. Tie chennile in securely.

2. Wrap chennile forward. Be sure to keep proper proportions.

3. Select two matching white duck quill fibers.

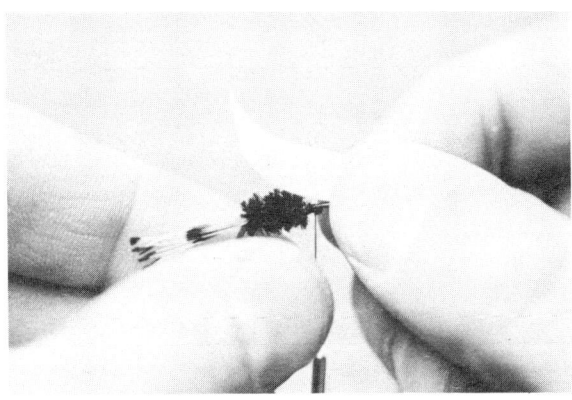

4. Measure wing as shown above.

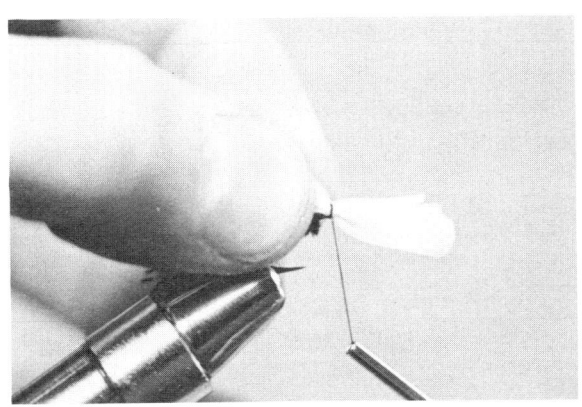

5. Tie in wing with curvature pointing up.

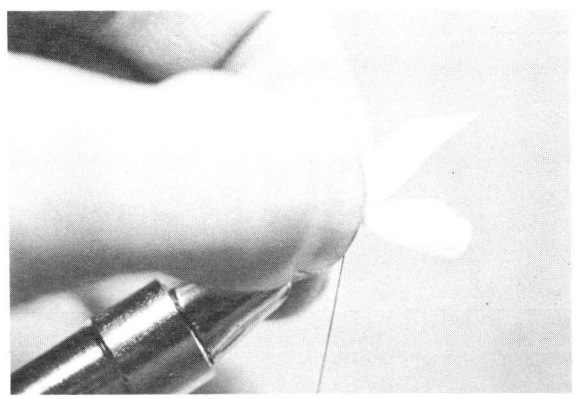

6. Push wings forward with thumb and finger. This is to cock the wing forward.

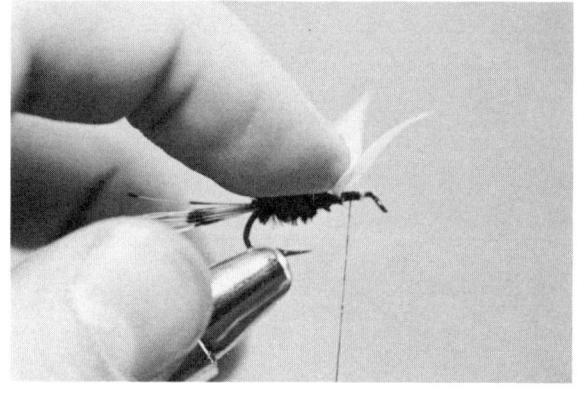

7. Use forefinger to divide wing again pushing wing forward. Be careful not to split wing.

8. Wrap thread behind the wings thus securing wings with the shank of hook. Drop a dab of head cement on each tip of wing.

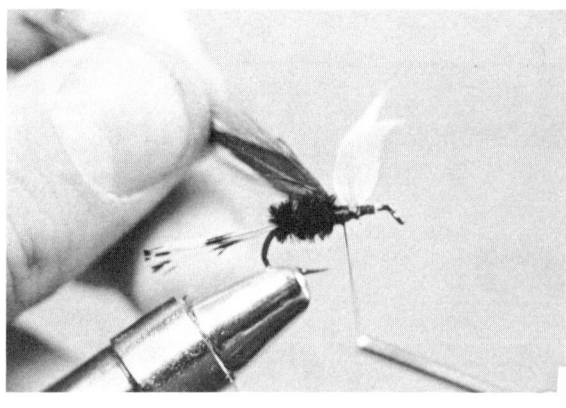

9. Tie in two brown neck hackles, or saddles. Color can vary from light to dark brown, depending on your preference.

10. Wrap hackle forward making sure that there are equal amounts of wrap behind and in front of hook.

11. Use thumb and finger to straighten wing out and make sure it is cocked properly.

Finished Fly

MOSQUITO

There is not a fisherman alive today who has not swatted this pesky little insect. Many people believe that one of the trout's favorite morsels is a mosquito. However, this is not entirely true. Trout do feed on Mosquito larvae. Seldom, however, do they feed on adult mosquitos. The question then remains, "Why does the mosquito dry fly work?" I believe it is successful because to the trout it represents other forms of aquatic life. It is a very attractive pattern to curious fish, and in small sizes represents a midge very closely. Many fishermen who have visited my shop have told me that the mosquito in sizes 8 and 10 brings them good luck when fishing large rivers. I suspect that it probably imitates a gray caddis rather than a natural mosquito. I would fish the mosquito in the usual dry fly fashion combined with some insect repellent to insure that the trout is the one who falls victim.

MATERIALS: Mosquito

HOOK: Mustad 94840 or 7957B.

SIZES: 8 to 22.

BODY: One dark and one light moose mane fiber.

WINGS: Grizzly hackle tips.

TAIL: Either grizzly hackle fibers or dark moose hair fibers.

HACKLE: Stiff grizzly neck hackle.

THREAD: Herb Howard prewaxed black.

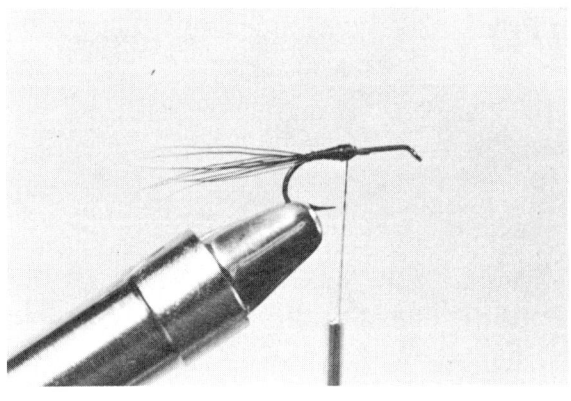

1. Tie on strands of dark moose hair and form a tapered thread body.

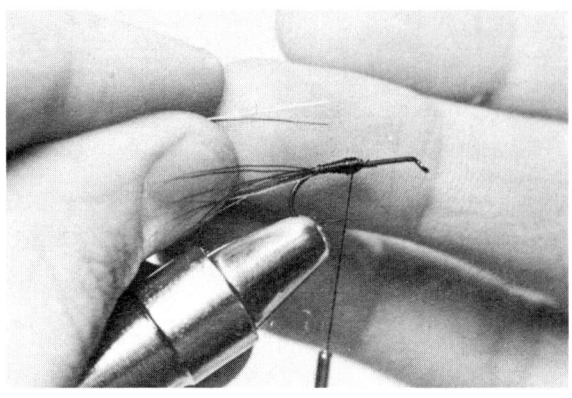

2. Select one dark and one light moose mane.

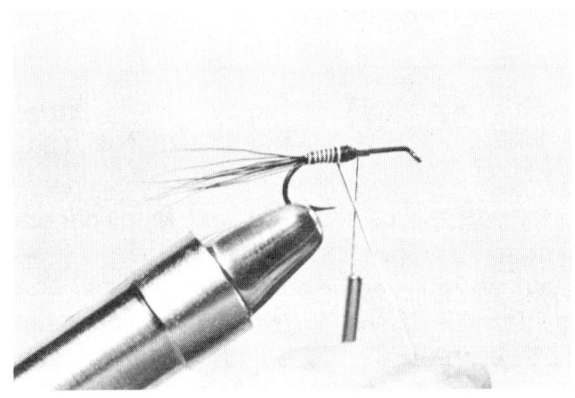

3. Tie on moose mane and wrap forward over tapered thread body, forming a light and dark quill.

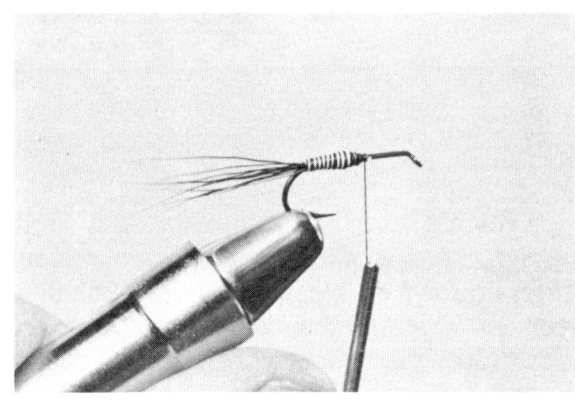

4. Laquer body with head cement. Be sure proportion matches above picture.

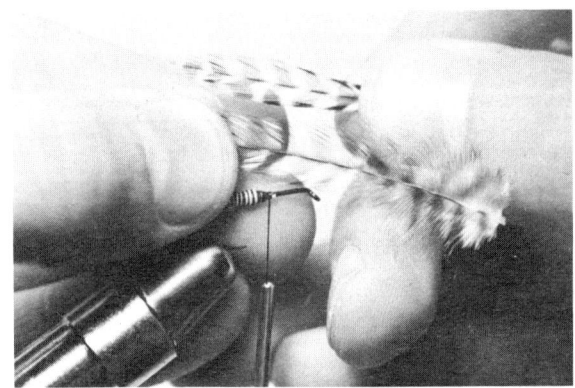

5. Select two grizzly hackle tips putting between thumb and forefinger.

6. Put other hackle between index finger and middle finger and middle finger and use other hand's thumb and forefinger to make hackle tips even.

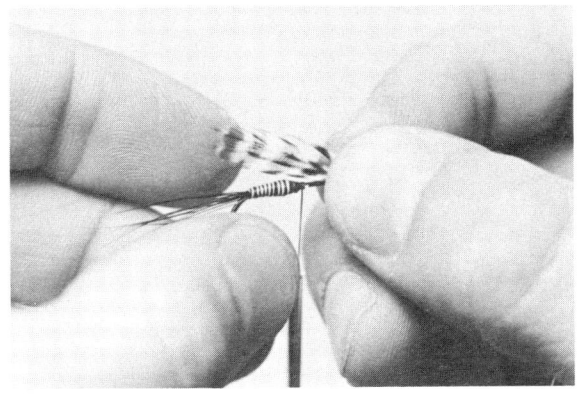

7. Measure and check proportions.

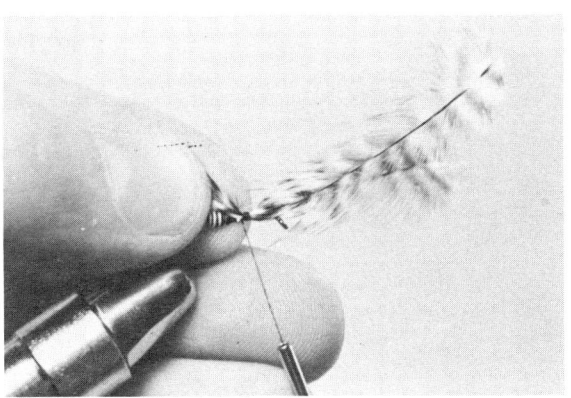

8. Tie on hackle tips.

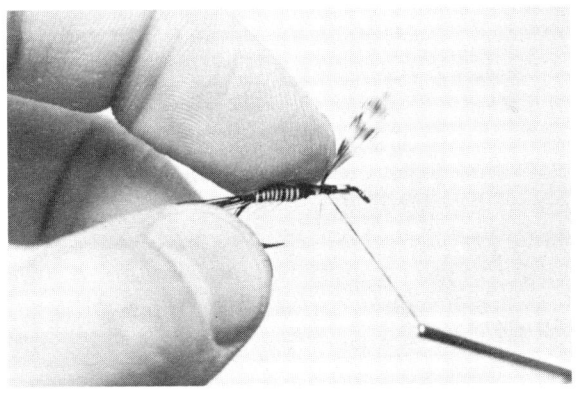

9. Use forefinger to push hackle tips forward to cock and divide them.

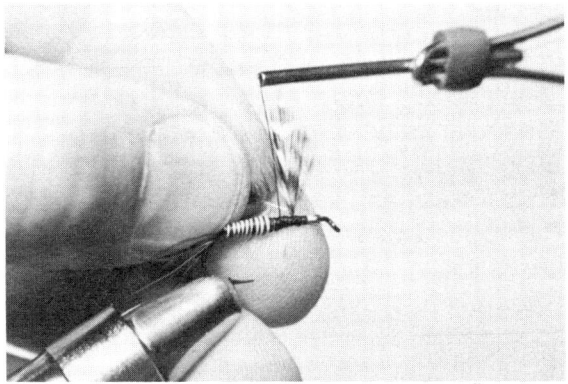

10. Tie on two grizzly neck or saddle hackles, depending on size.

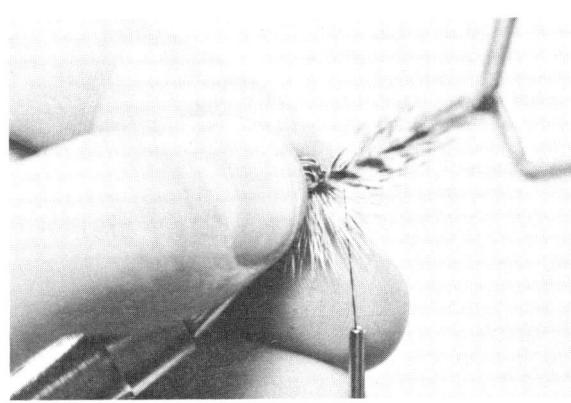

11. Wrap hackle forward making full, whip finish, and laquer.

Finished Fly

RENEGADE

This fly is one of the top rainbow trout flies in the West. It can be fished either dry or wet, but usually works best when fished dry. The Renegade could be described as a Brown Bivisible tied "fore and aft" style. Its light hackle tied on the front of the hook makes the fly extemely visible and a popular pattern for those who have trouble seeing a floating fly in rainbow trout waters. Although it is known as a rainbow pattern, it is effective on cutthroats, brown, and brook trout. There are many variations of the Renegade, such as the Double Renegade, with an extra Palmer-tied hackle in the middle of the fly. This particular variation is usually tied on long shanked hooks in sizes 4, 6, and 8 and has become a popular fly on the large Idaho and Montana rivers. Often each local area adds a little touch of variety to this fly. One can walk into almost every sporting goods store or tackle shop in the west and find Renegades for sale.

The secret of a good Renegade is good hackle, because (since it has no tail) the only thing that keeps the fly afloat is the hackle. A good quality peacock herl is important also to give the fly a nicely finished appearance. My experience has proved the Renegade to be a good river fly but not very effective in small springs. With its fore and aft hackling its floating quality is usually much better than the standard dry fly, thus making it a good fly for fast waters.

The Renegade can be just as effective if it sinks during the float and can be fished back as a wet fly, then worked dry by false casting and re-presented as a dry fly again. I am told it works in Colorado on the fast high-mountain streams by just casting it upstream and letting the current take it where it may. If it floats — fine; if it sinks, just let it keep going. In Montana, the fly is usually tied on #8 or #10 hooks with extremely heavy hackle and used as an attractor pattern over the many bouldered rivers. It really does not resemble any particular insect and is usually most effective when there is no hatch at all. These days, when good fly tying materials are hard to get, it is difficult to find good quality white hackle. My suggestion is to use an off-white or cream hackle. It may not look store-perfect but it will surely take more fish.

MATERIALS:	Renegade
HOOK:	Mustad 7957B or 3906 or 94840.
SIZES:	4 to 18.
TIP:	Gold tinsel.
BACK HACKLE:	Brown saddle or neck hackle.
BODY:	3 or 4 strands of peacock herl.
BODY:	Cream, off-white, or white saddle or neck hackle.
THREAD:	Either black monocord or Herb Howard pre-waxed black.

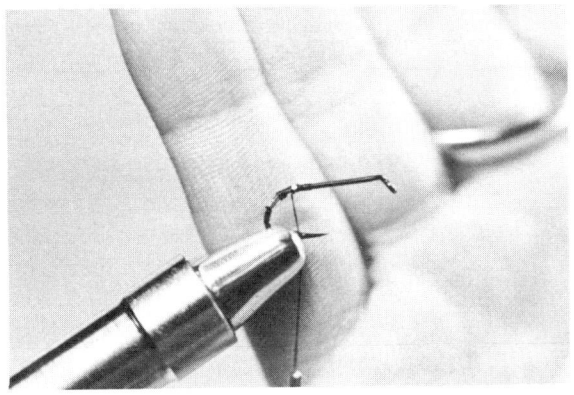

1. First tie on #14 gold tinsel forming a small tag.

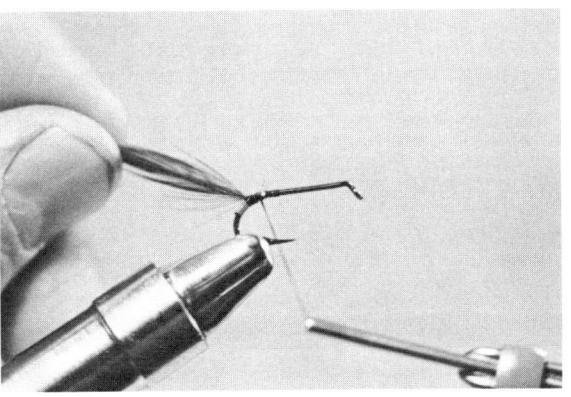

2. Tie on two medium brown neck or saddle hackles depending on size. Tie in securely.

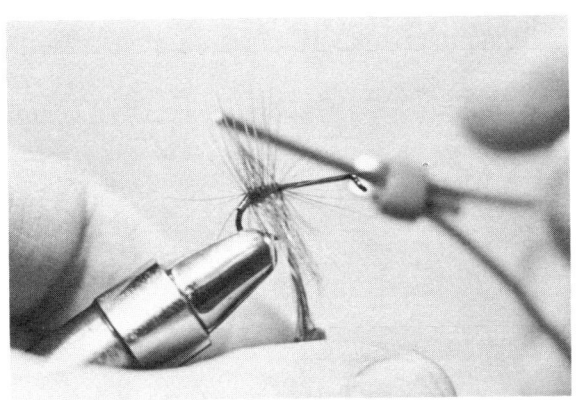

3. Wrap hackle forward and stop approximately where point of hook is, tie hackle off.

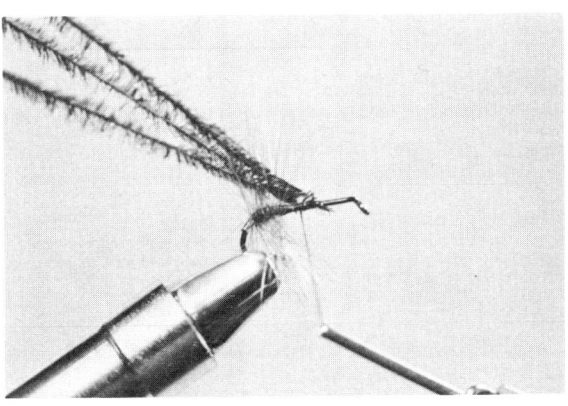

4. Tie from three to four strands of thick peacock herl. Tie to where brown hackle ends.

5. Wrap peacock herl forward and tie off. Be sure to leave room for next hackle.

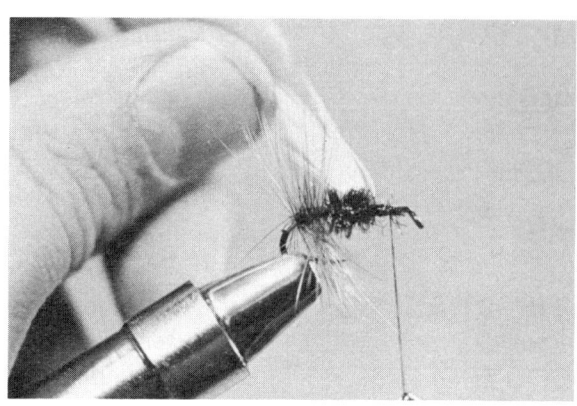

6. Tie on two white or light cream neck or saddle hackles.

7. Wrap light hackle forward. Tie off, laquer and whip finish.

Finished Fly

FALL RIVER SPECIAL

This pattern was first shown to me by a group of friends from California who use it to imitate small light mayfly hatches which occur on some of the spring creeks and rivers of northern California. It's design is very similar to the eastern Light Cahill, but with a few modifications. In sizes 16, 18 and 20 it can be a deadly pattern on the Henry's Fork or the Snake. I have even tied a number of these with light green bodies and used them to imitate small caddis hatches. Make a slight change by adding a dubbed cream fur body to ths fly and you have a western Light Cahill.

I have found that the important thing about this fly is to use stiff ginger hackle. Its thread tapered body makes it very insect-like and gives it more durability than a dubbed fur body. I tie this fly with genuine wood duck flank feathers only, and from all indications it is still the best material to use for the wing. If it is impossible to obtain wood duck, substitute dyed mallard sides. Try this pattern on some small spring creeks and see if it doesn't produce when there is a light cream mayfly hatch occuring.

MATERIALS: Fall River Special

HOOK: Mustad 7957B or for a lighter tie, Mustad 94840.

SIZES: 12 through 22.

TAIL: Five hairs of stiff light-colored elk body hair.

BODY: Tapered cream monocord.

WING: Genuine wood duck — lemon flank feathers (or dyed mallard).

HACKLE: Ginger — very stiff, extra-select. A light or dark ginger can be used.

THREAD: Cream monocord.

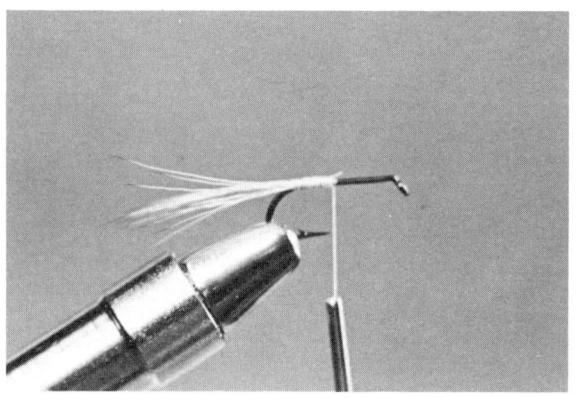

1. Tie on several strands of elk hair light ginger to light cream in color with cream monocord.

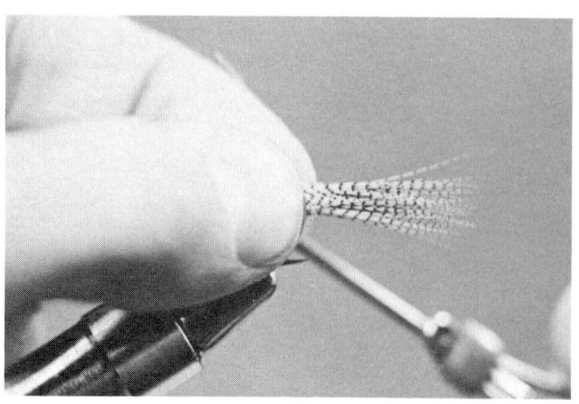

2. Tie on wood duck feather forward — about half way down shank.

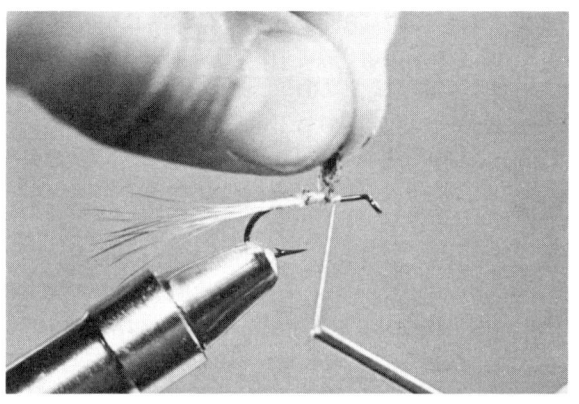

3. Pull feather up and wrap thread to front.

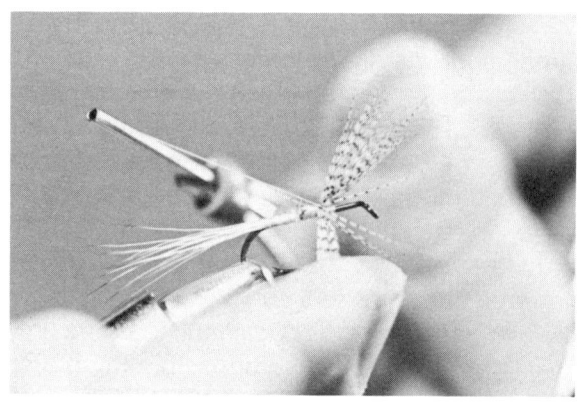

4. Divide wing in half.

5. Wrap circularly around wing closest to you then repeat process on other wing. Wings should look divided.

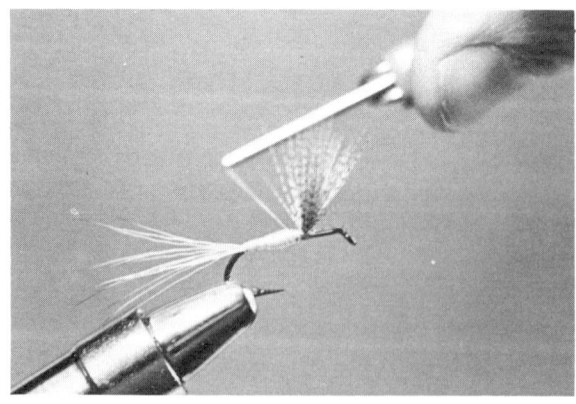

6. Wrap thread from back to front forming a tapered body.

7. Tie in two ginger hackles, a light or medium ginger preferred. Notice ends of vein are sticking between wings.

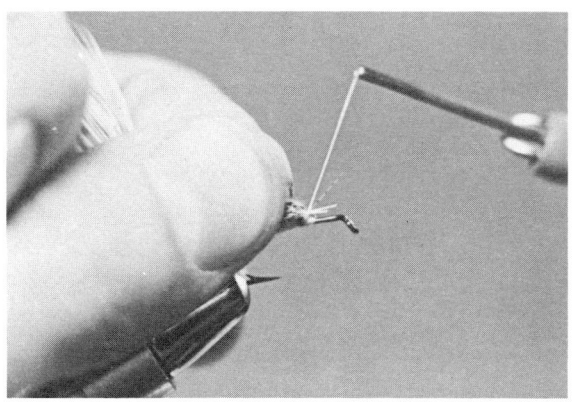

8. Tie down or trim hackle vein.

9. Wrap thread forward.

10. Start wrapping hackle and trim any hackle that strays.

11. Wrap hackle behind wing.

12. Complete hackle and whip finish.

BLACK MIDGE

The midge fly series is a popular collection of flies for the West. These small flies, usually tied in sizes 16 through 28, are found in most tackle shops throughout the Rocky Mountain area.

The fly I have featured in this series is the Black Midge which will give you the basis for tying most midge patterns. Almost all standard dry-fly patterns can be tied in the midge series. Many patterns are tied without wings in small sizes, and are intended to suggest color and form rather than detail.

The midge flies can imitate a number of insects. In western waters even in winter it is not uncommon to see trout rising to sparse hatches of dark midges. These flies often fall on nearby snow banks soon after hatching. The sight of these insects crawling around on the snow has given rise to the mistaken belief held by many that they hatch from the snow itself. Hence, the popular, but misleading name, "Snowfly", has been given these winter-born midges. As a matter of fact, in many tackle shops throughout the Rocky Mountains the Black Midge pattern (and some other midge patterns) are simply known as "Snowfly" patterns.

It is an important late-winter and spring fly and also an excellent spring-creek pattern. In the East, midge flies are important ties for low-water conditions of summer.

In my opinion, midges should be tied on a stout hook rather than on a light, wire hook that could bend out. This is important when fishing water that holds large fish. Too often I have seen a fly tyer using an extra fine wire hook to get the lightest possible fly. He finds himself very disappointed when a large trout straightens out the hook. The old theory which holds that large trout are caught with large flies is not altogether true in the West. There have been many expert fishermen who have landed six to seven pound fish on flies, size 18 and smaller.

Two of the finest small-fly fishermen I have had the pleasure of knowing are Jim Poor of Littleton, Colorado and Jim Kinker, of Jackson Hole, Wyoming. Both are experts in their field. Jim Poor's favorite stream, the South Platte River, is noted for its small-fly fishing. There is no question about his being king of the small fly in Colorado!

Jim Kinker is one of the many Wyoming anglers who ventures to the Henry's Fork of the Snake River, fishing its many hatches during June and July. He has become quite proficient at fishing the area with small no-hackle flies and midges. It takes a sharp eye and a keen sense of timing to hook a fish when it hits a tiny midge on the end of a long, fine leader, but Jim can do it as well as anyone I know.

Jim Kinker is a biologist, school teacher, and fishing guide, and has called upon his knowledge of aquatic life to help him with small fly selection. This has served him well while fishing the streams of Yellowstone Park. He often chooses the Black Midge when he fishes the Firehole and Madison. During the summer Jim is associated with me in our guiding operation and has become a well-known figure in the fishing world of the Jackson Hole Valley. From early April fishing on the Snake River when he is casting hackleless flies or midges, and on into the latter part of October when he is throwing heavily weighted Muddlers into the Snake River, Jim either guides or fishes steadily. We have worked together on many small fly pattern developments. Jim has made many suggestions that have proven indispensable, and we hope that you find our version of the Black Midge to your liking for those tiny fly situations.

MATERIALS: Black Midge

HOOK: Mustad 7957B, 94848, or 3906.

SIZES: 18 to 22.

THREAD: Herb howard black pre-waxed thread.

TAIL: About four or five fibers of dark moose hair.

BODY: Three strands of black ostrich herl.

HACKLE: Black select neck hackle.

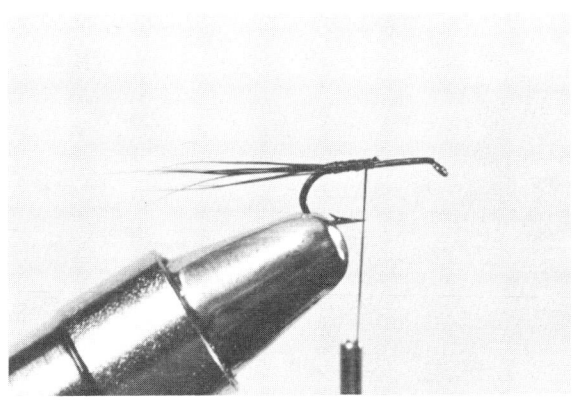

1. Tie on several strands of dark moose hair.

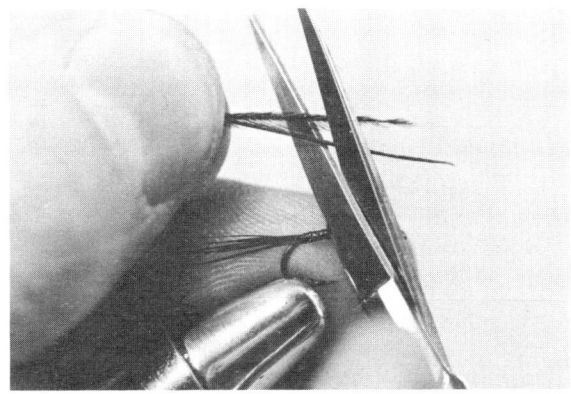

2. Take two thick ostrich herls. Trim to make even and tie on hook.

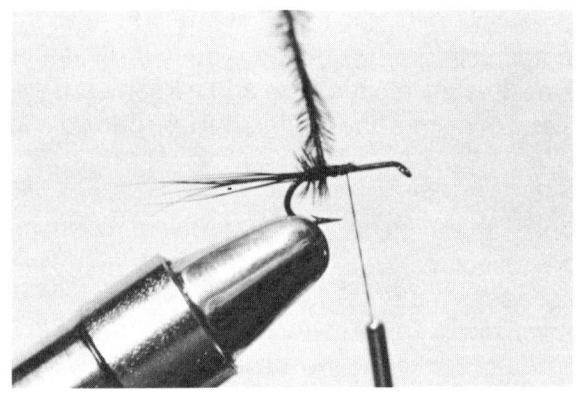

3. Wrap ostrich herl forward making thick body.

4. Here is the thick juicy body. Notice proportions.

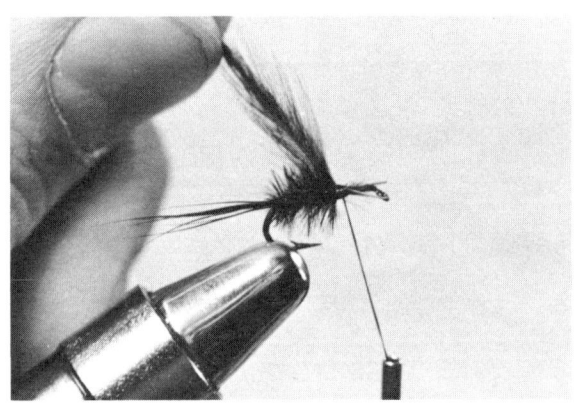

5. Tie on one or two black neck hackles, dry-fly style.

6. Wrap hackle forward. Does not necessarily have to be heavy hackle. Usually three wraps are sufficient. Whip finish and cement head.

Finished Fly

BLACK ANT

This adaptation of a terrestial insect has developed into a standard Western fly pattern. It performs effectively when fished an inch beneath the water's surface film, especially during the summer red and black ant hatches when the ornery, biting little critters fill the sky. Sudden mountain showers wash these ants and other terrestials into the water where their body construction allows them to float either on top or just under the surface. It is essential then, to fish them on a dead drift with no action at all. The ant which this fly imitates is the flying variety with translucent wings which power it through the air. When you spot one buzzing around your head try this black ant imitation. Several other imitations exist including a few with deer hair that are very provocative. I suggest you try several imitations to find which one tempts the fish in your area.

MATERIALS: Black Ant

HOOK: Mustad 3906 or 7957B.

SIZES: 8 to 20.

BODY: Black thread laquered.

HACKLE: Two black neck hackles.

TAG: Red laquer or red thread or floss.

TAIL: None.

THREAD: Either black monocord or any heavy black nylon thread.

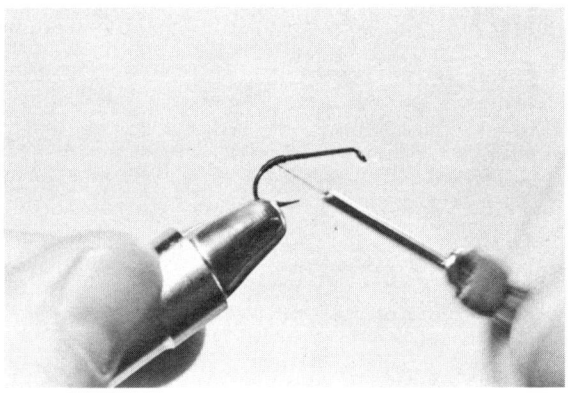

1. Start wrapping thread toward bend of hook.

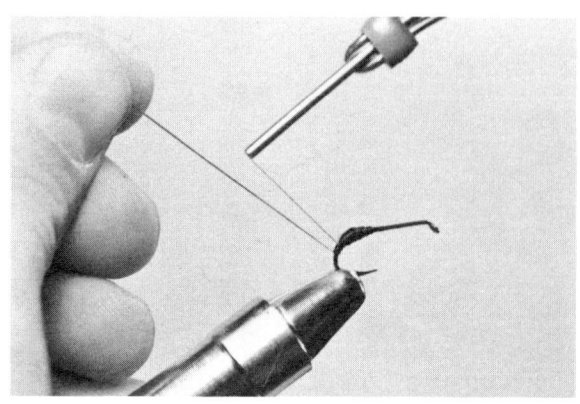

2. Wrap thread thick and add a tip of red floss and tie off.

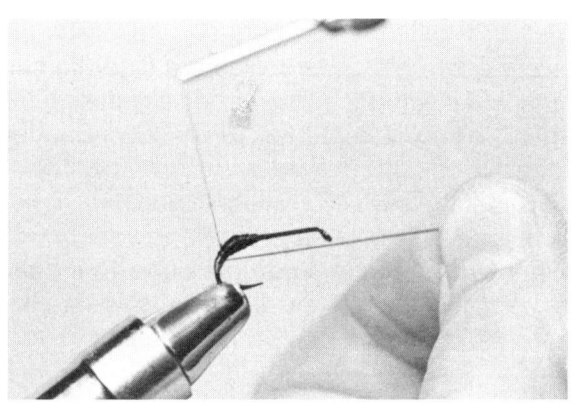

3. Continue after trimming floss off to build body.

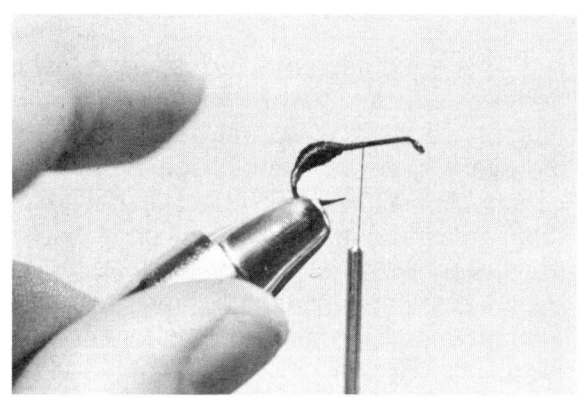

4. Complete body.

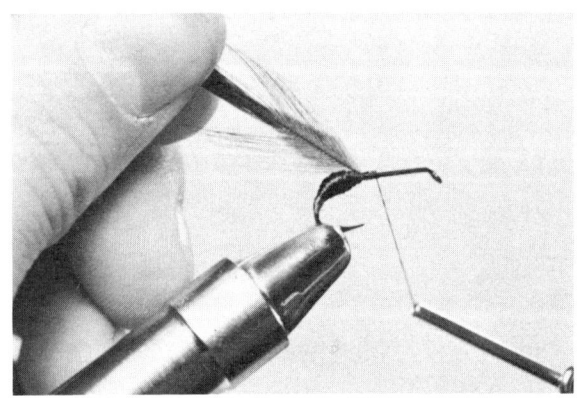

5. Add black neck hackle, one or two depending on desired thickness.

6. Wrap hackle forward dry-fly style.

7. Form head in proportion as above, whip finish.

8. Laquer both head and body thoroughly.

Finished Fly

BADGER SPIDER

Spider flies are very effective in the West — especially on a windy day when they skate across the surfaces of small creeks. These small flies are best used either on creeks and springs, or on ponds and lakes small enough to fly fish effectively. When tying this fly, the greatest consideration should be given to select hackles that are long and stiff enough to tip-toe across the surface film of any water you fish. This requires a high quality hackle that is usually found in a super select saddle hackle.

Some spider patterns are tied with tinsel bodies. I suggest tying them with either stripped peacock herl or stripped hackle veins that render a very insect-like effect with excellent floating qualities. There are spider hooks made, but if you do not have any of these on hand a good, light wire hook will do. Spiders can be tied on a standard dry fly hook if the fly is tied very sparsely.

The Badger Spider is an extremely effective fly in the Yellowstone area. I have found brown trout to be very vulnerable to it (much more so than rainbows and cutthroats). The largest brown trout that I ever caught fell victim to a number 16 Badger Spider tied on a Wright and McGill Eagle Claw up-eye hook, because at that time I could find no up-eye dry fly hooks available. It was not nearly as delicate as regular hooks made for fly tying but it served the purpose. I was 13 when I landed that 8½ lb. Brown!

MATERIALS: Badger Spider

HOOK: Mustad 9523 or Mustad 94833 or 94838.

SIZES: 10 to 22.

TAIL: Badger hackle barbules.

BODY: Stripped peacock herl, or stripped badger or grizzly hackle vein.

HACKLE: Extremely oversized badger saddle hackle of exceptional quality.

1. Tie on a badger hackle fibers forming tail. Strip one badger neck hackle using only the vein and tying the smaller end to the shank of the hook, laying down a thread base as shown above.

2. Wrap vein forward forming a quill body.

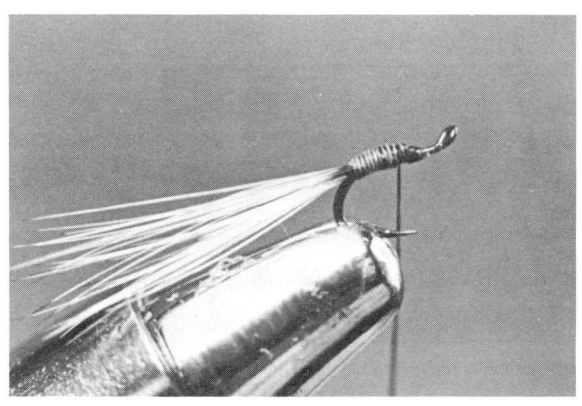

3. Tie off vein. Make sure there is plenty of room to tie on hackle.

4. Tie on one spade or extremely wide saddle hackle. Trim butt end so that butt of hackle does not block eye.

5. Wrap hackle forward. Do not under- or over-hackle the fly. Usually three wraps is sufficient. Tie off hackle, whip finish and laquer.

Finished Fly

BIRD'S STONE FLY

This stone fly imitation was tied by Cal Bird, of San Francisco California. It imitates an adult stone fly and as such, is one of the most realistic and renowned of all stone fly imitations. Although it may not be as widely used as a Sofa Pillow, it more often than not catches more fish. One of the reasons that its popularity has failed to overtake other Stone Fly imitations is that it is difficult to tie. I have tried to make the instructions as clear as possible so that it can be tied without undue effort. All the major fly shops of Montana handle this pattern, and usually recommend it as the best stone fly imitation.

Cal Bird made several stone fly nymph imitations along the same lines as his adult imitations. They are a good series of flies to have in your box if you plan to make the annual fly hatch on the Madison and Yellowstone rivers. A few of these Bird's stone flies will make your trip to Montana a pleasant and successful one.

I recommend that you use an STP French Fly Dressing on this particular fly. It does need a little help to keep it floating well, and this is the best thing I have found to give it the necessary boost. It is available in most fly shops and through several large fly material mail-order houses.

There is not any real secret in fishing the Bird's stone fly. Of course the major requirement is to have a stone fly hatch to work with. Many western rivers do have stone fly hatches which may be locally referred to as Willow flies, trout flies, salmon flies, or other various names. In Montana you might hear the name salmon fly more often than stone fly. These major hatches usually last for one to two weeks. It is good to check with the local guides on the usual time that they occur in order to plan to be there at the right time. The Bird's Stone Fly is the one to bring for these areas when the hatch is on.

MATERIALS: Bird's Stone Fly

THREAD: Black or orange monocord.

HOOK: Mustad 9672, or Mustad 79580, or Mustad 9671.

SIZES: 4 to 14

TAIL:	Two strands of heavy moose hair, laquered, or two stripped hackle veins.
BODY:	Orange wool or floss.
RIBBING:	Furnace or reddish brown trimmed saddle hackle.
WINGS:	Dark bucktail or fox squirrel tail.
HACKLE:	Furnace saddle hackles.
ANTENNAE:	Laquered moose hair — two strands, or two laquered hackle veins, stripped.

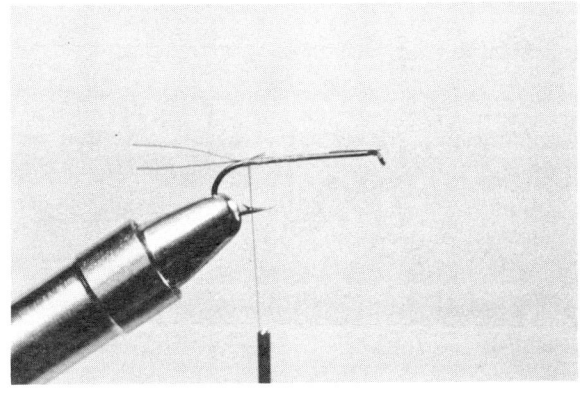

1. Strip two brown neck hackles leaving only the vein. Tie on divided as shown above.

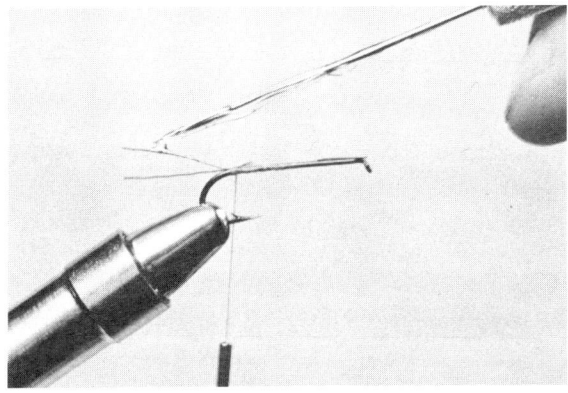

2. Laquer tail as shown above.

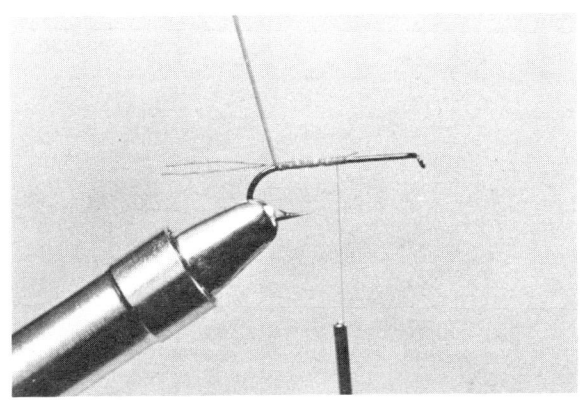

3. Tie on a four strand orange floss. Tie base at middle of hook.

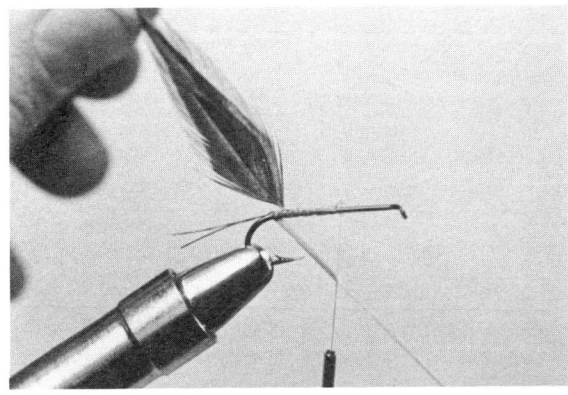

4. Tie two furnace saddle hackles in and make one wrap of orange floss behind saddles. Tie them in dry-fly style.

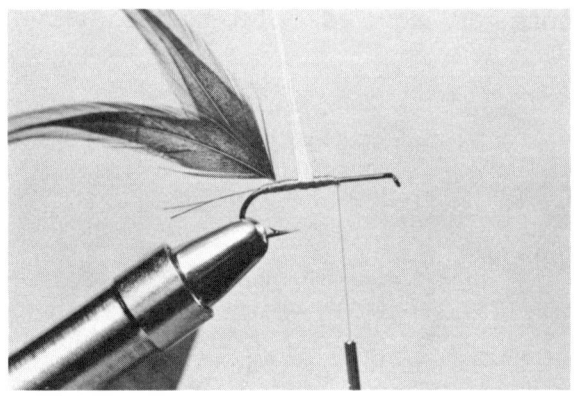

5. Wrap floss forward forming body.

6. Laquer body thoroughly. Notice proportions.

7. Wrap furnace hackle forward very thickly and tie off.

8. Trim hackle on sides. Trim hackle below and above fly.

9. Hackle should appear as shown above when trimmed.

10. Tie on brown bucktail and measure using only long fibers.

11. Tie down bucktail. Bucktail should not exceed tail in length.

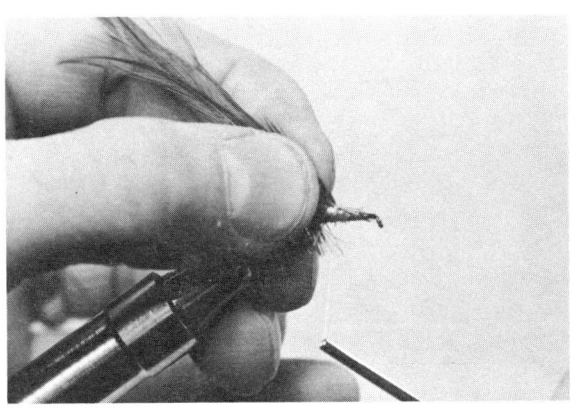

12. Tie on three to four furnace saddle hackles.

13. Laquer thread base thoroughly.

14. Wrap furnace hackle forward forming a thick hackle.

15. Tie on two heavy dark moose hairs for antennae as shown above.

16. Fly should appear as above. Whip finish and laquer.

17. Trim hackle off top and bottom, leaving only hackle protruding from sides.

Finished Fly

SOFA PILLOW

This stone fly imitation is one of the very most popular flies in the west today. On the Madison, Yellowstone, Gallatin, Beaverhead, and Big Hole rivers, its patterns are used for the spectacular stone fly hatches which occur there. It is tied in two different styles; the Standard Sofa Pillow, and the Improved Sofa Pillow. I tie the patterns in two colors — gray or brown. In northwestern Wyoming, the gray pattern is the more effective color, while in Montana the brown is more effective.

The Improved Sofa Pillow was first shown to me by Mrs. Pat Barnes, great lady and fly tier of West Yellowstone, Montana. This particular pattern is an extremely good floater and is becoming more popular than the Standard Sofa Pillow. During the large stone fly hatches that occur in Montana, the flies may vary in size from 2 inches up to as large as 3½ inches. At times they thickly carpet the top of the water and the hatch usually progresses upstream at the rate of a mile or more a day. Most stonefly hatches are usually in full swing from the third week of June to the first week of July. Don't miss this hatch, its an experience you never forget.

MATERIALS:	Brown Sofa Pillow
HOOK:	Black monocord.
HOOK:	9672 or 79580.
SIZES:	4 to 10.
TAIL:	Dyed red duck quill.
BODY:	Either red or orange floss, laquered.
WING:	Fox squirrel tail.
HACKLE:	Four extra-select Indian Brown or other saddle hackles.
MATERIALS:	Gray Sofa Pillow
THREAD:	Black monocord.
HOOK:	Mustad 79580 or 9672.
SIZES:	4 to 10.
WING:	Dyed yellow duck quill.
BODY:	Yellow floss.
WING:	Gray squirrel tail.
HACKLE:	Four select grizzly barred saddle hackles.
MATERIALS:	Improved Sofa Pillow
THREAD:	Black nymo or monocord.
HOOK:	79580 or 9672.
SIZES:	4 to 10.
TAIL:	Medium brown or light elk hair fibers.
BODY:	Orange wool or polypropolene.
RIBBING:	Brown saddle hackle palmer style.
WING:	Medium brown or light elk hair fibers.
HACKLE:	Four extra-select brown saddle hackle.

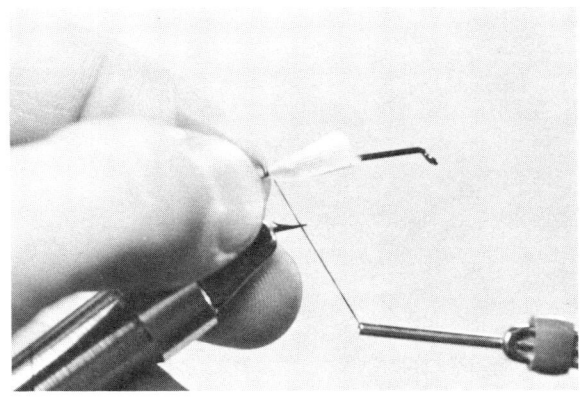

1. Tie on one red duck quill for tail with curve of feather pointing up.

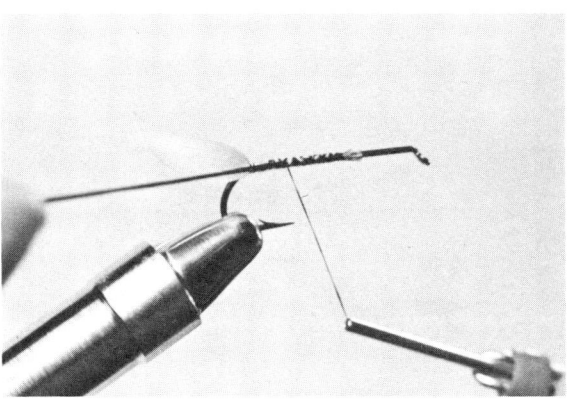

2. Tie on either orange or red floss.

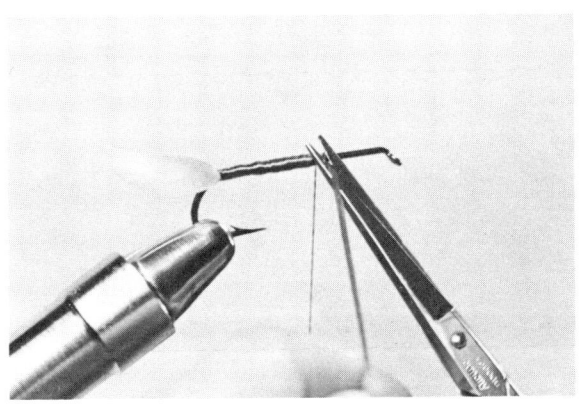

3. Wrap floss 2/3 down shank. Floss may be laquered at this point.

4. Select some fox squirrel tail and remove all short fibers leaving only the long. Measure. Tips of hairs should not exceed tail.

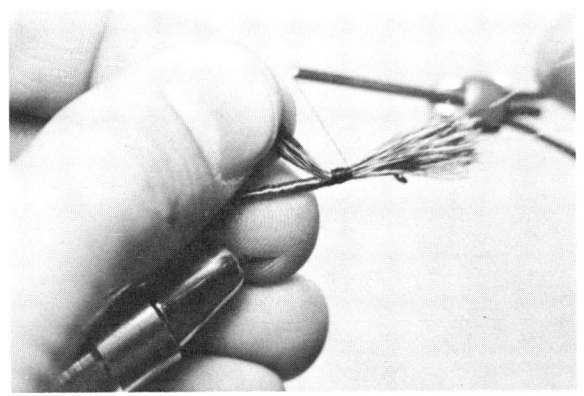

5. Tie down fox squirrel tail very tightly.

6. Tie in four Indian select reddish brown or medium brown saddle hackle, dry-fly style.

7. Add head cement on thread portion.

8. Wrap two hackles forward.

9. Tie off first two hackles. It is not necessary to get them extremely dense.

10. Wrap second two hackles covering spots missed by first two hackles giving fly fullness and body.

11. Take scissor points and pull out any hackles that may be pulled under. Whip finish, and laquer.

Finished Fly

HORNBERG

This fly fished either dry or wet is a legend in its own time. The origin of the Hornberg is questionable, but it seems to have been designed in the mid-western U.S. as a bass fly. It was then taken to Canada where it fooled the Canadian brook trout as well. It began its career as a wet fly but has since been developed into a diversified dry fly that imitates a number of insects, such as the caddis, stone fly, alder, and damsel fly. Originally the Hornberg was tied with jungle cock-eyes, but because of the recent embargo, these feathers are very scarce. I thus recommend a suitable imitation, and am illustrating one way to imitate the Jungle Cock feather for this fly.

The Horn fly's light construction lets it settle on the water quite gently in spite of its large size. When fishing it dry-style, cast it upstream and let it drift back on a dead float. Some anglers strip the fly back wet-style after it has completed its drift, dry it out, then re-cast it dry-style. It attracts restless fish at night too for it can imitate large moths. I have found that the Hornberg tied in sizes 14 and 16 is a great small caddis imitation. I often fish one particular river in Idaho, where I have found light-colored caddis hatches (almost of a white nature). There I use a Hornberg in sizes 14 and 16 with very dependable results.

MATERIALS:	Hornberg
THREAD:	Black Monocord thread or Herb Howard Prewaxed
HOOK:	Mustad 9671, 7957B, or 3906B
SIZES:	2 to 16
BODY:	Either gold or silver flat medium tinsel.
WINGS:	A down wing of yellow calftail or bucktail, and two outside wings of mallard breast.
CHEEK:	Black hackle tips topped with white hackle tips.
TAIL:	None
HACKLE:	Either grizzly or mixed brown grizzly saddle or neck hackle.

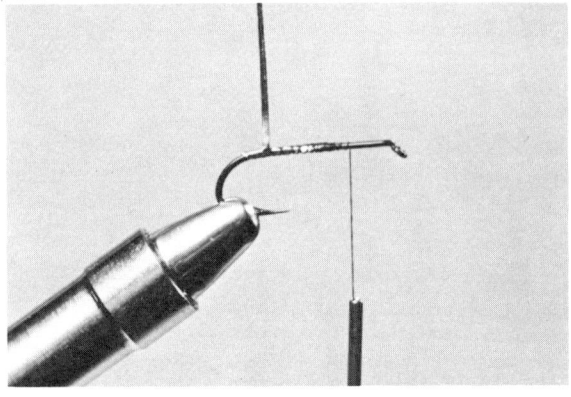

1. Tie down some medium gold tinsel and wrap forward.

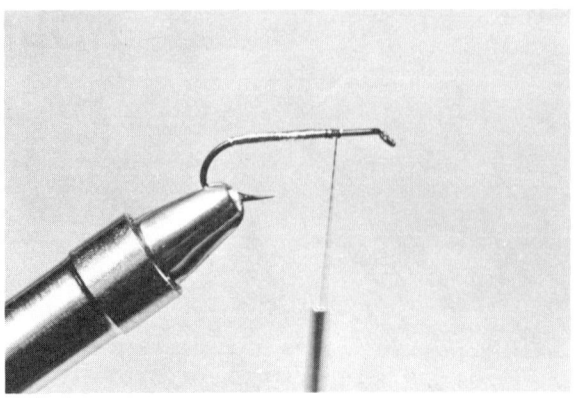

2. Wrap tinsel forward and stop, using proportions shown above.

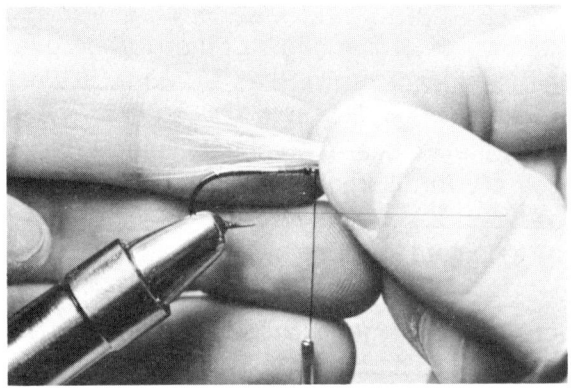

3. Tie in a small amount of yellow bucktail. Be sure to note length and not to exceed it.

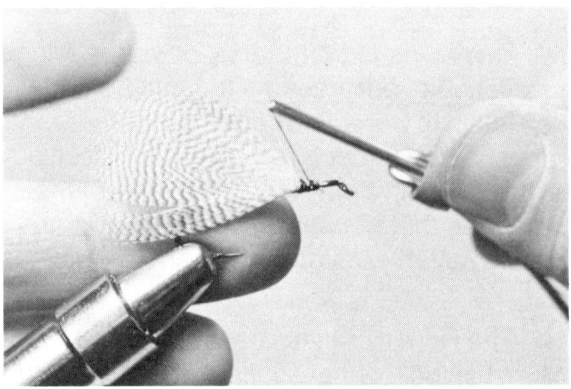

4. Tie on one barred mallard breast on one side and another mallard breast on the other side melding together. One length should not exceed the other. They should be matched.

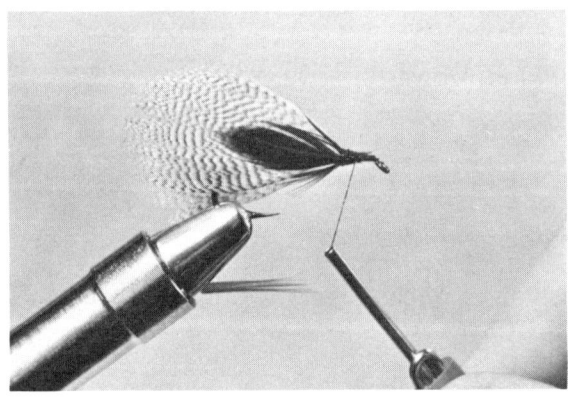

5. Tie in one thin hackle dyed black so it melds right along with the barbed breast feather. This should be repeated on the other side.

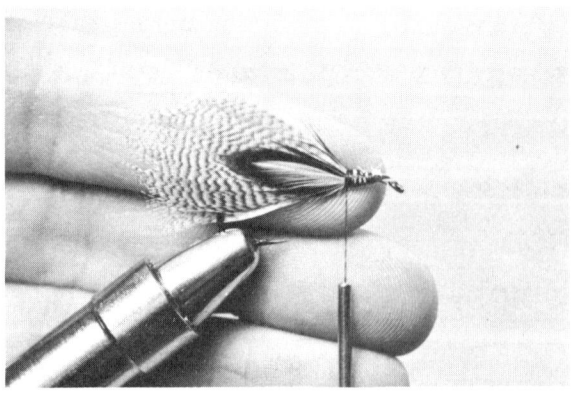

6. Tie in a small cream dry neck hackle right against the black. This will form an imitation jungle cock eye.

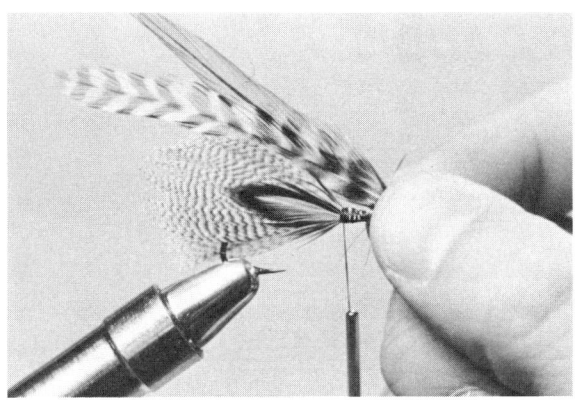

7. Take one medium brown and one grizzly hackle saddle, glossy side facing the rear (dry fly style). Tie on and wrap forward.

8. Make sure the hackle is tight enough to support a wing if you intend to fish the fly dry. (If you intend to fish it wet, reduce quantity of hackle.) Whip finish and laquer.

Completed Fly

KING'S RIVER CADDIS

This down-wing caddis fly was developed in California for the famous King's River. The late Buzz Buszek tied the fly for local California waters. He then sent samples to many areas of the West and heard that it worked on all streams where large caddis hatches occured. It functions tremendously if tied larger for the coastal rivers of Oregon, Washington, and California, and smaller for the spring creeks and rivers of Idaho and Montana. In sizes 16 and 18 the fish always mistake it for a real caddis on the insect-rich Henry's Fork River of eastern Idaho.

Many different body colors and hackle colors combine to make this a versatile fly for the Rocky Mountains. I suggest that you match the caddis colors for the area you plan to fish. I believe the caddis performs best if cast in the standard dry fly fashion. Sometimes it can represent a live caddis trying to escape imprisonment in the surface film if the rod tip is twitched to give the fly natural agitation. I have heard outstanding reports on the King's River Caddis tied in sizes 16, 18, and 20 for eastern rivers of New England, so I suggest that my eastern fishing friends try this pattern.

MATERIALS: King's River Caddis

HOOK: 9671, 3906, or 7957B.

BODY: Orange floss.

WING: Turkey Quill.

HACKLE: Brown neck hackle.

RIBBING: Brown neck or saddle hackle tied palmer style and trimmed.

THREAD: Large sizes, black monocord; small sizes Herb Howard prewaxed thread.

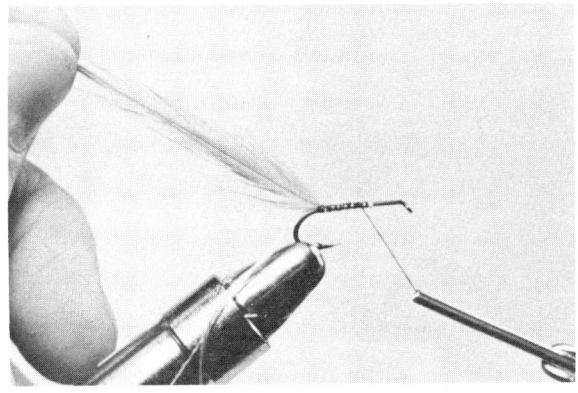

1. Tie in one medium brown neck hackle either yellow, or orange flat four-strand floss.

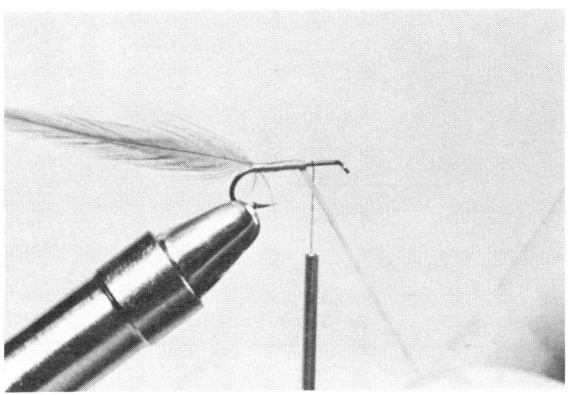

2. Wrap floss forward and tie off.

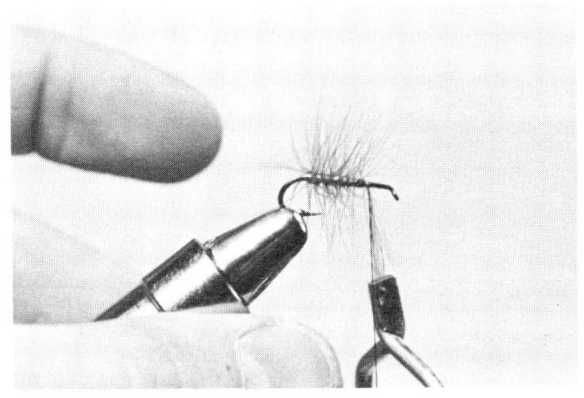

3. Wrap hackle forward Palmer-style, extremely tight.

4. Trim hackle both top, sides and bottom. Use forefinger of left hand to keep thread out of the way and from being trimmed.

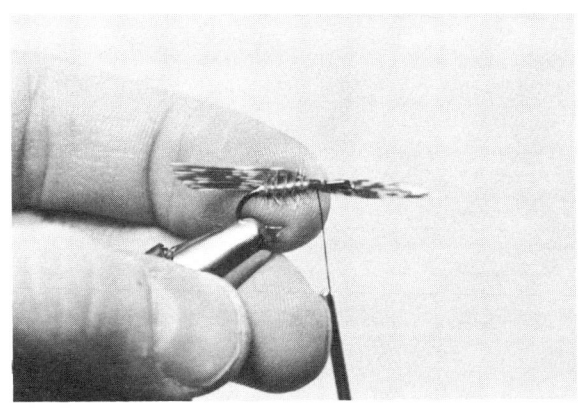

5. Tie on one side of mottled turkey quill. Tie on at tip of feather instead of base.

6. Tie on an equal amount of turkey quill again at tip matching turkey on other side.

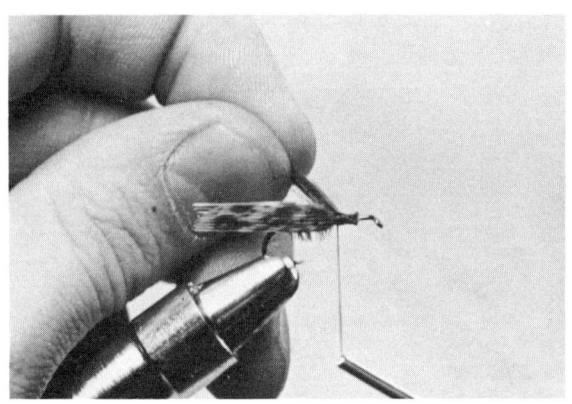

7. Tie on two medium brown neck hackles, dry-fly style.

8. Wrap hackle forward. Tie off trim, head cement and laquer.

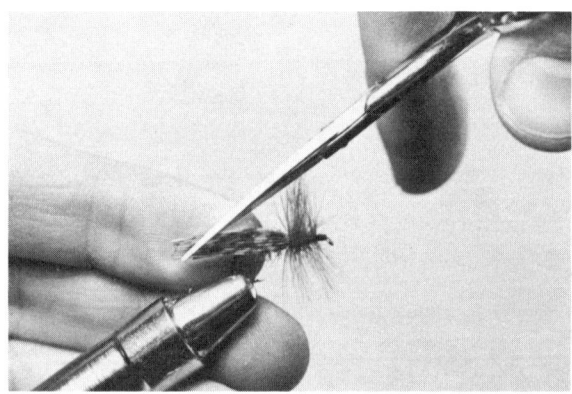

9. Trim turkey quill wing.

Finished Fly

COLORADO CAPTAIN

This version of the Captain was developed in Colorado by several amateur tiers and although throughout Colorado many fly shops carry it, few other areas have caught on to this useful fly. I consider it important in that it is a Westernized version of a popular standard pattern. Its style resembles the Royal Coachman and it should be fished accordingly.

Colorado fishermen have been instrumental in adapting many eastern flies for the West. One of the most important tyers doing this is Jim Poor of Littleton, Colorado. He has been called Colorado's fishing laureate and rightfully so. He has advised many of the world's fishing greats in his "Anglers All" tackle shop on the subtilties of tying flies for the Rocky Mountain area. He specializes in Colorado's South Platte River. Many of his friends claim that no one is more familiar with the South Platte than Jim Poor. His theories are widely accepted and his flies truly a work of art. Every year Jim makes an annual fishing expedition to Montana, Idaho, and Wyoming, but just outside his back door the South Platte offers one of the greatest challenges to fly fishermen. In my opinion he ties the finest small dry fly I have ever seen, in sizes 18 through 28. He is a wizard at tying and fishing these small wonders. Besides all that, his knowledge of nymphs is uncanny. I never cease to be amazed at how many good fly tyers and fly fishermen Colorado produces. Here in Wyoming, we receive annual visits from Colorado fly fishermen who bring many new patterns developed there. Every year a new one (such as the Colorado Captain) catches my eye.

Another good Colorado fly that has been introduced to me is the Colorado King tied by George Bodmer, who operates a fine fly fishing shop in Colorado Springs. George has indoctrinated many new anglers to the sport of fly fishing in Colorado Springs, an area which was previously untouched. Fast gaining a national reputation, George's Caddis flies are highly renowned in Colorado. You will find his Colorado King pattern in the fly pattern dictionary at the end of this book, on page 245. I recommend that you try the Colorado Captain, and other Colorado designs for the West. Jim Poor has claimed to me that these flies work just as well on the East Coast. With a little modification, and a little experimentation on your part you can discover a whole new world of eastern fishing.

MATERIALS:	Colorado Captain
THREAD:	Black monocord.
HOOK:	Mustad 7957B or 94840.
SIZES:	8 to 18.
TAIL:	Several strands of golden pheasant.
TIP:	Gold tinsel.
BODY:	Three strands of black ostrich.
WING:	White calftail, small diameter, tied upright and divided.
HACKLE:	Select reddish brown hackle, or neck hackle for small sizes.

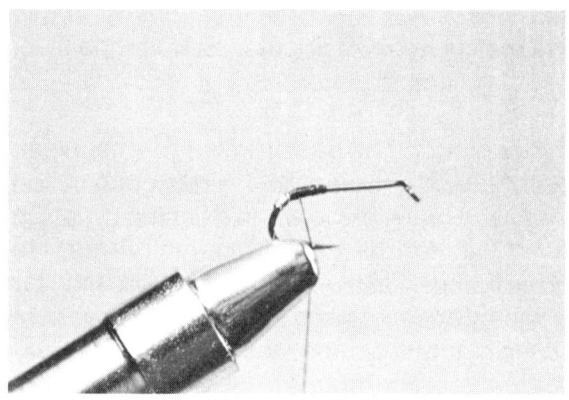

1. Tie on a gold tag of #16 gold tinsel.

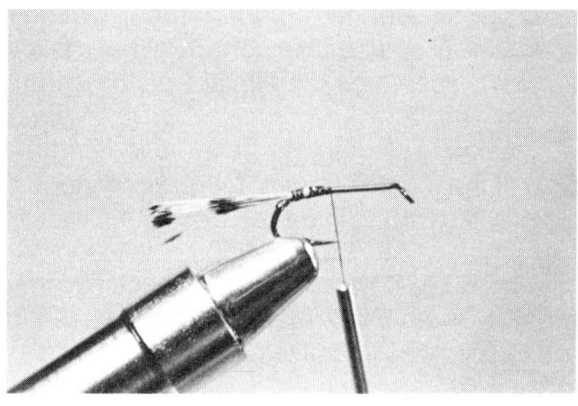

2. Tie on several strands of golden pheasant tippets.

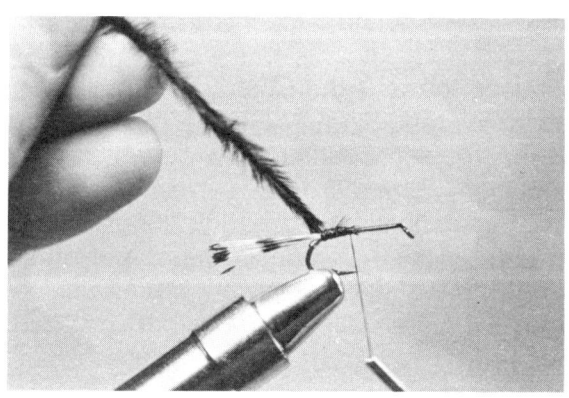

3. Tie on two to three strands of black ostrich herl.

4. Wrap herl forward forming thick furry body.

5. Tie on white calftail.

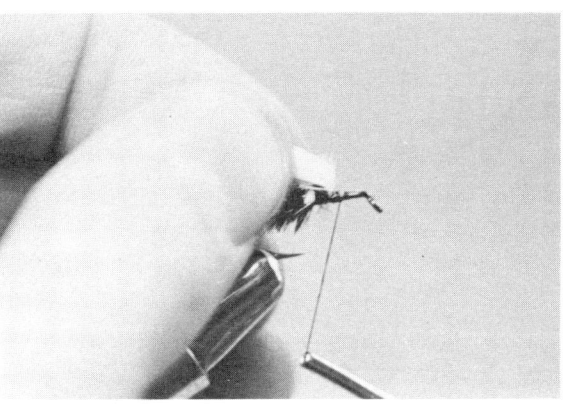

6. Pull back on hair and wrap thread forward.

7. Divide wing and "x" thread between wings — see instructions page 111-113.

8. On wing fartherest from you wrap circularly wrapping thread tightly around it securing it to the base. Then wrap thread around wing facing closest toward you.

9. Tie on and wrap brown saddle hackles, medium brown to red.

Finished Fly

JOE'S HOPPER

    This fine grasshopper imitation traces its ancestry to the state of Michigan. Its acceptance spread West and it has become a standard imitation for grasshoppers. Primarily fished as a dry fly, it deceives fish as a wet fly too, since it represents a small minnow fished this way. A bit of Mucilin on the wings and hackle creates buoyancy; thus large sizes can also be used as stone fly imitations.

    Joe's Hopper performs best during the grasshopper season from the middle of August to the first of September. In small streams with high, grassy bank and slid off into the stream. With a slight twitching of the line the grasshopper will do the hopper stroke like its live counterpart.

    The Joe's Hopper is a great fly for drift fishing in any Western river. On large ones where the current is heavy and deep cast the fly directly upstream and let it float motionless keeping a tight line. Also, when cast downstream ahead of the boat it will float like a cork. It is large enough to be watched by even a poorly visioned angler.

    As for tying the Joe's Hopper, good stiff brown and gray saddle hackle greatly enhances the fly's buoyance. The heavy turkey wings should be laquered either before or after tying this fly. The best method is to spray the whole quill and dry it, then cut two wings from the opposite sections of the same quill. This fly also tricks eastern fish in small sizes, 12 through 16; because, in these sizes it can imitate a caddis fly.

MATERIALS: Joe's Hopper

HOOK: Mustad 79671 or 9672, sizes 4 through 16.

BODY: Yellow chennile or wool.

WING: 2 matched turkey quill sections.

TAIL: Red hackle fibers.

RIBBING: Brown saddle hackle (trimmed).

HACKLE: Brown and grizzly saddle hackles mixed.

THREAD: Black monocord.

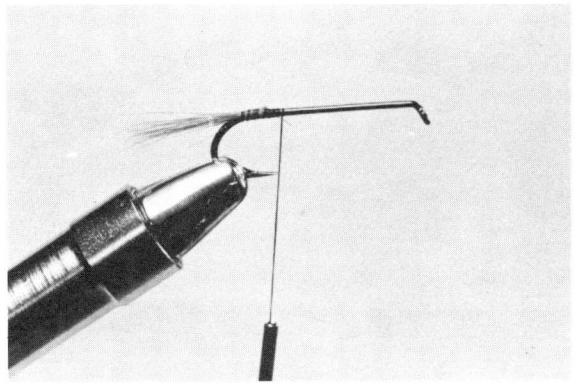

1. Tie on red neck hackle fibers.

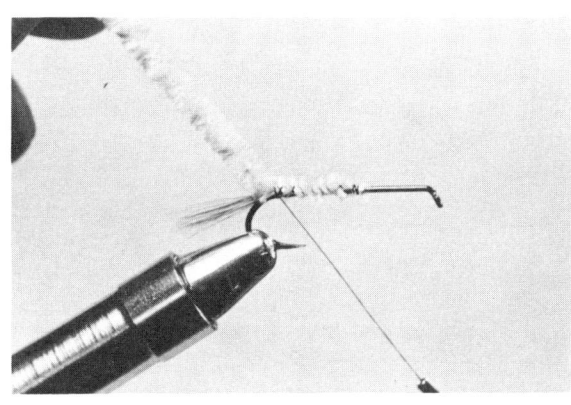

2. Tie on yellow chennile. It is important to tie base chennile at least ½ way down hook to eliminate any lumps in body.

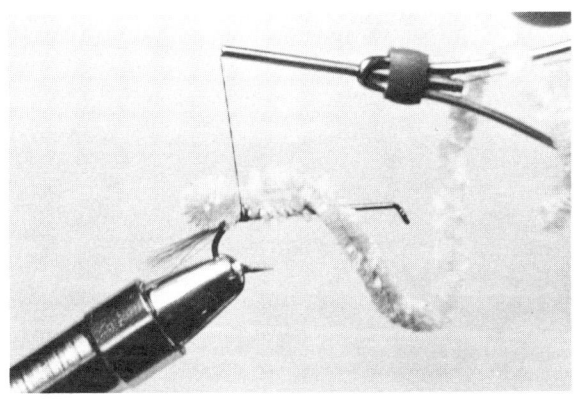

3. Form loop and tie down.

4. Tie in brown saddle hackle. Leave strips of chennile hanging.

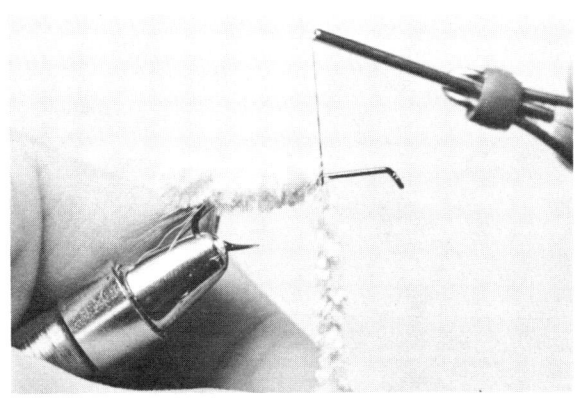

5. Wrap chennile forward. Notice loop of chennile which forms an extension of body. Tie off chennile.

6. Wrap saddle hackle forward very thickly. Tie off and trim.

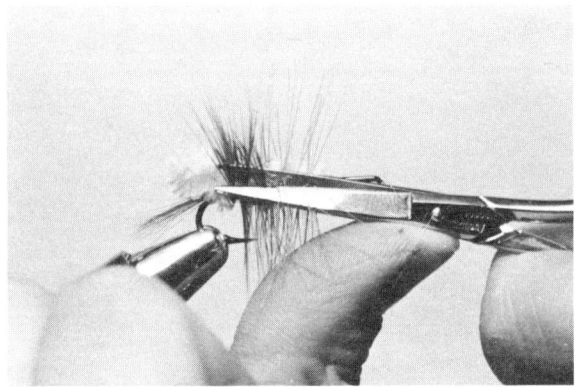

7. Using thumb to guide scissors trim hackle tight on sides of fly.

8. Tie on one laquered turkey quill. Notice how finger is holding quill next to body.

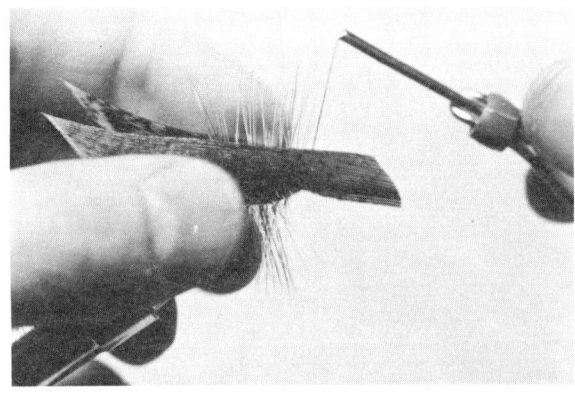

9. Tie on a corresponding quill on other side again thumb and forefinger holds them together. Tie down tightly.

10. Tie in one brown and one grizzly saddle hackle. Tie both in tightly and use thread to smooth base for hackle.

11. Laquer thread base.

12. Wrap hackle forward, tie off, trim and whip finish.

13. Trim ends of laquered turkey forming final product.

Finished Fly

Special Hair Fly Section Dry Flies

Step by Step Instructions

HUMPY

Sometimes known as a "goofus bug," the Humpy is probably one of the finest hair flies ever tied for Western trout. Many people claim to have been the first to have tied the Humpy. That question has yet to be settled, and even today there are several traditional methods of tying this fly. People in California used what was fondly called a "Horner's Deer Fly", invented by the late Jack Horner, the famous California fly tier. It resembled the present-day Humpy in many ways but had some slight differences. The name, "Humpy," probably originated around Jackson Hole in Wyoming.

The Humpy's best qualities are its buoyancy and its ability to imitate numerous types of insects. In large sizes it can represent stone flies and large gray caddis flies. In smaller sizes it can imitate various small caddis hatches and even delicate mayfly hatches. Anglers tie it in a wide range of sizes from size 2 for Salmon, to 24 for the most finicky trout. Its ability to "keep on floating after many drownings," makes it a useful fly for those who enjoy fishing heavy, fast water.

The Humpy originally sported a deer hair tail, body, and wing, and grizzly hackle. It usually had a red, yellow, or black body. In Jackson Hole, where I live, one of every two flies sold is a Humpy.

In 1967 I took a close look at the Humpy and decided to try to improve on the basic pattern. One of its faults was that when the fragile deer hair tail was destroyed, the fly could not float upright, and thus, had to be discarded. I also concluded that the hair commonly used for bodies and wings was too coarse and hollow so it split after only a few fish, again making the fly unusable. Originally, the fly came in only one color: basic gray with a red, yellow, or black body. First I gave it a tail made of elk hair. Dark brown in color, it was considerably stiffer yet more flexible, so it held with repeated use. I later found moose body hair even better and more readily available. I then experimented with several body hairs other than deer. I found that light elk created an excellent body and made the fly cream color, thus adding a new dimension. Next I experimented with several types of deer hair and discovered that hair from either a young doe or fawn that had been killed early in the season had more natural oils, was smaller in diameter, and held together more securely. Hair from older deer killed in late winter was much too coarse and made the tying extremely difficult.

About that time grizzly hackle became difficult to obtain and seemed poor in quality, but there was a great abundance of good Indian select saddle hackles. So, I experimented with Badger saddles for hackle. For two years I tried both grizzly and badger hackle and decided there was no noticeable difference in their fishtaking qualities. Even now, I still offer both grizzly and badger hackles to my customers. My preference leans slightly toward the badger as being the stiffer hackle.

Dan Bailey, who lives in Montana, mixes brown and grizzly hackle for his Humpys which he calls "goofus bugs." (Their popular name in Montana.) A few years ago, Mrs. Ramona Bressler, of Jackson Hole, Wyoming, developed an all black Humpy tied with dyed-black deer hair. This pattern took large trout in places one ordinarily wouldn't dream of using a Humpy. One of her black Humpy creations took a six lb. cutthroat from a clear quiet beaver pond — certainly not traditional "Humpy water." Recently, I have experimented with blue dun, brown, and ginger hackles for Humpies and found that they produce in certain situations.

In large sizes the Humpy is a good high-rider on the large powerful rivers of the West. I have talked to people who have fished Oregon's Deschutes River; California's Kern River; East Walker River; rivers in Nevada; New Mexico; Colorado's Gunnison; and the major rivers of Montana. All of them had favorable reports about having fished with the Humpy. Every year the Humpy becomes more popular throughout the United States. A year ago I had a letter from a customer who had fished in New Zealand and swore that the only flies that were successful were some of those "Old Snake River Humpies," all chewed up from a past season's fishing.

I have found that a Humpy in sizes 8, 10, and 12 works well for drift fishing from a boat which we do often in Western rivers, because it has more flotation than most dry flies. It drifts easily downstream from a moving boat and floats much longer than an average dry fly. When fished upstream from the bank it usually floats through the roughest areas and takes fish in water not normally touched by a dry fly. In small sizes 14 to 24 (and tied sparsely) it is amazing how effective this fly can be. I have used it on small spring creeks where there is hardly any current, and believe it or not, it can catch fish. Sometimes when all the small no-hackle and light-tie dry flies have drawn a blank, these small Humpies have worked for me. To this day one of my favorite small dry flies is a number 16 or 18 sparsley tied, badger-hackled gray Humpy.

MATERIALS: Humpy

HOOKS: Mustad 7957B.

SIZES: 2 through 24 (for lighter ties, Mustad 94840 sizes 8 to 16).

THREAD: Monocord, either black, yellow, red, orange, flourescent green or flourescent orange.

TAIL: Dark elk leg hair or moose body hair. (If none of these are available as stiff as possible deer hair.)

BODY: Deer hair or cream colored elk hair.

WING: Tips of the hair used for the body become the wings for this fly.

HACKLE: Grizzly; grizzly and brown mixes; badger; ginger; cream; blue dun; or black.

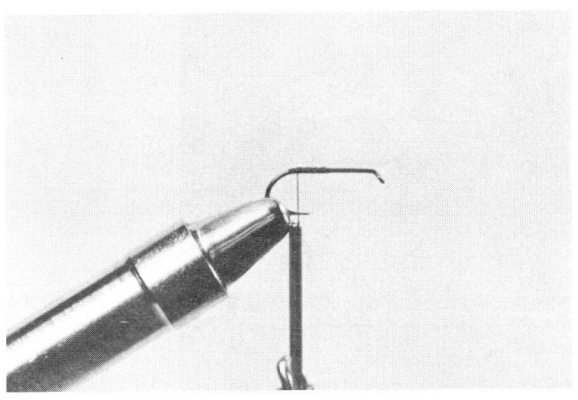

1. Wrap thread on shank forming a base to tie on tail.

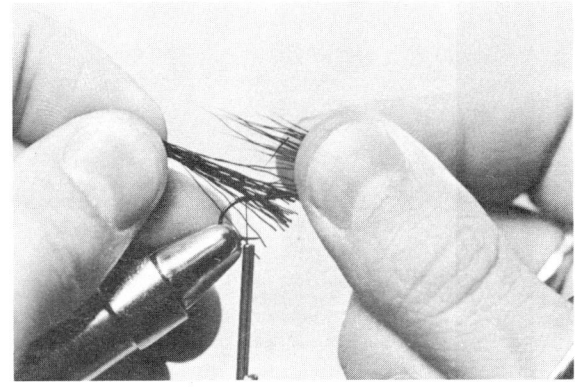

2. Remove small fibers leaving only the long even ones of dark moose as shown above.

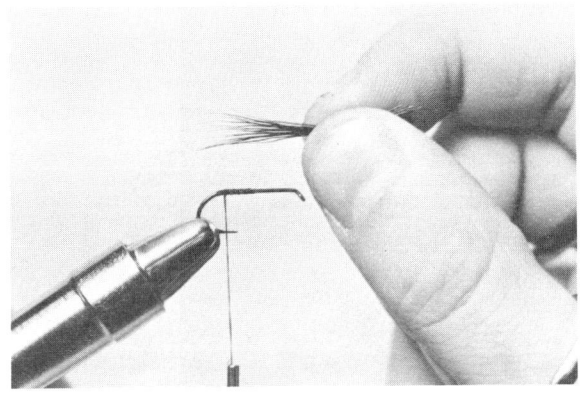

3. Moose tail should look like this. Note that elk should also be used or a dark stiff deer.

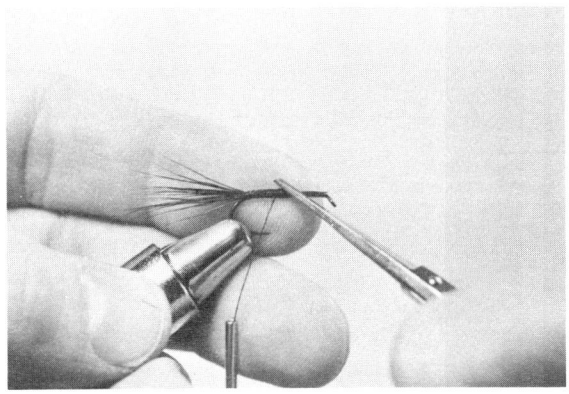

4. Tie on tail and trim. Make sure that tail is tied down tightly.

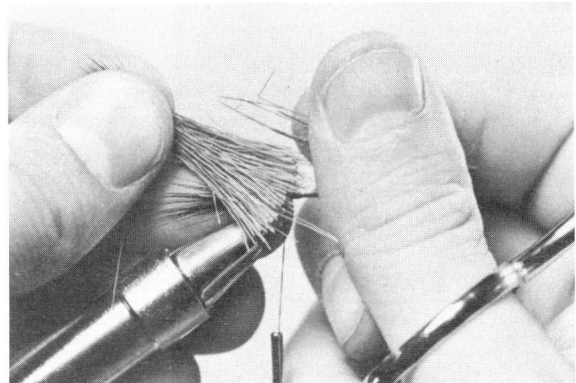

5. Remove all small fibers of deer hair as shown above. This is best accomplished by holding with thumb and forefinger of left hand the long end of the hair, while thumb and forefinger of other hand pull shorter hairs out.

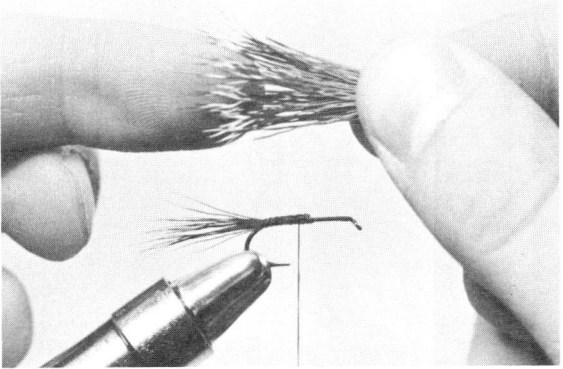

6. Use forefinger of left hand to remove any shorter hairs or fibers that may still be in the tips of the hair. This is best accomplished by moving the finger back and forth separating the fibers so that the shorter ones may drop out. Notice that the thumb and forefinger of right hand are securing the base of the hair.

7. Take deer hair and measure to make sure that deer hair slightly extends beyond the tail that you have already tied on. Notice that thread is tied down ½ way down hook.

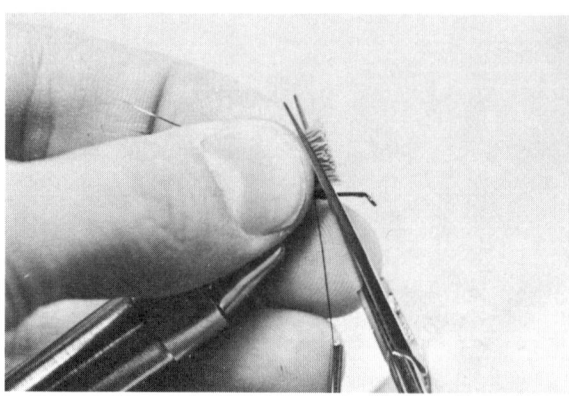

8. Keeping the hair in place reverse fingers and trim more off base. This should be ½ way down the hook. The minute the hair is trimmed, tie immediately to base of hook as shown in next step.

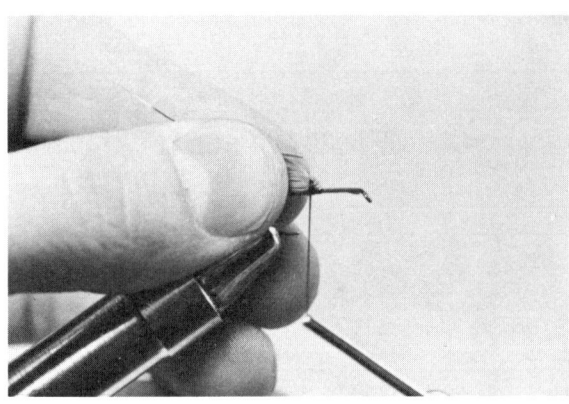

9. Hair is being tied on ½ way down shank of hook. . . . It is tied loosely at first, with every succeeding turn tighter. Thread should proceed toward rear or tail of hook.

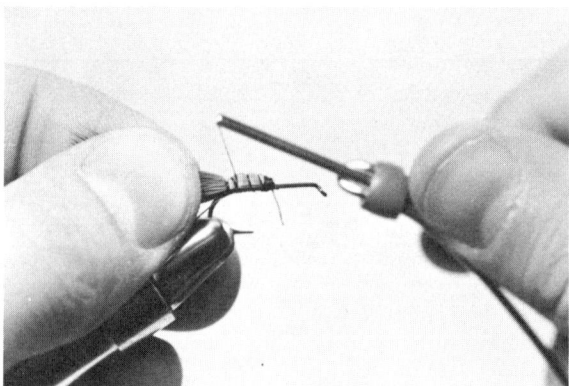

10. As you can see thread is being tied back and forth from the end of the hook toward where the hair was first attached.

11. Continue to wrap thread until there is no remaining deer hair showing. Notice that the deer hair ends and the body begins is directly up from the end of the barb.

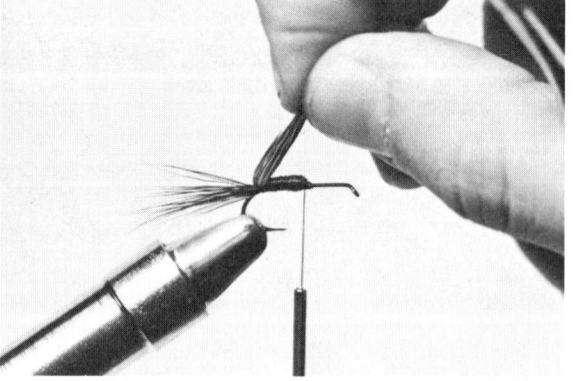

12. With thumb and forefinger of right hand pull the deer hair straight up giving it a slight twist.

13. Pull deer hair forward toward eye of hook. With left hand move bobbin to other side of fly making sure that the thread matches where the hair was originally tied on the shank of the hook. Pull thread directly down with left hand, as shown in next step.

14. As you can see the thread has been pulled down tightly forming a hump. This hump should not be loose but should be pulled tight. If you have a large hump that is not proportionate to the hump in the picture you are using too much hair.

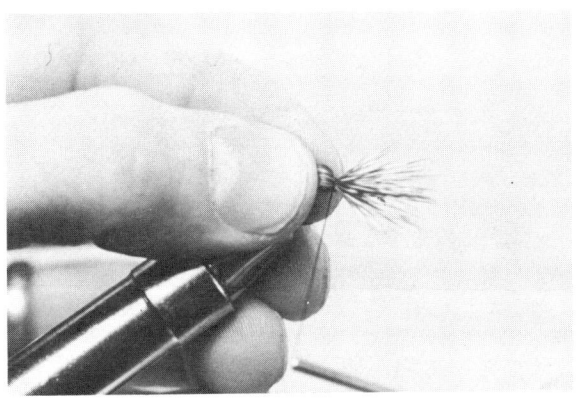

15. Wrap thread with right hand securing the deer hair to the hook with more wraps.

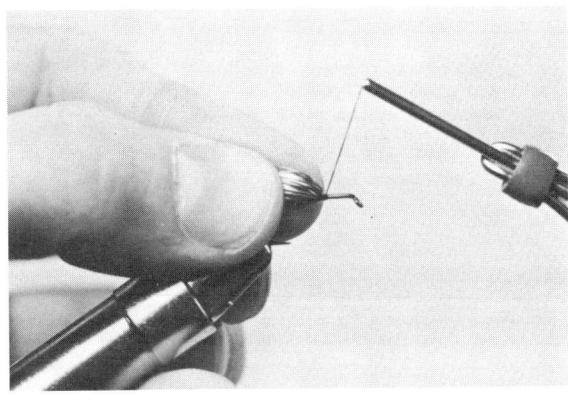

16. Wrap in front of hook pulling deer hair back. This will keep the body from sliding forward. The remaining hair will be used to form wing.

17. Divide wing using a criss-cross method, wrapping thread from front to back then reversing it wrapping it from back to front.

18. Wrap from front to back securing wing. Use thumb and forefinger to cock wing back up.

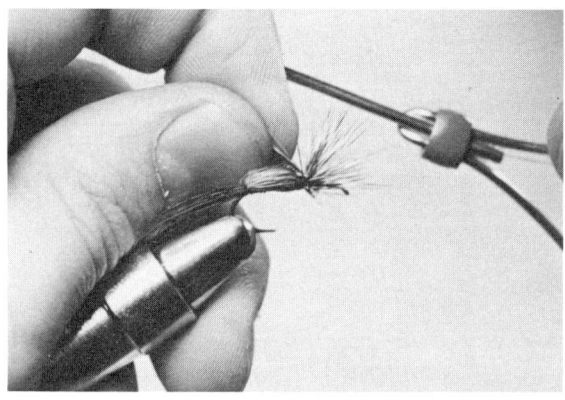

19. Tie on two saddle hackles these may be either badger, grizzly, ginger, or brown, depending on your choice.

20. With thumb and forefinger, slide both hackles together. Then attach hackle pliers.

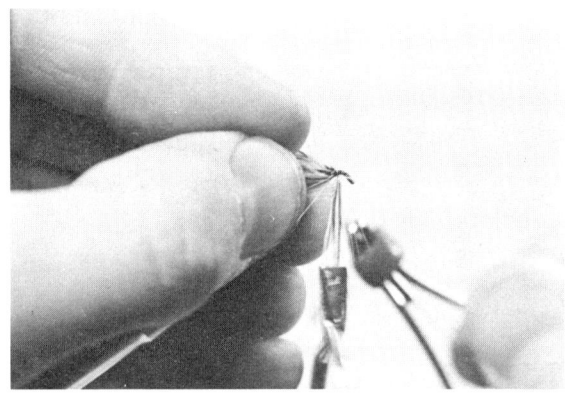

21. Wrap evenly making even wraps with hackle behind wing and then continuing forward wrapping in front of wing. Wing should be in middle of the complete hackle.

22. Pull back on wing and hackle. Tie off, whip finish and laquer. It is important that this fly is not crowded at the head. Otherwise it will float on top of its head rather than floating properly.

Finished Fly

ROYAL HUMPY

In my opinion this fly is the greatest dry fly in the West today. I have yet to find a place where it fails. In small sizes, such as eighteen and twenty-four it is the most deadly western spring creek fly that I know. In the Henry's Fork of the Snake River, the Royal Humpy has taken rainbows that exceeded seven pounds. It has also accounted for a seven pound brown from Yellowstone's Lewis River as well as several six pound cutthroats from Wyoming's Snake River. Reports from Montana claim that it is the best heavy-water fly for brown trout that the fishermen there have found. The fly has existed for only four years and the reports of its success are still flowing in. In sizes 10 through 14 it is one of the most highly visible and buoyant dry flies now tied.

Although I am the first one to have tied the Royal Humpy, I cannot take credit for its invention. I worked out the mechanics of tying the Royal Humpy, but the man responsible for its existence is a former guide, friend and companion of mine, the late Charles Ridenour.

Charlie worked for me during the last few years of his life. A native Pennsylvanian, one time collegiate wrestling champion, and a graduate of Penn State University, he was an avid fly tier and fly fisherman. Charlie left me his collection of wonderful, old fishing books which includes a first edition copy of Ray Bergman's TROUT. He left behind a vast collection of wonderful memories of times spent on the river and at the tying bench, but one of the most important things Charlie left me was the idea for the Royal Humpy.

One day we were floating along fishing and talking about flies. I was rowing while Charlie was casting a humpy against the bank. He turned to me and exclaimed, "My gosh, I can't see that fly, my eyes are just getting too old. If only I had tied on a Royal Wulff I could see it!" I quickly reminded him that he had tried the Royal Wulff prior to tying on the Humpy, without a single rise. This situation was very unusual on the Snake since the Royal Wulff is one of the most productive patterns there. He leaned over, looked at me and mused, "You know, I've been thinking for several years, the two best flies on this river are the Royal Wulff and Humpy. If someone could just work out a combination of these two, it would be a fly with great fish-taking qualities and I'll bet it would be a heck of a floater."

I gave some thought to Charlie's idea but stored it in the back of my mind. A couple of weeks later I was fiddling around in the shop when Charlie walked in and said, "By golly, I tried to tie that new fly we talked about, but I just can't get the wings to stay anchored on the deer hair. Sometime I will have to get you to tie it for me." I could see the problem Charlie had in tying the fly. Although he was an expert fly tier, he was somewhat lacking in the patience which is essential for tying a new fly. Again, I pondered his ideas for the new fly and made a mental note to try tying it someday.

Two weeks later Charlie died leaving me a bookcase of fine fishing books and the idea for a new fly. After his death I thought about doing something that would be a fitting memorial to him. I considered hanging his old guiding cap in my shop with a plaque dedicated to his memory. But that just did not seem to be the thing. So, three months later I finally sat down to tie his Royal Humpy. As he had put it, that would be the only logical name for the fly.

That was in 1970 and now the Royal Humpy is a reality and a winner among flies.

MATERIALS: Royal Humpy

THREAD: Red or yellow monocord.

HOOK: Mustad, 7957B or 94840.

SIZES: 6 to 24.

TAIL: Several fibers of dark moose hair.

BODY: Light gray natural deer hair.

WINGS: White calf-tail. Divided upright.

HACKLE: Stiff brown saddle or neck hackle, a reddish tinge if possible.

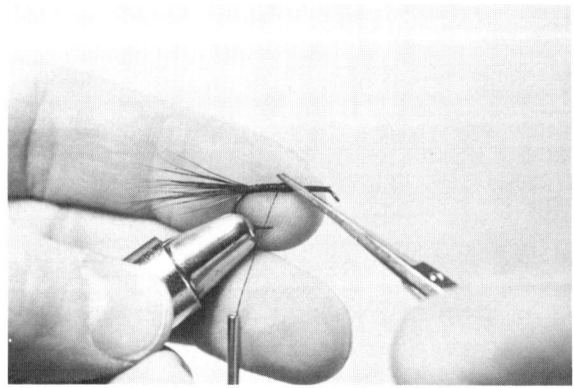

1. Tie several strands of moose hair.

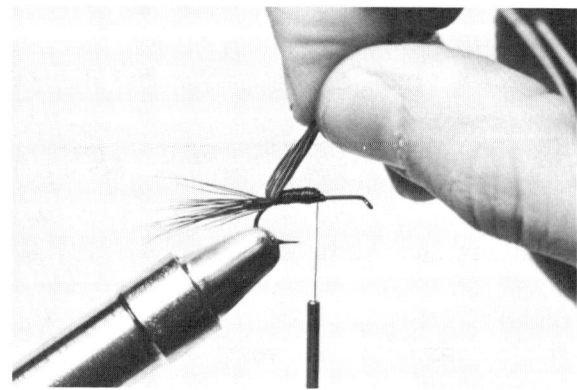

2. Tie deer hair in on shank as per Humpy instructions on pages 81-83.

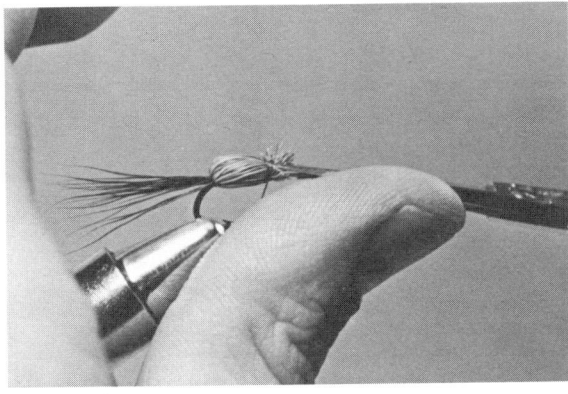

3. After trimming wing, guide scissor points with thumb trimming excess deer hair.

4. Wrap thread over deer hair so you have an even base for the wing.

5. Making sure tips of calftail are even, tie on tightly (tips of wing pointing forward over eye)!

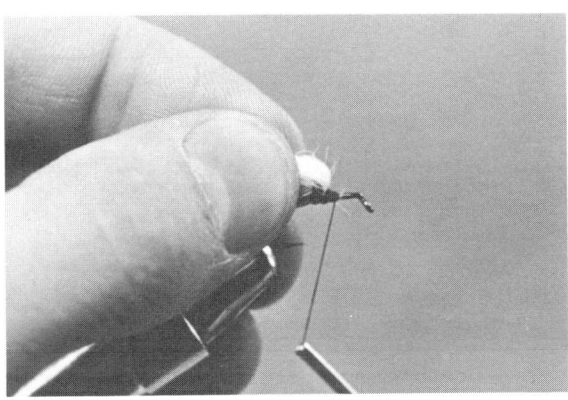

6. Tie in front of wing using thumb and finger to pull back wing. This will keep the wing from sliding forward.

7. Use finger to push wing forward. Take thumb and finger of both hands and divide wing.

8. Wrap thread between wings from front to back.

9. Wrap from back to front dividing wing from other side. This method should be repeated. It is called "Xing."

10. Wrap circle of thread clockwise around the wing; wrapping up and around wing giving a base to thread and tying it tightly.

11. Wrap around other wing, the wing closest to you in same fashion. It is good to hold onto wing and wrap around, releasing wing.

12. As shown previously, continue to wrap around closest wing.

13. With thumb and finger push wings together and trim butt.

14. Tie in two medium brown hackle and make sure that wings are tied tightly.

15. Wrap tying thread forward toward eye.

16. Wrap hackle forward making sure that there is an even amount of hackle behind and in front of wing. Whip finish and cement head.

Finished Fly

PARACHUTE HUMPY

It is the old favorite Humpy tied parachute style, and it is a goodie! The advantage of the parachute tie is that the fly can land on the water with a soft gentle touch! rather than the normal "kerplunk" of a regular humpy. This fly is becoming popular in the West and in several areas of the East. A good amateur tier can easily tie this fly which is the superior floater that he often needs for brushy, heavy streams. There, a good-floater is necessary to slip over the deep pockets found under overhanging branches. The Parachute Humpy is also buoyant on boulder-strewn rivers where average dry flies cannot float. The Parachute Humpy is just the ticket to draw out fish you may not realize are there.

You can tie this fly in several different colors and sizes. Tied with green deer hair it becomes a terrific green drake imitation. Its silhouette on the water makes it appear more natural than many of the heavy deer flies tied these days.

One secret in tying this fly is to drop a little polyurethane cement on the hump and a little on the white wing. This adds a great deal to its durability, for the fly does have the tendancy to come apart at the hump when not treated with the polyurethane.

I consider the parachute humpy to be one of the best boat-flies we have today. It can be cast quite easily from a moving boat, yet provides such visibility that a rank beginner can see it. One of its drawbacks is that in large sizes it does have much air resistance and under windy conditions careful technique is required to cast it correctly. A heavy-butted leader designed for heavy dry flies is a real asset in casting this one. If you have read FISHING THE DRY FLY AS A LIVING INSECT by Leonard Wright, you might consider using some of his theories and methods with the Parachute Humpy. You might find it interesting and very rewarding.

MATERIALS:	Parachute Humpy
THREAD:	Red, yellow, black or green monocord.
HOOK:	Mustad 7957B or 94840.
SIZES:	8 to 20.
TAIL:	Several fibers of moose body hair, or dark deer hair.
BODY:	Either natural deer hair or a variation of dyed deer hair colors.
WINGS:	White calftail (single upright wing).
HACKLE:	Mixed grizzly and brown; badger; ginger; or grizzly hackle. I suggest a nice wide hackle (tied parachute style).

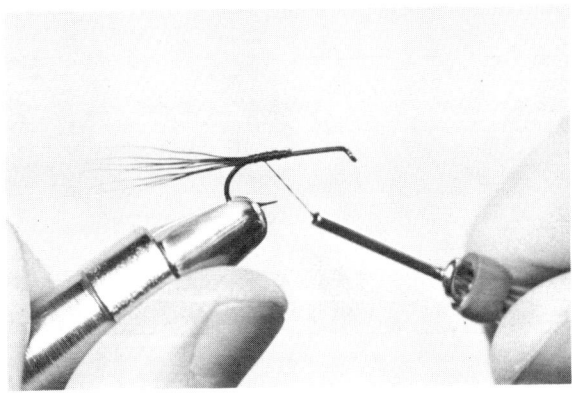

1. Tie in several strands of dark moose hair. Tail should be the length of shank.

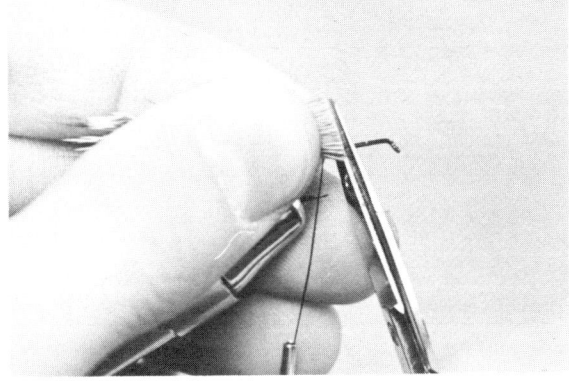

2. Trim deer hair even at base as shown above. (Before this make sure all deer hair tips are even.)

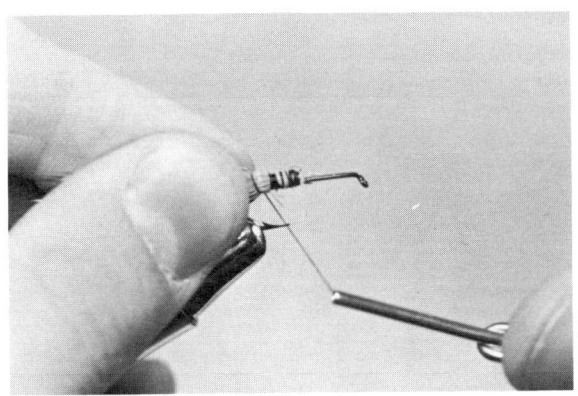

3. Tie down base of hair and wrap forward, tying down hair very tightly.

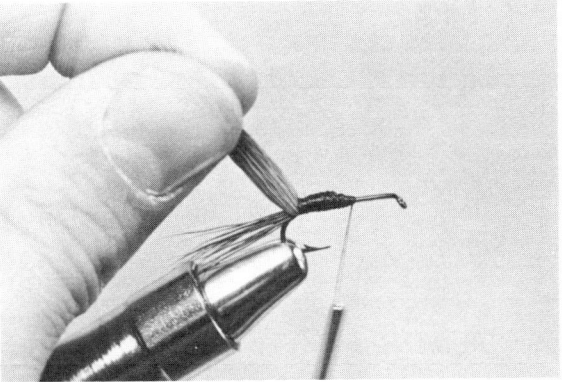

4. Wrap tie thread back and forth over deer hair, making sure that all deer hair is covered. Notice from photo that thread stops just slightly above end of barb. Thumb and finger are gripping hair separating it from tail.

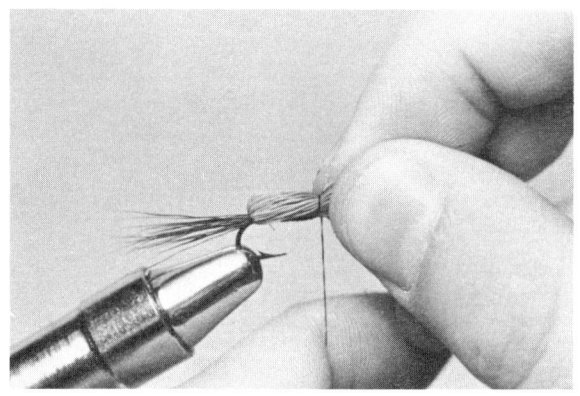

5. Pull hair forward with a slight twist using the left hand with the thread. Pull straight down.

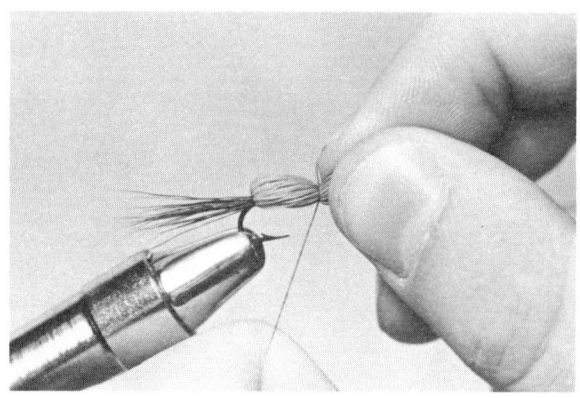

6. This shows thread being pulled tight forming hump. Wrap several wraps at this point.

7. This shows anchoring body securely. Notice excess hair sticking forward.

8. Trim hair and wrap solidly anchoring body. This hump should not be too heavy. If it is, the thread will cut into the hair and the hair will break, ruining the body.

9. Tie in light calftail tips pointing forward over eye. Make sure that hair is tied in securely.

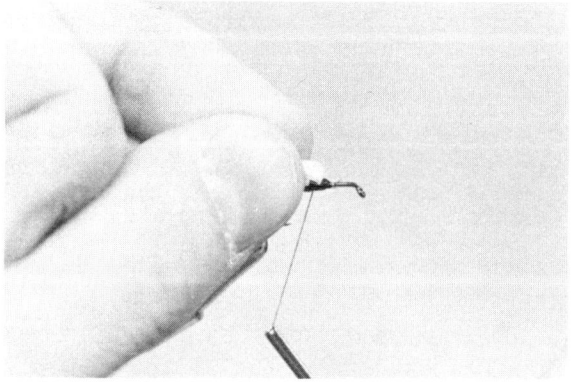

10. Make several wraps in front of wing. Notice how thumb and finger are holding wing back.

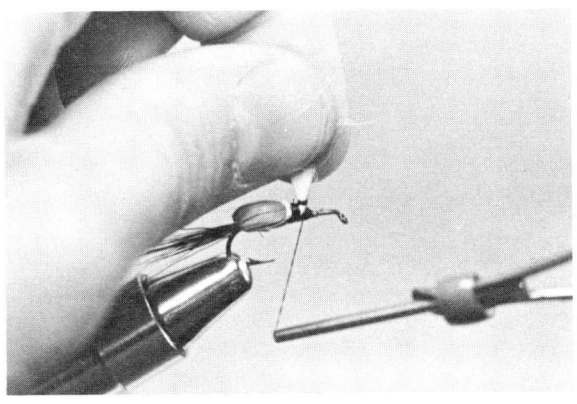

11. Start wrapping clockwise around wing. Notice how thumb and finger are holding wing.

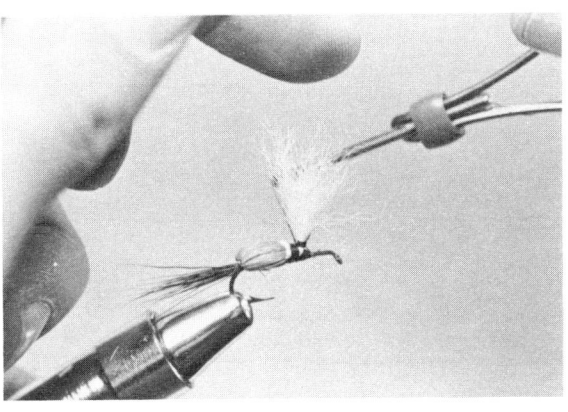

12. As you are going around wing thumb and finger are alternately releasing and gripping wing so that thread is wrapped firmly around base of wing.

13. Shows thread-wrapped upwing. It is important to note that a firm thread base is formed for hackle to be wrapped on. It is important to make it as shown (not too large or too small).

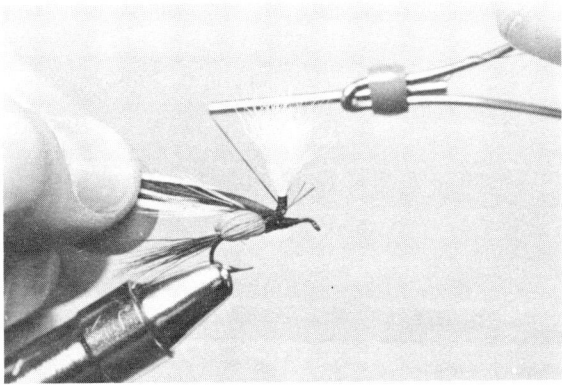

14. Tie in two badger saddle hackles. Notice two hackle veins are tied in a manner so that they can lie up along wing.

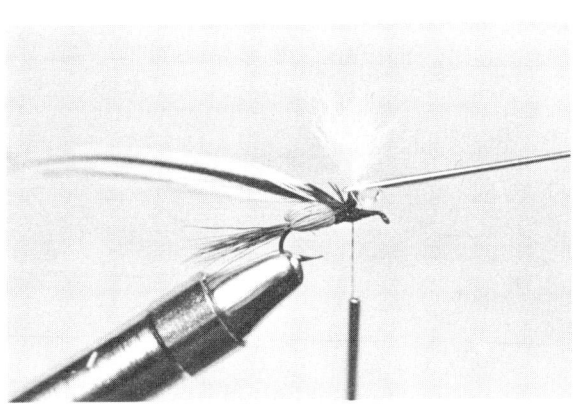

15. Laquer thread base on wing thoroughly and let dry at least four or five seconds.

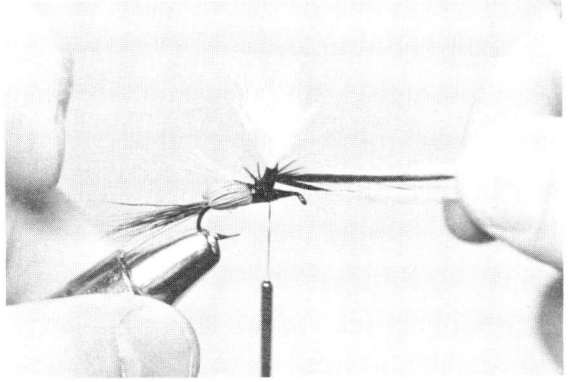

16. Grasping hackles with the thumb and forefinger, make one wrap of hackle clockwise around base of wing tight against the body. Attach hackle pliers.

17. Hackle should be wrapped evenly from body base up to top of thread and back down again.

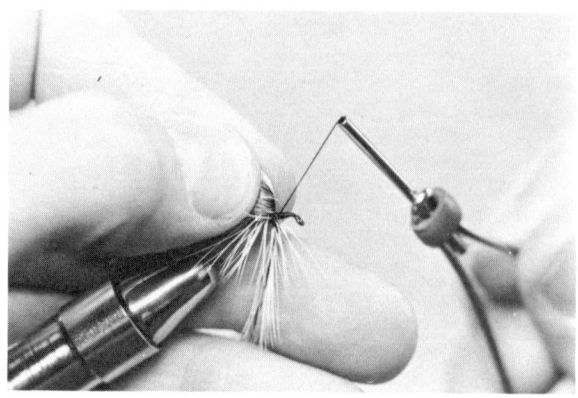

18. Pull back on hackle and wing and tie down. This prevents the forward hackle from being tied down. Notice thumb and finger. Whip finish and head cement.

Finished Fly

ADAMS IRRESISTABLE

The Irresistable has been a well known fly in the United States. This clipped deer-hair-body fly has been one of the top floaters available to the dry fly fisherman. This pattern has been improved upon and redesigned by several tiers. One of the most notable improvements on the Irresistable was made by Hank Roberts of Boulder, Colorado. His Adams Irresistable has become popular throughout the Rocky Mountain area. He was one of the first tiers to give a successful taper and trim the Irresistable's body. In my younger years I learned the proper method of designing, trimming and imparting good floating characteristics to this fly by watching several of his tiers at work. For the past fifteen years I have worked at making further improvements on the Irresistable and I have learned several tricks that will help you tie it.

One of the most important factors in tying a good Irresistable is to use top quality hair. I have found that Caribou hair is probably the easiest to tie. Although it may not be as durable as deer hair, it is much easier to trim to shape than most deer hair. When using deer hair it is essential to have very coarse, thick hair primarily from a small doe or a young buck that has been killed in the early fall. The hair should be taken from the rump area, and not along the back. Any portion of the hair toward the legs also would be desirable. When tying the Irresistable it is necessary to have an extremely durable and sharp pair of scissors, such as the Thompson Adjustable scissors in order to clip the deer hair. Most sharp pointed Solingen steel scissors will not stay sharp enough to tie very many flies. An English pair of scissors marketed by Veniard and Sons has large finger holes and are easily held. (This firm has a catalog for American fly tiers.) They have sharper points than the Thompson Adjustable, but they are not quite as durable.

An important thing to remember when trimming the Irresistable, is to taper it from the back to the front. It should be tapered quite dramatically distributing the bulk toward the middle of the fly. Most people who tie the Irresistable have a tendency to make the body too long, crowding the hackle too far toward the head. Because of the bulk of the body material, extreme care must be exercised to properly proportion this fly. It has the tendency to tip over on its head if it is not balanced properly. I suggest that you study the following pictures very carefully in order to learn the proper proportions. It is also good to use slightly oversized hackles on the Irresistable and make the tail slightly longer than usual in order to balance the fly and support the heavy weight of the body.

When fishing the Irresistable try some small sizes such as 16, 18, and 20. These can be extremely effective in small springs and streams where other flies fail. I like to fish with large sized Irresistables for the heavy rivers of the northern Rockies such as the Madison, Snake and Green. In California it is considered a special fly for the coastal rivers. Reports from Oregon say that the regular fishermen of the Dechutes and Rogue Rivers name the Irresistable as one of their top flies. I have provided in the dictionary in the back of this book, several other variations of Irresistables that you will want to try in your area of the country.

MATERIALS: Adams Irresistable

THREAD: Nymo for the clipped hair body. Black monocord for the hackle and wings.

HOOK: I prefer Mustad 7957B over all others I have tried.

SIZES: 4 to 20.

TAIL: Dark moose hair fibers or brown neck hackle fibers.

BODY: Gray Caribou hair or coarse gray deer hair.

WINGS: Grizzly hackle tips.

HACKLE: Brown and grizzly mixed saddle or neck hackle.

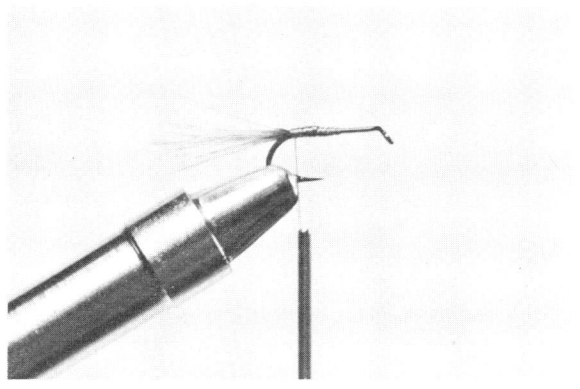

1. Tie on several fibers of brown neck hackle. Tail should be the length of hook.

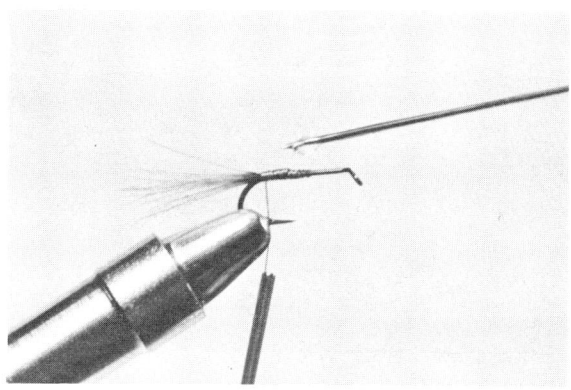

2. Drop on head cement on thread base which is formed after tying on tail.

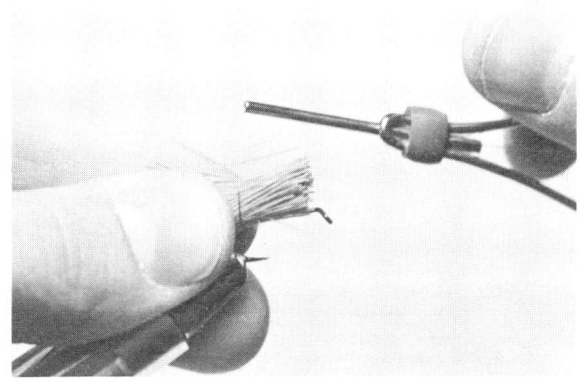

3. Trim a bunch of deer or caribou hair. Trim both ends so that hair is easy to work with. Lay hair directly on top of hook. Start to wrap.

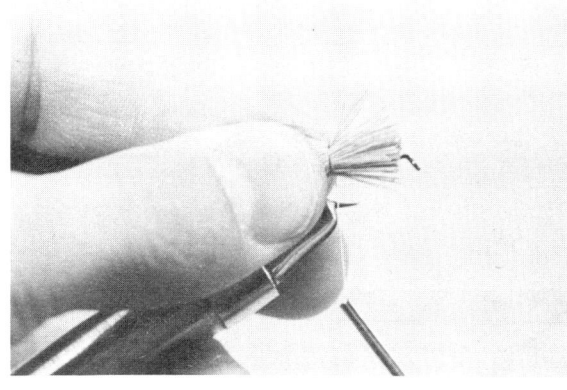

4. Pull down on first wrap. This wrap should be done where the tail begins. (On the base of the hook or approximately at where the rear end of the hook barb.)

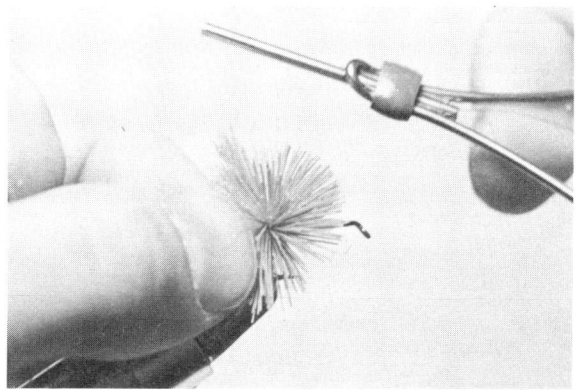

5. Pull tight on hair.

6. Wrap another wrap. Pull even tighter. Hair should spin slightly.

7. Wrap another wrap. Pulling tightest.

8. Lay a second bunch of hair on top of hook against first bunch as shown above.

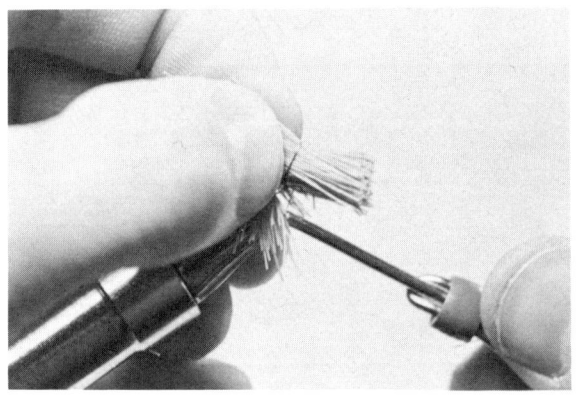

9. Spin hair by pulling down hard on thread.

10. Wrap another time pulling down tighter.

11. Wrap one final time pulling the tightest yet without breaking thread.

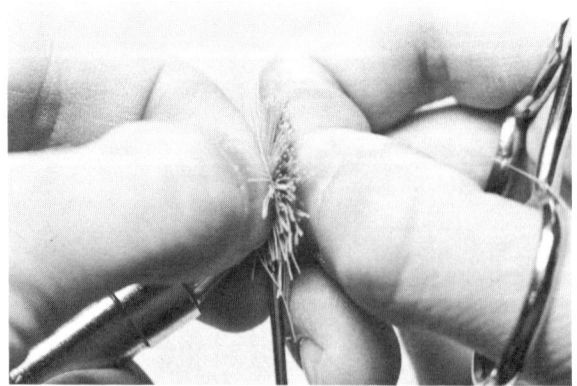

12. With thumb and finger of both hands push both clumps together making hair very tight.

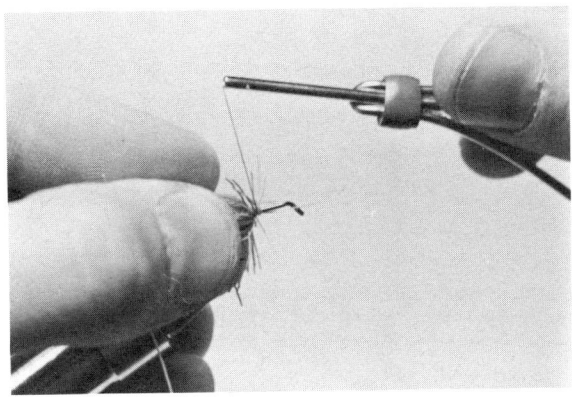

13. Wrap two or three turns of thread in front of the clump of hair.

14. Check your proportions! Match the above picture!

15. Half hitch and tie off.

16. Remove fly from vise.

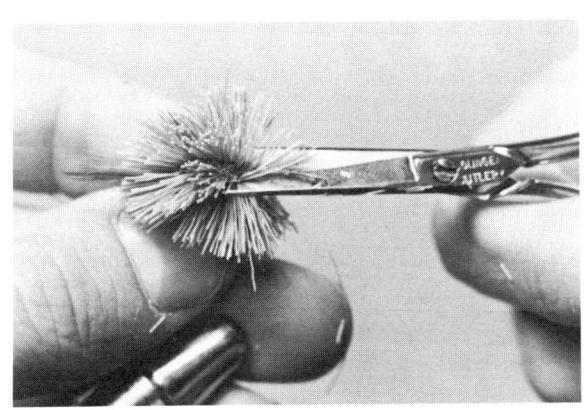

17. Trim under barb hair flat towards tail of fly.

18. A continuation of Step 17.

19. Trim hair towards tail on top of body, tapering as per picture of Step 25.

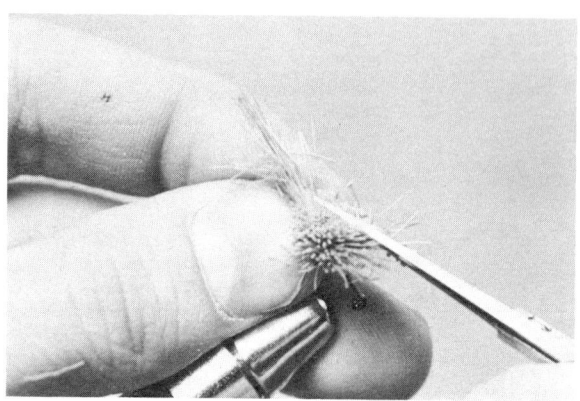

20. Continuation of Step 19.

21. Work trimming along sides of body. Be sure to keep taper!

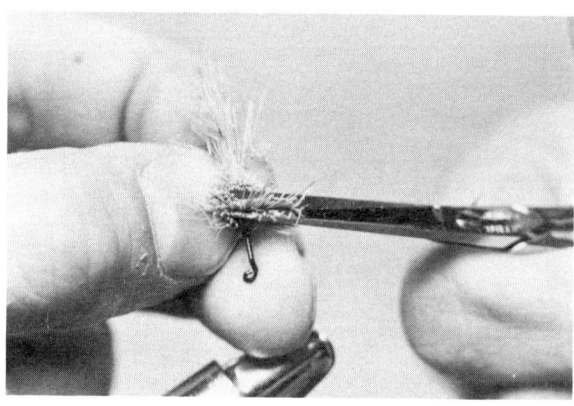

22. Keep trimming all loose stands of hair. Keep taper according to Step 25.

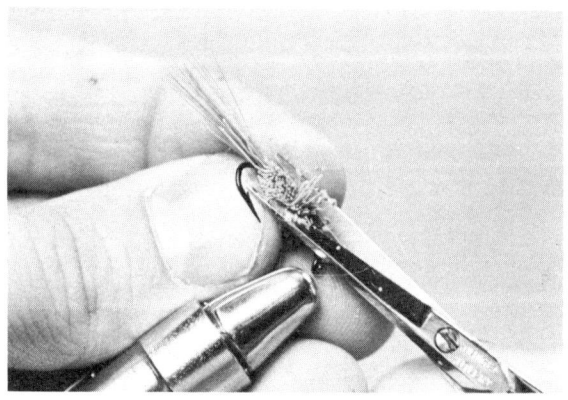

23. Continue to trim and taper.

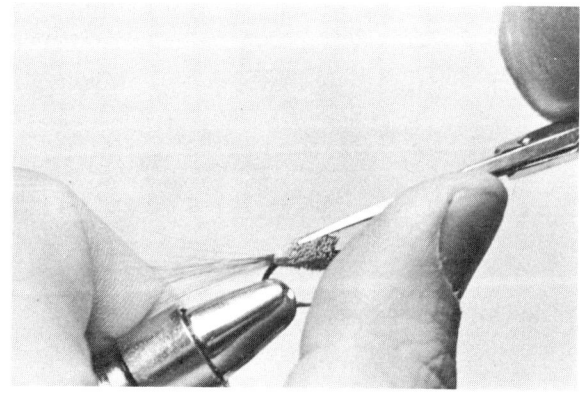

24. Using thumb guide scissors to make final taper.

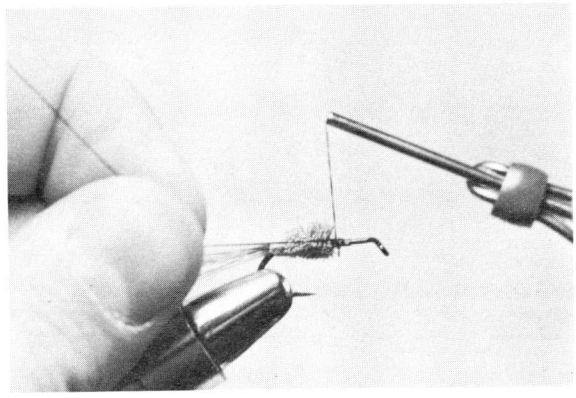

25. Tie on black monocord. Notice taper and proportions. Be sure to match them.

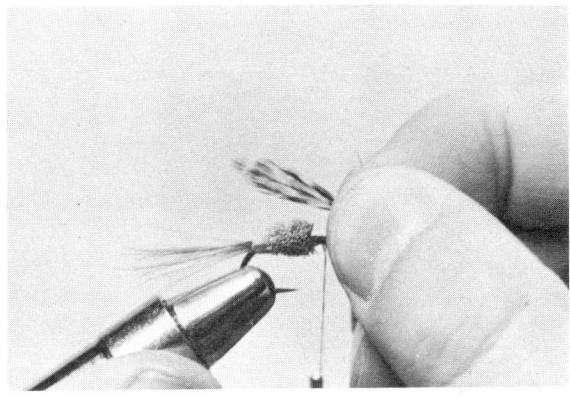

26. Select and match two grizzly hackle tips.

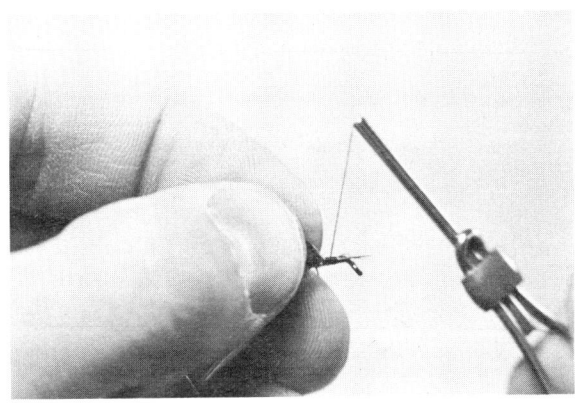

27. Tie on two matched grizzly hackle tips.

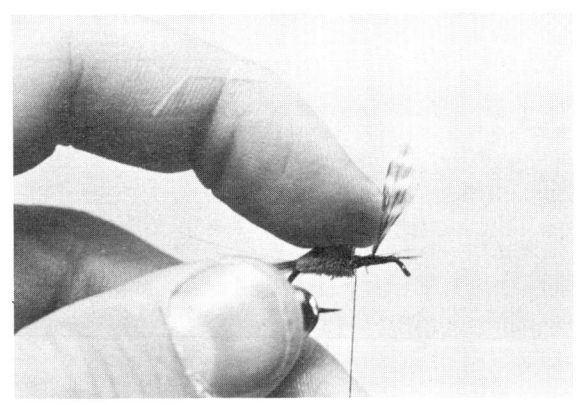

28. Use forefinger to divide hackle tips.

29. Wings should be divided like above picture.

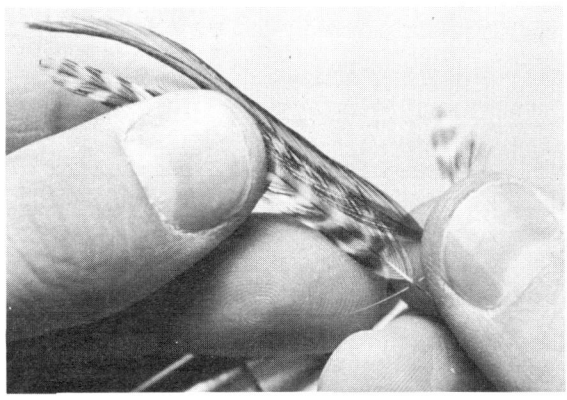

30. Select one brown and one grizzly saddle hackle or neck hackle. Brown should be reddish or deep brown. Grizzly should be well-marked.

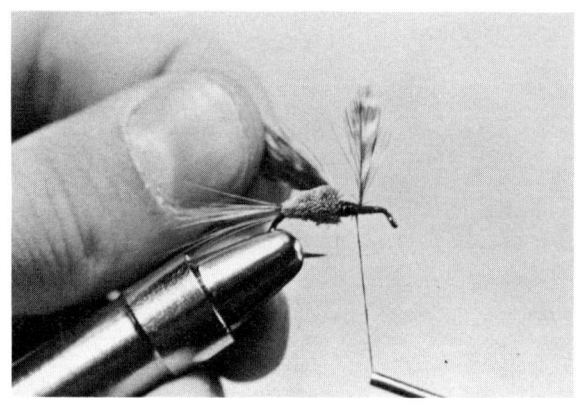

31. Tie in hackle.

32. Wrap straight up and down. Again tie behind the wing and in front of wing. Be sure to leave plenty of room for head. Tie off, whip finish and laquer.

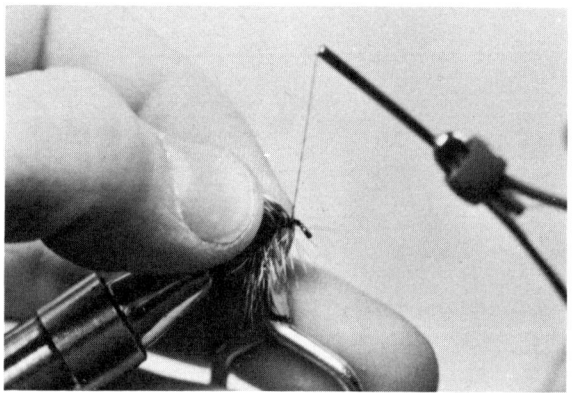

32. Tie off hackle. Whip finish and head cement.

Finished Fly

BLUE DUN IRRESISTABLE

The Blue Dun Irresistable is considered the standard tie among the variations of the Irresistable fly. First tied on the East Coast, it is basically a Grey Wulff pattern with a clipped deer hair body. Many western tiers consider it one of the better irresistable patterns. I find it particularly effective in sizes 14 through 18. I like it when the Caddis hatches start here on our heavy rivers. A lot of our Caddis insects are very small and it is hard to float a small dry fly in the heavy water of the Northwest. This particular Irresistable renders the proper coloration for our caddis, and will be very buoyant in small sizes.

I like the Blue Dun Irresistable for fishing the Teton River in Idaho, especially in a size 16. This particular river is a slow-moving, mossy-bedded paradise for both the dry fly or nymph fisherman. It is a place where the hatches come off from early morning until late evening. So many different types of insects hatch here that it would take an entomologist to catalog all of them. When I have fished this river I have had great luck with this fly. I have even sunk it and fished it in the film as you would a nymph with great success.

It doesn't even look like a nymph when wet, but one day four years ago I was able to hook fifteen fish in less than one hour, all on the Blue Dun Irresistable — fished wet. A couple of years later, on Western Wyoming's Salt River I tried it wet-style fishing it as I would a nymph on a dead drift. Where nothing else had worked prior to this, I began to catch trout! It seems to be an odd method, but it has worked for me. Don't be without one in your box (and try it wet once in a while).

MATERIALS: Blue Dun Irresistable

THREAD: Nymo for clipped hair body; black monocord for wings and hackle.

HOOK: Mustad 7957B.

SIZES: 6 to 18.

TAIL: Dark brown elk hair.

BODY: Clipped caribou or light gray deer hair.

WINGS: Dark brown elk divided.

HACKLE: Medium Blue Dun. Saddle hackles on large sizes, and neck hackles on small sizes.

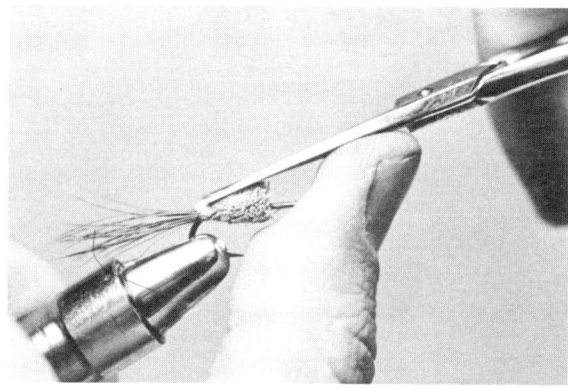

1. After tying on tail and trimming body as shown in the previous Irresistable, please refer to pages 95-100. It is important that this body is trimmed and tapered.

2. Tie on a bunch of medium brown elk hair. (Experience will tell you how much.) It is important to tie not too much. It is better to be slightly sparse than too heavy.

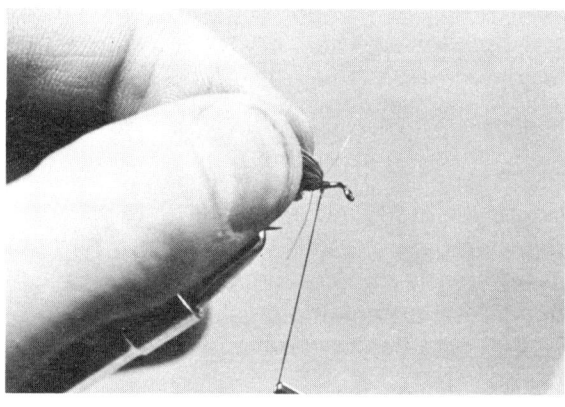

3. Tie at least four to five wraps of thread in front of wing to keep it from sliding forward.

4. Trim butt of hair that remains from tying on the wing.

5. Divide and wrap wing as shown on pages 122-123.

6. Tie on two medium blue dun saddle or neck hackles depending size. Be sure to secure them tightly.

7. Wrap hackle forward making sure that wing is in the middle of hackle. Usually about two wraps on each side on this particular fly is enough.

Finished Fly

PARACHUTE IRRESISTABLE

It is difficult to discuss a fly that you have invented without sounding as if you are tooting your horn a little. So I will try to keep the bragging to a bare minimum! I believe that this fly will become more and more popular in the coming years. It's drawback is that it is a hard pattern to tie, as most amateurs have some trouble tying both the Irresistable, and the Parachute. One thing to consider when tying these or other hard patterns, is that the fish are not always as critical of our fly-tying as we are (thank the Lord)! Tackle some of those hard flies! The best thing to remember is to tie the fly in the *correct proportions* so that it can float well and present a fairly good outline to the fish's eye. Keep in mind that it does not have to be tied perfectly to catch fish . . . just well enough to hold together while it is catching them!

The Parachute Irresistable is best fished in the heavy water for which it was designed, because it is visible even in poor light. Its deer hair body and parachute design give it the properties of superior flotation. Besides being a fine trout fly, in large sizes it also is an excellent bass bug! It can be tied in red, green, and yellow and fished as one would with any deer hair popper.

I prefer this fly in sizes eight and ten on the Madison River. Many of my customers who fish here have claimed that this fly worked in extremely fast water where nothing else could even float. I like mine tied with very stiff, wide, saddle hackle. In large sizes it can be difficult to cast in heavy wind. I do suggest that you use a leader with a heavy butt section to aid in casting this particularly heavy dry fly. It can be tied with various combinations of body colors and hackles. You should use your imagination or refer to the fly pattern dictionary for the many possible variations. I hope that you will tie this fly and let me know your results. Keep in mind that it is a fast water fly.

MATERIALS: Parachute Irresistable

THREAD: For the hair body: Nymo nylon thread. For parachute wing and hackle: Black monocord.

HOOK: 7957B or Mustad 94840.

TAIL: Brown hackle fibers.

BODY: Clipped gray deer hair.

WINGS: Light calftail (single, up-right wing).

HACKLE: Brown and grizzly neck or saddle hackle, mixed (tied parachute style).

1. Tie on deer hair or caribou hair as per instructions given previously for Irresistable, on page 97. For this fly it is important to add a third bunch of hair to make the body longer than that of the standard Irresistable.

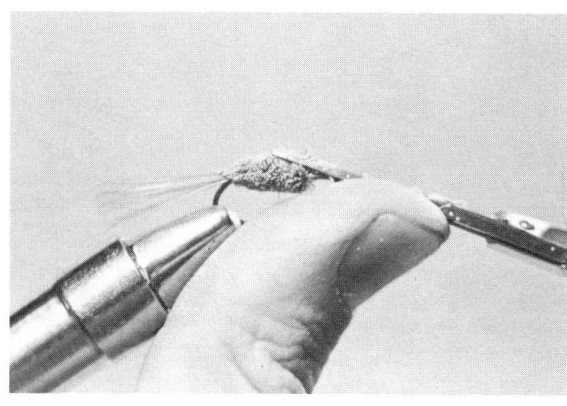

2. Half-hitch and remove fly from vise. Trim and taper as per instructions on pages 99. Make sure body has been trimmed. It should be tapered from tail to front.

3. Tie on even strands of white calftail. Tie forward over eye.

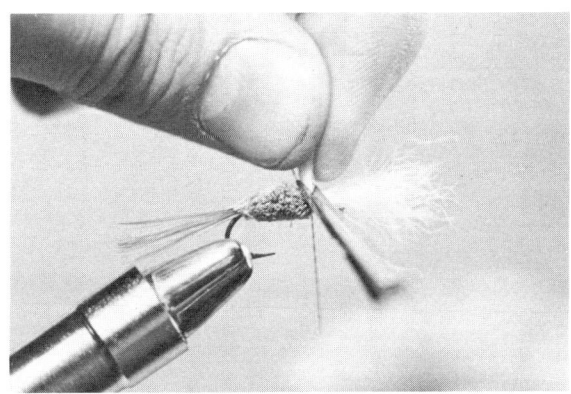

4. Trim butt of calftail.

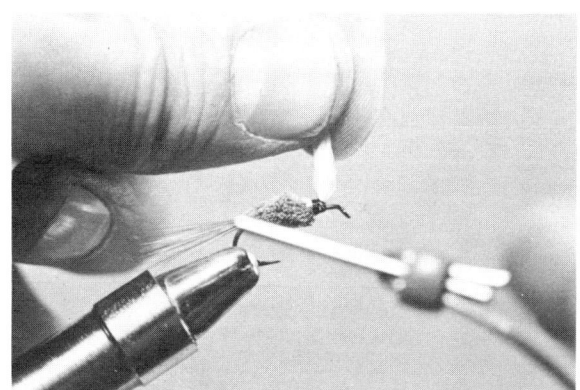

5. Pull calftail back toward tail, and start wrapping clockwise around calftail.

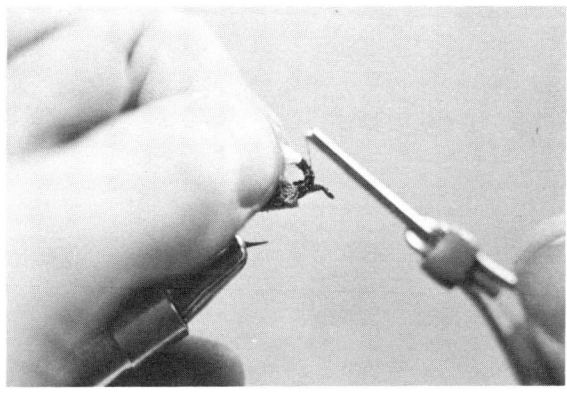

6. Continue to wrap around working the thread up. A good, firm base is essential.

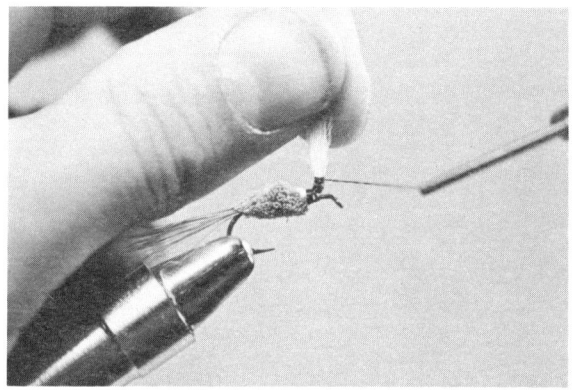

7. Test wing to make sure that it is tied in properly before finishing. Notice how all white has been covered with thread and wing is secured to shank.

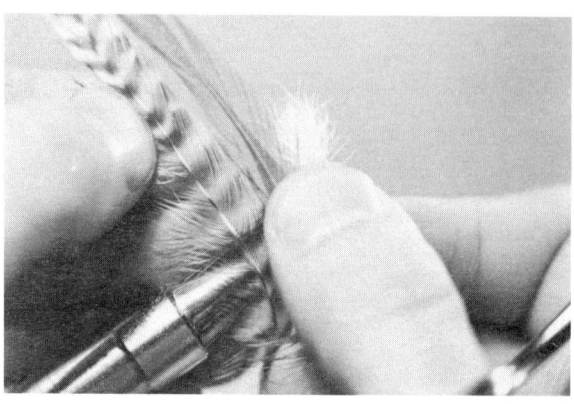

8. Select one gray and one wide brown neck hackle or saddle hackle.

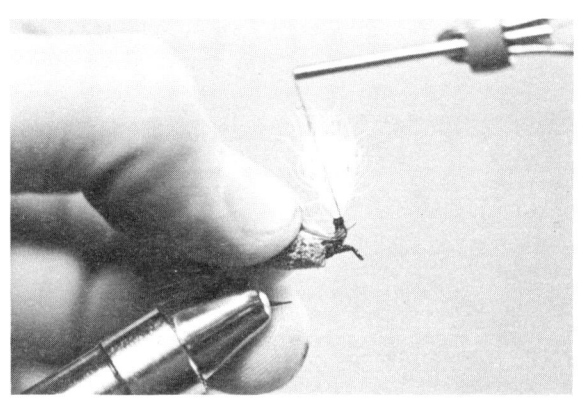

9. Tie in both hackles with dull side down.

10. Laquer threaded portion of wing thoroughly.

11. Wrap hackle circularly, clockwise around wing working up base evenly.

12. Then work hackle down the base until it meets the body. Tie off, whip finish and laquer.

H AND L VARIANT

This fly was President Eisenhower's favorite. Its white wings make it very visible and because he could see it so well, his fondness for it was well known among his angling friends. His boxes were packed full of H & L Variants and on his favorite fishing streams in Colorado he took as many trout as any fisherman using another fly. Its popularity has spread throughout the West, and it is now a widely used pattern both in Colorado and Montana, and gaining adherents throughout the other western states.

Many of the local anglers around West Yellowstone, Montana claim that it is the best mayfly imitation for their area. It has been nicknamed by many guides the "Dude Fly" because it is so visible and easy to fish, for people who have trouble seeing the standard dry fly.

One thing to remember when tying the H & L is to find good furnace saddle hackle. I recommend Indian select saddle hackles. The white calftail wings make the fly extremely buoyant and visible. It is also important to select good calftails for tying the fly. Out of a batch of one hundred calftails, usually 60% of them are passable for use, but about 40% will be soft and fine. These are the ones to look for. Find dense fine hair, which you think can be tied down with ease. Some of the calftails are long-haired with each hair wide in diameter, and thus they are very difficult to work with. This is always discouraging for the beginning fly tyer. I find it usually pays to buy calftails in bulk quantities rather than singley. When ordering them through the mail you should specify that you are tying dry flies and need dense, one inch to two inch hair for the tail. Many people use extra long calftail for streamers, and without specifying, you may get hair that is completely unusable for your needs.

Besides being an excellent trout pattern, the H & L Variant is probably one of the best whitefish dry flies that we have in the West. Tied in sizes 16 and 14 it is a killer on the Rocky Mountain whitefish which inhabits many rivers in the West in large populations. In the Snake, Green, Madison, Big Hole, and New Fork Rivers and other smaller streams throughout the West, the populations vary from an overabundance to only a few. Sometimes shunned by trout fishermen, cussed, and maligned they have still made many a trout fisherman's day when the trout were not biting. Whitefish often fly more avidly to a fly than do trout, thus making them a nuisance to the fisherman who is interested only in trout. The Whitefish can be an important game fish however, and a source of hours of pleasure. It is not uncommon to catch thirty to fifty whitefish on a good day. Usually their fighting qualities are not as good as a trout's but some waters such as the Wind and Pogo Aggie Rivers in central Wyoming contain whitefish of such super vigor that just to hook one provides thrill enough to satisfy any angler. In the cold, winter months when trout fishing is not open, many areas have winter whitefishing seasons. Sometimes you can catch whitefish on nymphs, or on warm days in the winter they can even be caught on dry flies. This lengthens the fly fishing season quite a bit, helping fishermen practice skills for the upcoming summer season. Either as a whitefish or a trout fly the H & L Variant is one hell of a fly and should be among your hair-wing fly collection.

MATERIALS: H & L Variant

THREAD: Black monocord and for small sizes, black Herb Howard pre-waxed.

HOOK: Mustad 7957B or Mustad 3906, or Mustad 94840.

TAIL: White select calftail, small diameter fibers.

BODY: First couple inches stripped peacock quill, the other section peacock herl fibers, not stripped.

WINGS: Divided upright white calftail, again small diameter full calftail.

HACKLE: Furnace, Indian select saddle hackles on large sizes, furnace neck hackle for small sizes.

1. Tie white calftail making sure that all hair tips are even. Tail should be the length of the shank. Tied in very tightly.

2. Trim some nice even white calftail making sure that all short fibers have been removed and all the remaining fibers are nice, even, and thick. Use this proportioning to get proper wing size. Notice where thumb and forefinger are on the calftail.

3. Reverse wing and tie it over eye, midway down shank. Thumb and finger should be placed at same spot on hair as were the thumb and finger were in previous photo. Tie down wing tightly.

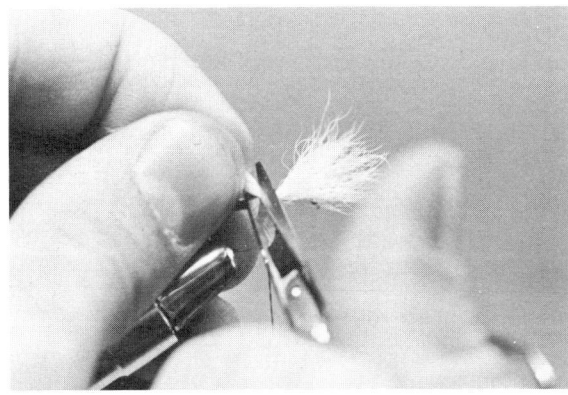

4. Trim butt of hair.

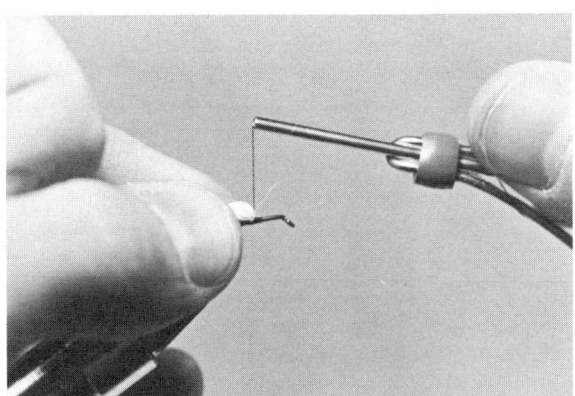

5. Wrap in front of wing so that wing does not slide forward.

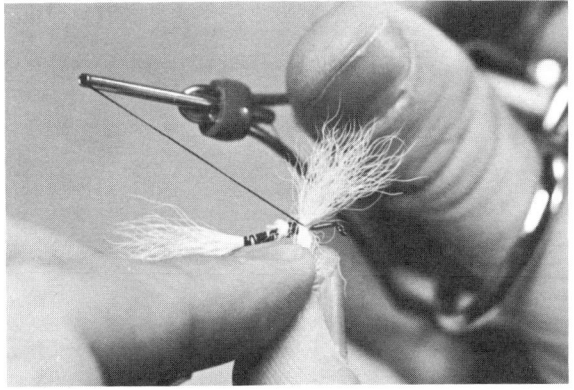

6. With thumb and finger of left hand, divide wing and make one wrap between wings.

7. With thumb and finger of left hand, pull wing apart again and from back to front wrap between wing.

8. Repeat the last two steps. This forms an "X" pattern and the method is called "Xing".

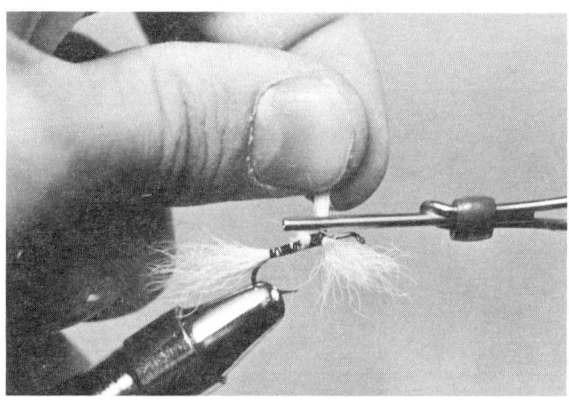

9. With thumb and finger of left hand, hold wing farthest away and start to wrap thread around clockwise.

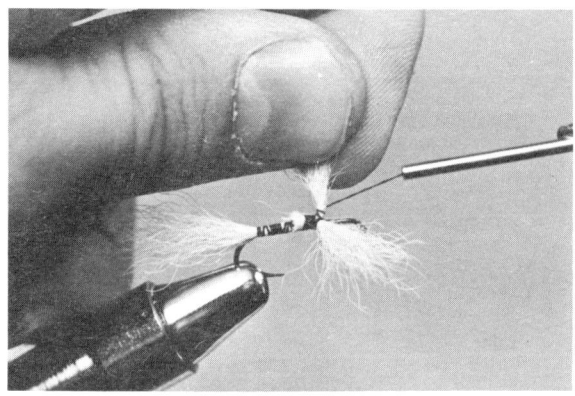

10. Continue to wrap around wing.

11. Wrap wing until a firm base of thread is secured.

12. Again, with thumb and finger of left hand clockwise wrap around wing closest toward you. This wing will be harder to wrap than the one furthest away. It sometimes happens that the thread will slip off. By wrapping loosely at first, this can be eliminated.

13. Continue to wrap thread around wing. You must release thumb and finger to complete each wrap.

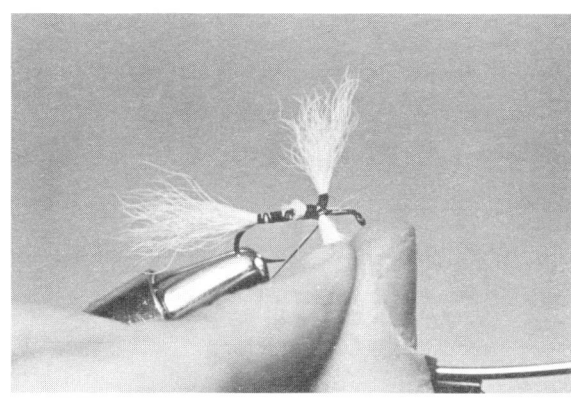

14. Put fingers back and again make another wrap. Continue this process.

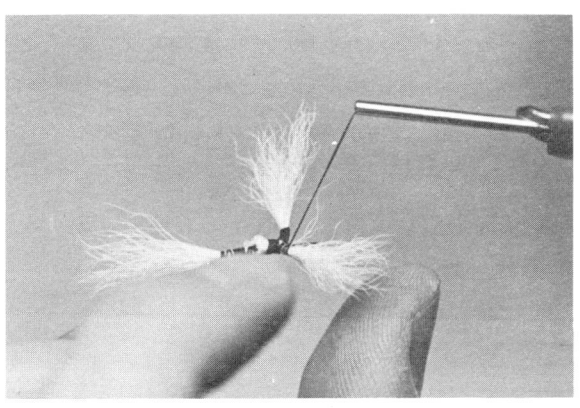

15. The wrapping forms a good solid base.

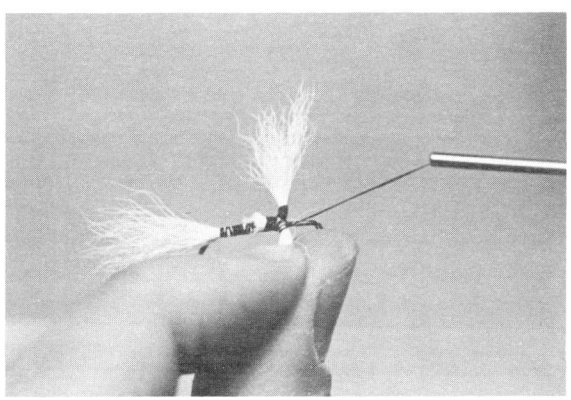

16. Continue to wrap thread around the wing securing it.

17. After both wings have been wrapped with thread, bring tying thread back to where butt of hair has been trimmed.

18. With thumb and finger pull wings together.

19. Wings have a divided effect shown above.

20. Wrap thread and cover all white at butt end and continue to wrap until a nice, smooth tapered thread body is made.

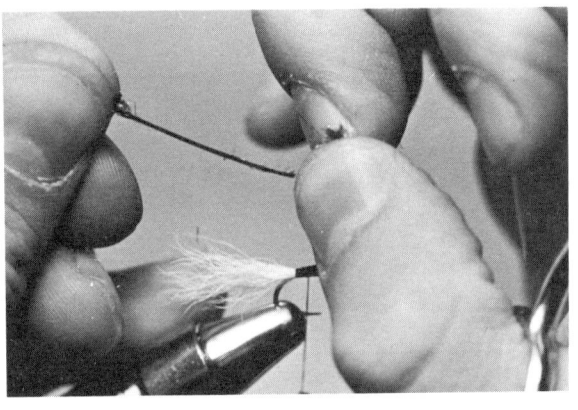

21. With thumbnail and finger of right hand strip herl off of peacock quill. Approximately two inches will suffice, leaving the rest of the quill with herl on it.

22. Tie on quill and wrap forward.

23. As you wrap forward a quill body will be formed. Then after the quill runs out a herl tuft will be formed. Tie off peacock herl leaving plenty of room for hackle.

24. Tie on two either brown or furnace saddle hackles. Notice that thread is being wrapped between wings tying down vein.

STREAMERS

Mylar Mickey Finn

Light Spruce Fly

Buck Royal

Silver Hilton

Little Rainbow Trout

Black Ghost

Red Ant

Marabou Streamer

WET FLIES

Blue Dun Squirrel Tail

Rio Grande King Wet

Western Coachman

Carey Special

Wooly Worm

NYMPHS

Zug Bug

Hare's Ear

Mosquito Larva

Fledermaus

Dark Caddis

Muskrat

Stone Fly

Montana

Grande Stone Fly

Tellico

Fresh Water Shrimp

Light May Fly

March Brown

25. Wrap hackle forward. There should be an equal number of wraps behind and in front of the wing, so that the hackle is equal and the wing is in the middle of the hackle. Tie off head, whip finish and laquer.

26. Laquer quill body.

Finished Fly

ROYAL WULFF

Lee Wulff, the famous fly tyer, fisherman, and film maker revolutionized fly fishing and fly tying with his Wulff series. These flies were one of the first ever invented using hair instead of natural feathers for wings and tails. These patterns catch trout, salmon, and steelhead, and are now used the world over. Probably no one series of flies has ever gained more popularity and become so widely accepted as the Wulff patterns. They are some of the most dependable fish-catchers ever tried.

I once asked Lee what his Royal Wulff represented. He puzzled a moment and replied with a smile, "Well, I don't think they represent any one natural insect, but more a dessert, something after the main course, a little like Strawberry shortcake. That's it, that's the best way I can describe my Royal Wulff, it looks like strawberry shortcake — something great big and juicy floating down to a large trout!"

In the mountain West the Royal Wulff represents the flying red ant hatches that appear during the months of August and September. Fished on small springs in sizes 14 and 16 it is deadly. Also on larger rivers during the last two weeks of August this fly in sizes 8, 10, and 12, is one of the best for Wyoming trout's dessert!

MATERIALS: Royal Wulff

HOOK: Mustad 94840, 7957B, or 3906.

SIZES: 6 to 20

BODY: Three of four wraps of peacock herl followed by red floss then by three or four more wraps of peacock herl.

WING: Divided white calftail tied upright.

HACKLE: Brown saddle hackle (or still neck hackle on small sizes).

HEAD: Black monocord.

TAIL: Dark elk hair, or moose hair (fairly thick).

1. Tie in some dark brown elk for tail or some dark moose hair for tail. Tail should be length of shank. Make sure that this tail is tied in and the butt of the tail should not exceed ½ the length of the shank.

2. Tie in some white calftail. Be sure to remove all short fibers leaving only long even fibers. For aid in doing this please refer to page 111.

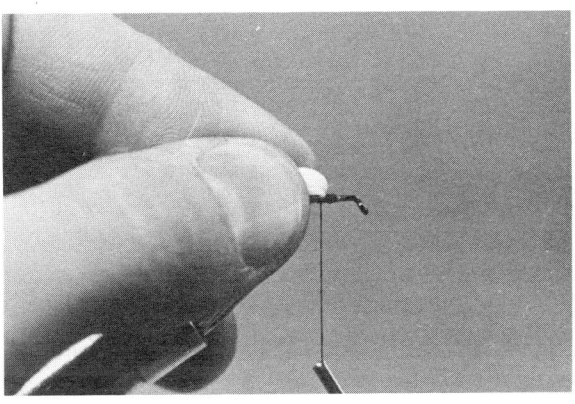

3. As shown above, be sure to tie in the wing on top of the hook, approximately ½ way down. Tie wing in very tightly. Next tie in front of wing, to keep the wing from sliding forward.

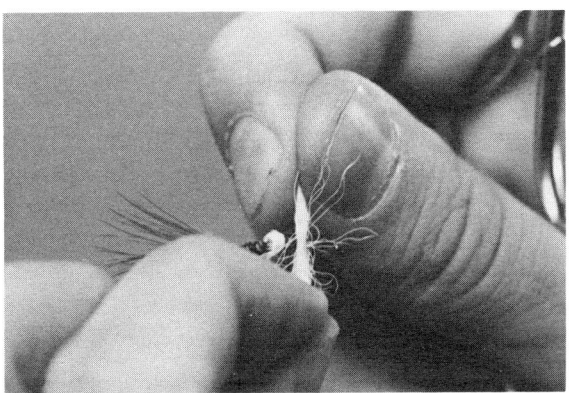

4. Divide wing in ½ with thumb and forefinger or right hand and thumb and forefinger of left hand.

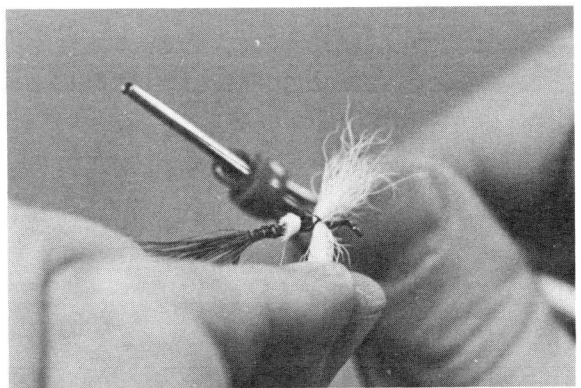

5. Then from front to back wrap one wrap between wings and wrap under, and from front side of the hook wrap thread from back to front again. This is called "Xing" the wing. This method should be repeated about three times.

6. Wrap circularly around wings. For mere detail please refer to page 112. Then wrap circularly around wing closest to you. With thumb and forefinger of left hand squeeze wings together making them upright and divided.

7. Be sure to tie behind the wing, making sure that the wing has been securely tied to shank of hook. Then wrap thread back to the tail and attach two peacock herl strands.

8. Wrap peacock herl forward forming a small butt, then tie in red floss. Notice that remaining strands of peacock herl have not been trimmed. This will be left to tie on the next butt of herl.

9. Wrap floss forward leaving room to tie off peacock herl forming the second segment or butt. In this case the two remaining strands were not thick enough and we added another strand so that the second butt would be thick, as the first butt. We then wrapped it forward and tied it off.

10. Tie in two saddle hackles, a dark brown is preferred. On smaller sizes a dark brown neck hackle, usually three or four are necessary. Wrap hackle forward with equal wraps behind and in front of the wing, depending on the area to be fished to determine how heavy the hackle should be.

Finished Fly

GRAY WULFF

Another of the Wulff patterns, the Gray Wulff is a popular fly in the Rocky Mountains. Basically a hair-wing Blue Dun, it usually floats where a plain Blue Dun cannot. It is one of the most beautiful of all flies, and one of the simplest to tie when the basic methods are mastered. The method below is the basic one for tying the White Wulff, Ginger Wulff, and Blonde Wulff as well as the Gray Wulff.

One important thing for tying the Gray Wulff is the selection of elk hair. Although you can use deer hair, the elk hair is more durable and produces a more effective pattern. The best growth on the elk for proper Wulff hair is below the rump along the back legs, or on the front legs just above the knee. It is important when ordering elk hair to specify that you are tying hair-wing patterns such as the Wulff patterns, and have the supplier select hair that is at least 1½ inches long, but not over 2½ inches. The longer the hair, the more difficult it is to work with.

The Gray Wulff is tied with Blue Dun Hackle. It can vary from a light blue dun to a medium dark blue dun, according to the preference of the tyer. I prefer a light badger hackle dyed blue dun. I have heard that the new photo-dying method as described in Eric Leiser's new book, FLY TYING MATERIALS, makes an excellent blue dun color for the Gray Wulff. I particularly like the badger because a dark strip remains after the dying. It blends so well with the elk hair wing that it looks very fishy. I believe that you must have good hackle for tying the Wulff patterns. Most large sized Wulffs should be tied with saddle hackles. Some of the best are Philippine or Indian select saddle hackles. These are available through many companies and are sold specifically as Indian or Philippine hackles. This saddle hackle is narrow, usually for sizes 14 to 8, and makes the stiffest hackles for Wulffs or other hair flies. Out of an average bunch of strong saddle hackle about 60% is unusable for dry fly hackling, either because the hackle is too wide or too short. But the quality supplied is superb, so it is worth the extra expense and time to select the right hackles from the rest.

One thing to remember is not to use dyed brown calftail. I have seen several Wulffs tied with this material, but in my opinion they do not look as convincing, float as well, or take the fish as often as the regular-tied Gray Wulff.

The Gray Wulff should be fished as a standard dry fly. One thing to remember is that the Wulffs were designed to float superbly in heavy water. If you have nimble fingers and sharp eyes, tie it in small sizes, 18 through 24, it can be a fine slow-water pattern. You can vary the amount of material used for the fly according to the area you plan to fish. The heavier the water, the stiffer the hackle, and the fuller you should tie the fly.

On dark days you may have trouble seeing the Gray Wulff. This is one of the few drawbacks of the fly. But, on the fast-moving western rivers, when you might normally tie on a Blue Dun or a Quill Gordon, give the Gray Wulff a try.

MATERIALS: Gray Wulff

THREAD: Black monocord.

HOOK: Mustad 7957B or Mustad 94840.

SIZES: 6 to 22.

TAIL Dark brown elk hair.

BODY: Gray wool or muskrat dubbing or rabbit gray dubbing.

WINGS: Divided. Elk hair — dark brown to medium brown.

HACKLE: Light blue dun or a rusty blue dun or badger dyed blue dun. Indian select saddle hackle for large sizes, for small sizes, neck hackle.

1. Tie on some medium brown select elk hair forming tail. Tail should not exceed length of shank.

2. Select a bunch of medium brown elk hair that has good dark tips and barred coloration. It should be tied loosely at first increasing the tension as one ties, until wings are tied in securely. This should be done about midway down the hook.

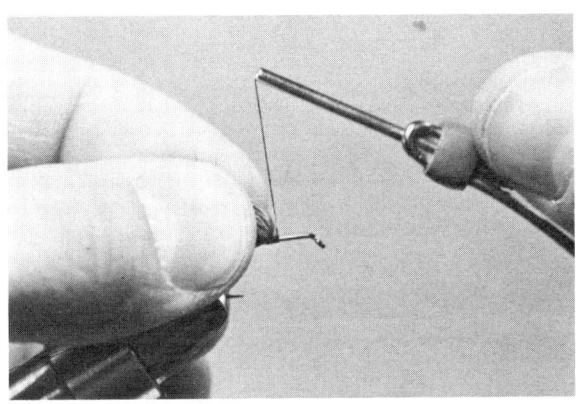

3. Wrap in front of wing so wing cannot slide forward.

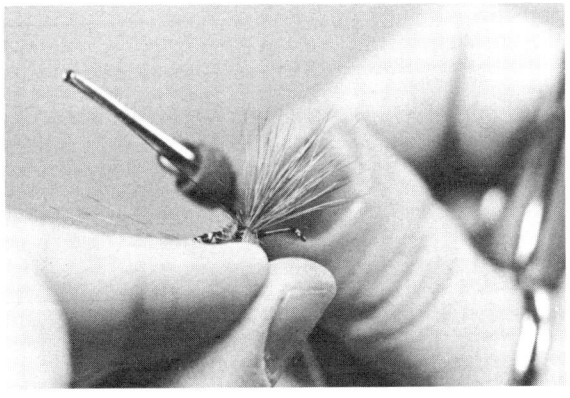

4. Divide wing in ½ with thumb and forefinger and one wrap in between.

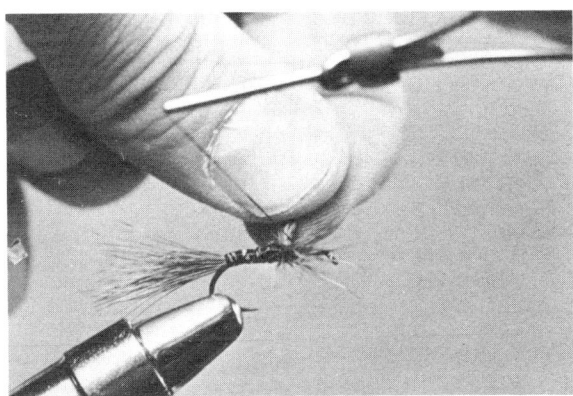

5. Wrap in a "x" pattern, thread back and forth between wing.

6. Wrap circle of thread around base of wing farthest away from you.

7. Wrap circularly again around wing on the wing closest to you.

8. Between thumb and forefinger squeeze wings together.

9. Use forefingers to straighten wings and divide them.

10. Notice how wing is divided and cocked evenly.

11. Dub on some gray muskrat or rabbit fur.

12. Wrap dubbing forward tapering as shown above.

13. Tie on two select Indian dyed badger or dyed cream blue dun color. Tie base of hackles in securely.

14. Wrap blue dun hackle forward wrapping it an even amount behind and in front of wing.

15. Tie off head, whip finish, and head cement.

DEER HOPPER

In recent years many imitations of the fabled grasshopper have sprung up. Several good copies such as Whitlock Hopper, Dan Bailey's Hopper, and Hank Robert's Deer Hopper have entered the fishing scene. I have developed my own hopper, which is somewhat representative of the others, has excellent buoyancy, and is one of the few which floats upright with dependability. It tantalizes fish where creeks have deep undercut banks, and on rivers, such as the Green and Madison, which have heavy, fast water and rapids. Many grasshopper patterns have the problem of floating on their sides, which subtracts from their representational qualities. But, the way this fly rides could fool even a grasshopper!

MATERIALS: Deer Hopper
HOOK: Mustad 9671 or 9672.
SIZES: 6 to 12.
BODY: Clipped yellow deer hair.
RIBBING: Brown saddle hackle.
TAIL: Either brown or red hackle fibers.
WING: Brown mottled turkey quill.
HACKLE AND HEAD: Clipped grey deer hair.

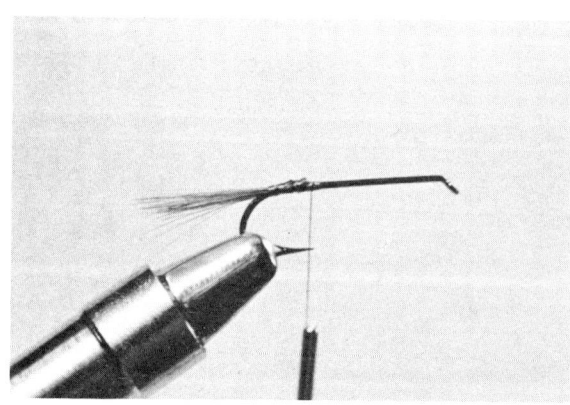

1. Wrap several fibers of red hackle forming tail.

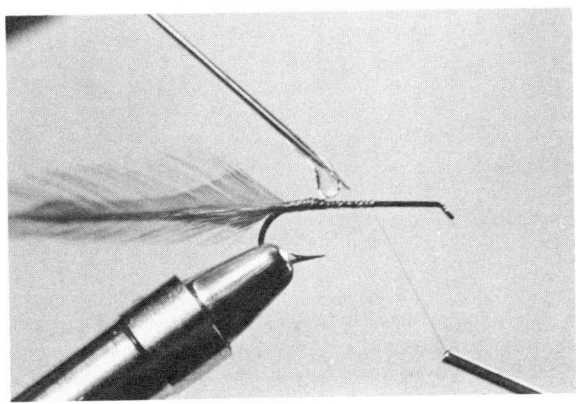

2. Tie on one reddish brown saddle hackle and laquer thread as shown. Thread has been wrapped in middle of hook giving good solid thread base. Then return thread back to tail.

3. Lay bunch of dyed yellow deer hair on top of hook. Tie on as instructions used in Irresistable using the proper thread method. See pages 97-100.

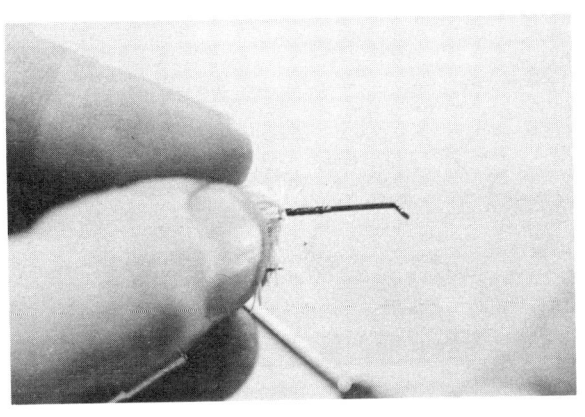

4. Wrap two or three turns of thread in front of the first clump of hair.

5. Tie on second clump of hair as first clump.

6. Spin hair by pulling down hard on thread.

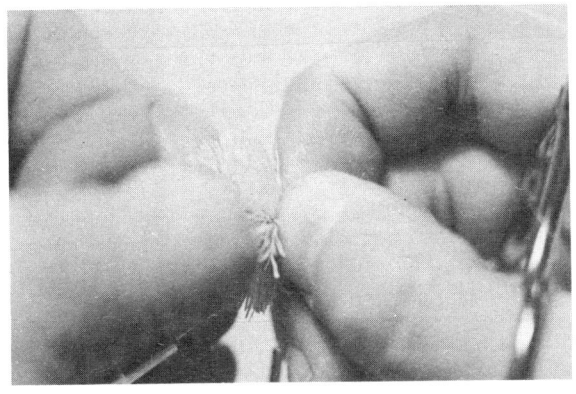

7. With thumb and finger of both hands push both clumps together making hair very tight.

8. This shows hair spun. Judge to see if proportions are either smaller or larger than the photo. This particular proportion needs another group of hair.

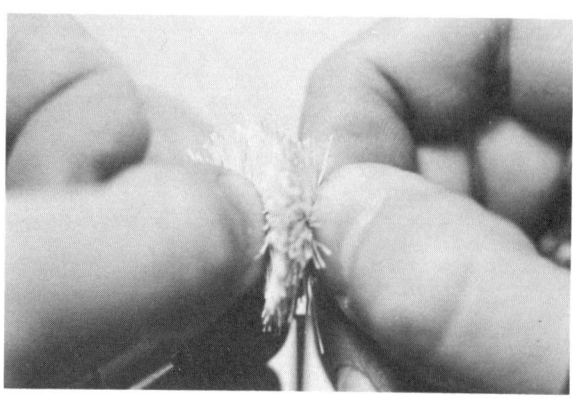

9. Tie in third group of hair and tie in with thumb and finger of both hands to push this clump of hair in tightly.

10. Half hitch and tie off.

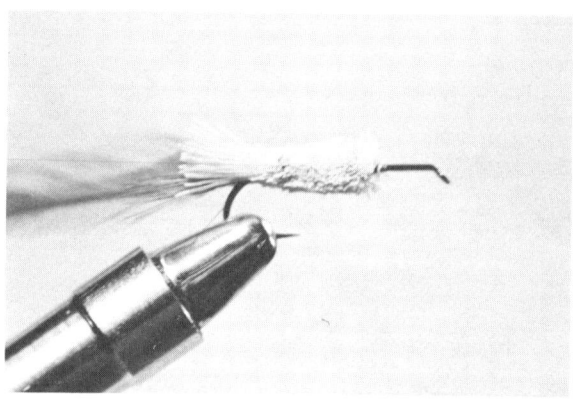

11. Trim hair as above leaving a butt end of hair as shown trailing over tail.

12. Wrap brown saddle hackle forward palming hair body.

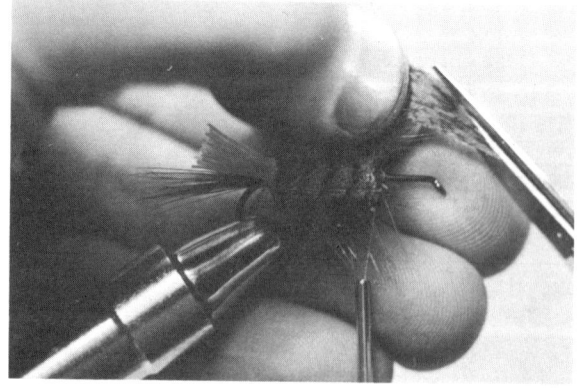

13. Select one turkey quill that is a dark mottled brown.

14. Using forefingers of both hands lay quill flat against body with curve down and tip pointing up.

15. Tie in wing, very tightly so that it does not stick straight out or down.

16. Tie in a matching wing on the frontal side. Notice that thumb and finger are pushing wing up against body.

17. After tying in wing lay down a base of thread and drop head cement on that.

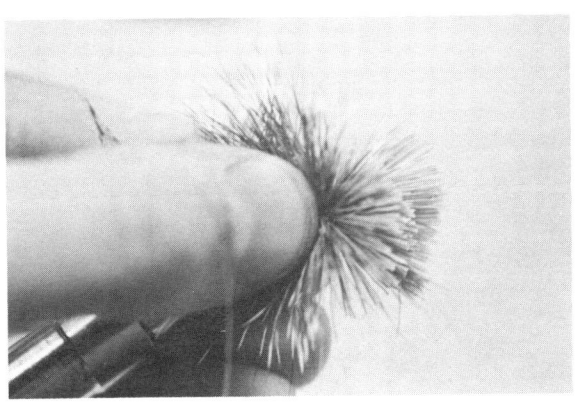

18. Tie in some light brown or light gray deer hair. Lay first wrapping thread over hair loosely then next wrap tighter until the third wrap is tightest. Tie in another group of hair on opposite side of hook up against wing. For further instruction in tying this type of head, refer to Muddler Minnow instruction on pages 159-160.

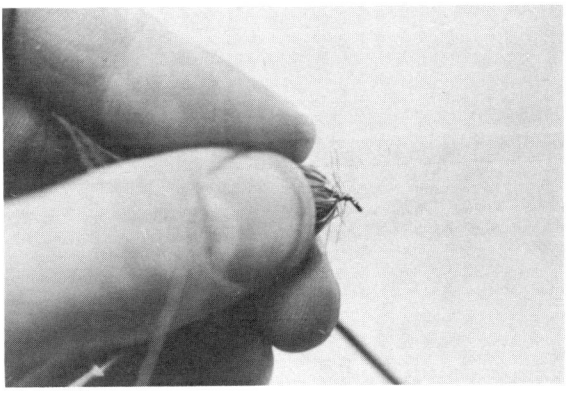

19. After tying on hair on other side, wrap thread forward to eye and pull back on hair forming head. Whip finish head and laquer.

20. Use thumb and finger to push down flattening hair on top and bottom of fly.

21. Trim hair off of bottom of fly until it is flat.

22. Trim hair off of sides, as shown.

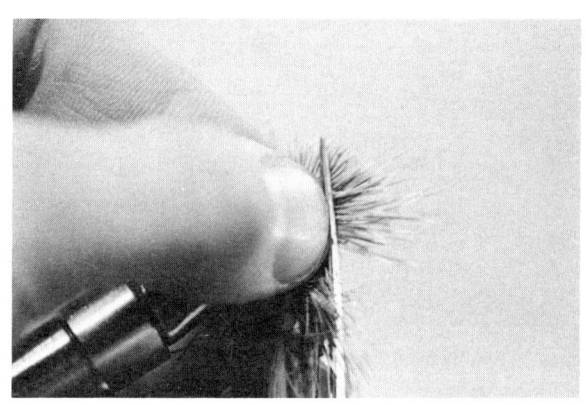

23. Trim hair off other side as shown.

24. Trim hair off top.

25. Trim hair closer off top in a circular fashion from left side to right side. Refer to the finished product to get an idea of how to trim head.

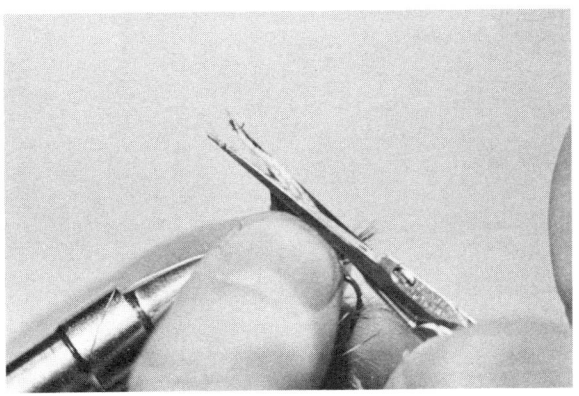

26. Trim wing so that both sides match. Hair should be trimmed at a 45° angle.

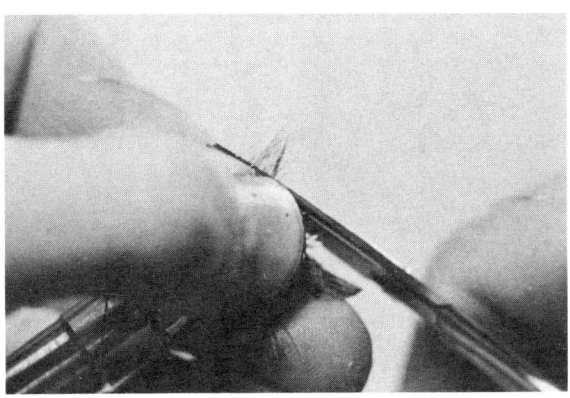

27. Trim hackle under and on top of fly. Hackle should be trimmed so it exceeds body and wing, approximately ⅛ inch. Check finished product for exact trimming size.

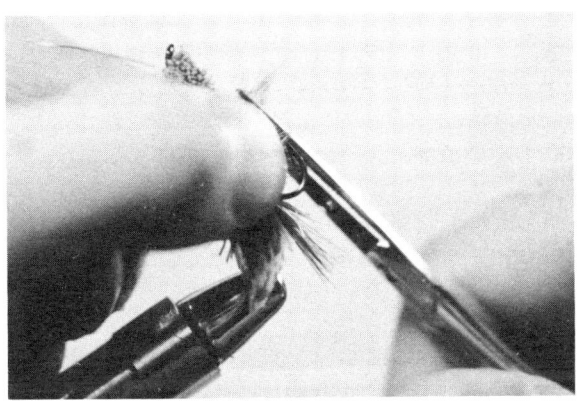

28. Trim hackle from bottom of hook approximately even with hook point.

29. Here is trimmed fly. Notice that head is trimmed flat and hackle is trimmed so it just exceeds top of the wing and the bottom of the hook. Notice how head is round.

30. Again another view showing how wings are sloping up. They imitate the legs of grasshoppers to a wary trout.

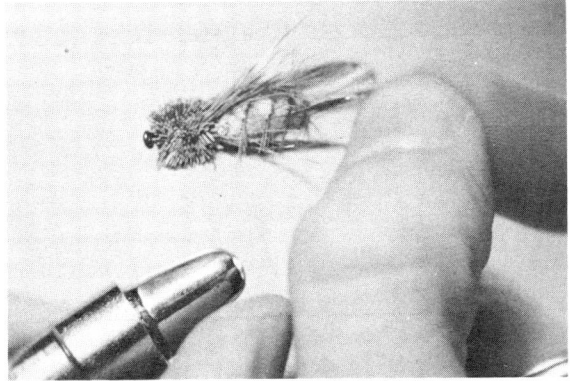

31. You can see how the bottom of the fly is trimmed flat. Notice wings and see how they look identical to legs of a grasshopper.

BUCKTAIL CADDIS

This is a famed Northwestern pattern fashioned to imitate the many caddis and stone fly hatches in the Rocky Mountains. Tied mainly in larger sizes, (#6-10) it skims the top of the water and thus is a popular standby for the many guides in Idaho, Montana, and Wyoming. Highly visible, and bobbing on the surface, this caddis pattern knocks off some very large trout.

It is usually tied with an orange body and brown hackle, but can be tied with either gray or cream hackling depending on the hatches occuring. Customarily it is not very consistent on small springs or lakes, but has an advantage on heavier rivers, such as the Madison, Snake, Big Hole, and Misssouri. It best exhibits its qualities when fished with the Standard dry-fly method of laying the fly upstream and letting it float down gradually. Also, it can be fished downstream casting a slack line and letting it drift deep beneath the willow trees. This can be dangerous as you can use up many flies this way, but after you land one large trout a few lost flies are easily forgotten.

MATERIALS: Bucktail Caddis

THREAD: Black or orange monocord.

HOOK: Mustad 9671 or 9672 or 7957B.

SIZES: 4 to 14.

TAIL: None.

BODY: Either yellow or orange wool or floss.

HACKLE: Furnace select saddle hackle.

RIBBING: Palmer furnace hackle, should be a nice, select long saddle — one only.

WING: Brown bucktail, a soft bucktail, usually best to get from base of bucktail.

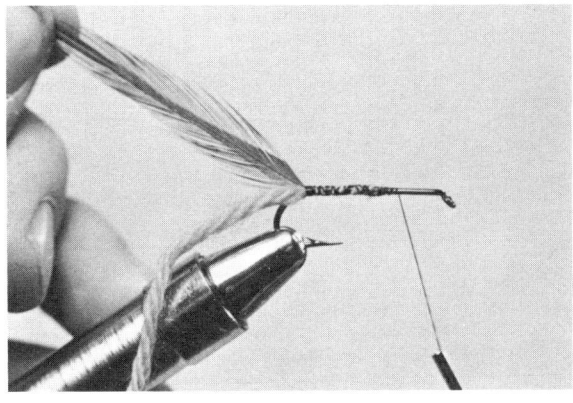

1. Tie on orange wool, then tie in one brown long select saddle hackle.

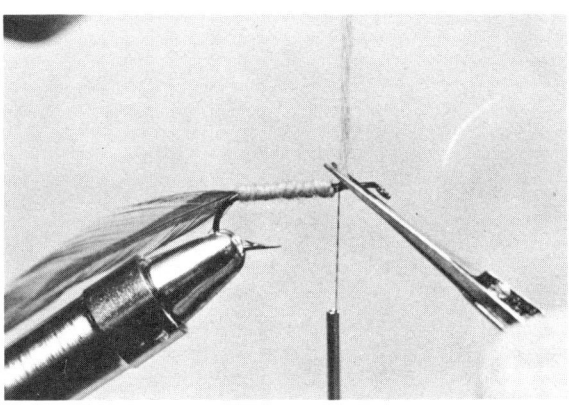

2. Wrap orange wool forward evenly and trim.

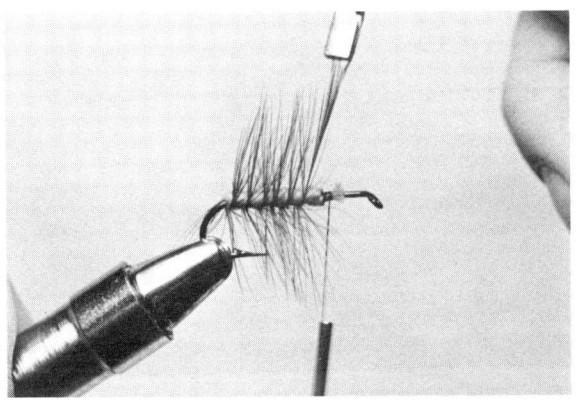

3. Palmer tie brown saddle hackle forward, dry fly style.

4. Tie on one extra select medium brown Indian saddle hackle. Tie down securely.

5. Wrap hackle forward making hackle very thick.

6. Select brown bucktail, preferably from the base of the bucktail that is very soft.

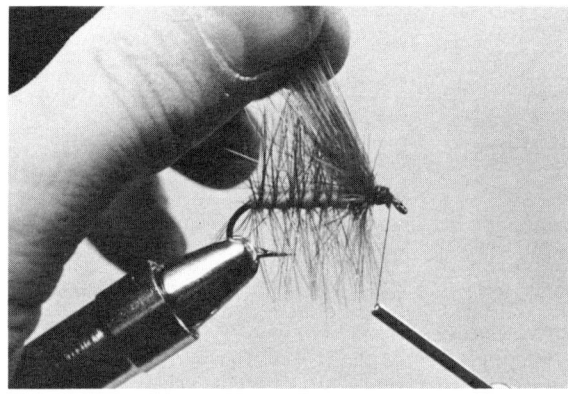

7. Tie down bucktail and in this case trim the base of the bucktail. You can also leave the bucktail as you would on a muddler, leaving it a full thick head; or you can tie off whip finish and laquer as in the picture.

Finished Fly

PARACHUTE ROYAL COACHMAN

This is probably the standard parachute pattern which is used by more people than any other. It is a great fly when absolute visibility is necessary. Besides being very visible, it is also very effective. In our area of Wyoming the Royal Wulff pattern is tied dry style to imitate the many flying ant hatches in the Jackson Hole Valley. The Royal Wulff and the Parachute Royal Coachman are both excellent fish-takers during the months of August and early September. I like sizes 14 and 16 for the smaller creeks and 10s and 12s for the large rivers.

The Parachute Royal Coachman is effective for fishing from a boat for someone with poor eyesight or on a day with lots of glare. The white wing of the Parachute stands up and is easy to follow in fast water.

I believe that Parachute flies would be more popular if they were not so difficult to tie. In the following instructions I will try to simplify the tying. An important thing to remember is that it does take a lot of practice to get them to turn out the way you want. You cannot just sit down and wrap three or four and expect perfection. I suggest that you tie quite a few just for practice. The more you tie, the simpler the fly becomes, until pretty soon it is just as easy as putting on any other wing or hackle. I wish you the best of luck in tying it and hope that you will give it a try to discover what a great fly it really is.

MATERIALS: Parachute Royal Coachman

THREAD: Black monocord

HOOK: Mustad 7957B or 94840

TAIL: Dark brown elk hair or dark moose hair.

BODY: Segmented peacock herl, red floss and then peacock herl again.

WING: White calftail tied single wing, upright.

HACKLE: Brown saddle hackle for large flies, neck hackle for small flies, tied parachute style.

1. Tie in dark moose or dark elk hair.

2. Tie in white calftail so that all the hairs have been made even, for further help refer to pages 107. Be sure to tie down wings tightly. Make it slightly longer than you would on a normal Wulff fly.

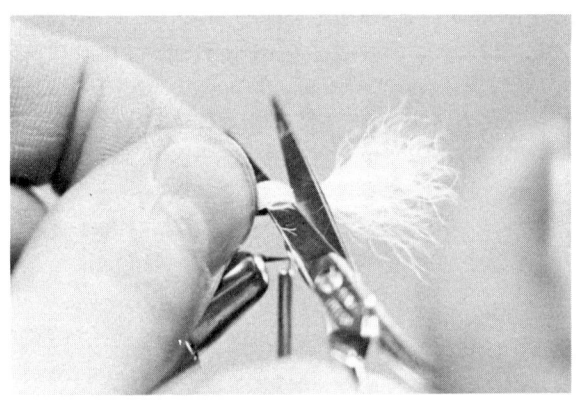

3. Trim butt of wing.

4. Wrap in front of wing, keeping it from sliding forward.

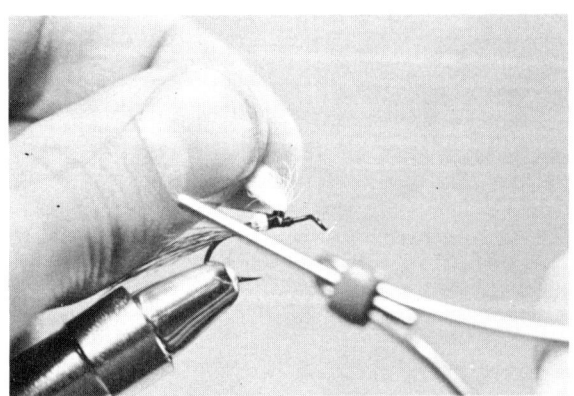

5. Wrap clockwise around wing holding the wing with thumb and forefinger, then,

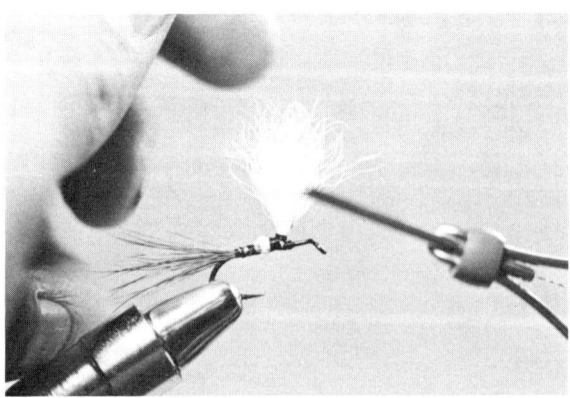

6. Releasing thumb and forefinger.

7. This is the proper base of thread which should be on the wing. Notice how the thread has been wrapped back toward the tail and wrapped forward toward the eye. Be sure to memorize the proportions as it will help you in the future when tying parachute flies.

8. Tie in two strands of peacock herl.

9. Wrap herl forward, forming butt.

10. Tie on red floss and wrapping forward, forming small red segment. Use the main butt of peacock herl as shown in next step to tie off final butt.

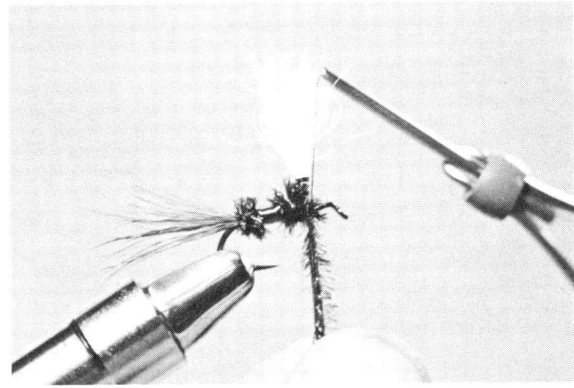

11. Notice how peacock herl was wrapped in front and behind butt and is tied off in front of the wing.

12. Tie on butt of hackle so that the butt will run up the wing. Notice carefully in picture. The hackle should be tied with shiny side facing up.

14. Wrap hackle from base of wing up to where the thread ends and then wrap back down toward base. It is important to have saddle hackles or neck hackles long enough to complete this task. Then tie off and whip finish and laquer.

13. After tying butt securely in, laquer as shown above.

Finished Fly

PARACHUTE GRIZZLY WULFF

The concept of the parachute fly is not new, but in recent years it has taken on national prominence. Its construction makes the fly the most gently riding and finest floating dry fly anyone could ask for. On springs where the presentation must be the most delicate possible, these flies shine. The parachute concept is incorporated into many of the Swisher-Richards dry fly patterns of the no-hackle concept. They provide the most flotation for the least amount of wrapped hackle.

As far as wing material is concerned, I particularly like calftail because it lends visibility. Light elk is also a good material. Of the large sized parachute flies I am partial to good, wide saddle hackle. On the small flies it is important to get hackle that is slightly oversized to provide good support and balance to the parachute fly.

The Parachute Grizzly Wulff is one that was originated in California and has gained steady popularity throughout the Rocky Mountain Area. The fishermen in California (especially in the northern part of the state) use this fly to imitate the many may fly hatches in their areas. Some of these flies are tied on sizes 6 and 8.

A person from the east would be amazed to see the sizes of the may flies that hatch on the spring rivers of northern California. It is no wonder that large rainbow and browns are found there. It is generally conceded that coastal areas, such as in Oregon and Washington as well as Idaho produce the largest rainbow trout in the country. The steelhead trout is the seafaring version of the rainbow. The inner regions of these three states have a multitude of crystal-clear spring type rivers. Many of these rivers are privately owned and therefore not accessible to the general public. Perhaps this is why they are not as well-known as rivers such as the Madison and Snake, in Montana and Wyoming. There are several fly fishing only, or limited-take rivers in all these states. One of the most popular is Hot and Hat Creek of California. The Grizzly Wulff is popular there as well as in many different spots throughout the west. In small sizes I recommend it for small eastern limestone streams. Anywhere that you might notice a mayfly hatch that resembles this fly, give it a try.

MATERIALS:	Parachute Grizzly Wulff
THREAD:	Monocord, yellow
HOOK:	Mustad 7597B or 94840
SIZES:	6 to 20.
TAIL:	Dark elk hair or dark moose hair.
BODY:	Yellow floss (laquered).
WING:	White calftail (single upright wing).
HACKLE:	Brown and grizzly mixed, saddles for large sizes or neck hackle for small sizes (tied parachute style).

1. Tie white calf wing as in previous instructions on page 134. Tie dark moose hair for tail and in pieces of four-strand yellow floss.

2. Wrap floss forward both in front and back of wing. Notice taper in body. A normal fly would use yellow thread but for demonstration purposes black is used here.

3. Lacquer body thoroughly.

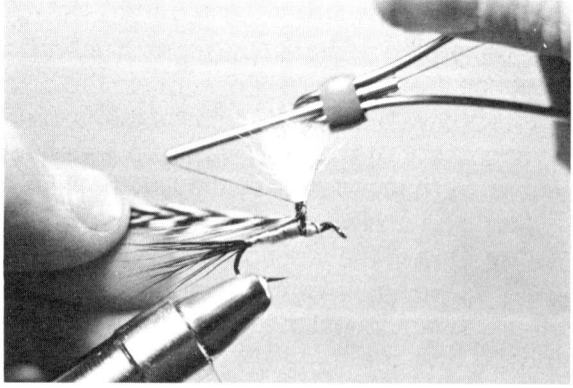

4. Tie in one grizzly and one brown hackle, both together. Notice how vein is being tied upwing.

5. Laquer, pull hackle away from wing while laquering. Let dry about three or four seconds before wrapping.

6. Wrap one turn of hackle around wing with hand. Attach hackle pliers and continue wrapping.

7. Wrap up the base of thread. Stop. Wrap back down the base of thread.

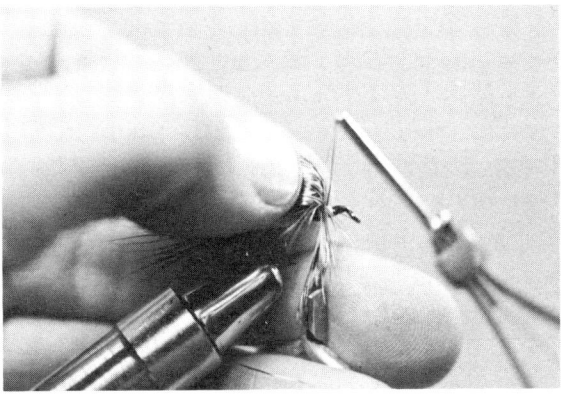

8. Tie off hackle when hackle has reached body. Whip finish, cement head, and check for balance of fly. Use scissor points to take out any hackle that might have gotten tied down. A touch of laquer on base of wing would not hurt.

Finished Fly

PARADRAKE

A few years ago two men revolutionized fly tying by introducing some dramatic new patterns. Carl Richards and Doug Swisher had good theories and their No-Hackle® flies instigated serious thinking about more natural insect imitations. I have tested their patterns and found them successful in certain western areas with waters similar to those of the Midwest where these flies were developed. There are two important fishing areas in the West which have become strongholds for the Swisher-Richards® patterns. One is the Henry's Fork River in eastern Idaho, the other is Armstrong Spring Creek near Livingston, Montana. Many of their studies concerned these particular areas, and their patterns are as effective here as any fly tied locally.

My experience with the Swisher-Richards patterns dictates that they are more adapted to the slow-moving water of rivers and small creeks. But much western fishing occurs on heavier water and does require specific western flies with more bouyancy. I suggest that you pick up a copy of Swisher and Richards' SELECTIVE TROUT to learn their useful new patterns. It is an excellent book and explains more about their patterns than I ever could. I am illustrating the Paradrake as a fine example of their work and a pattern which is a real fish-getter during the Green Drake hatches on the large streams of the West.

MATERIALS: Paradrake

HOOK: 94840 or 7957B.

SIZES: 8 to 20.

TAIL AND BODY: Dyed or natural gray deer hair: light or dark elk hair — depending on body color desired. I prefer elk as it is a bit tougher and stronger than deer hair. Also dark moose is adequate.

WINGS: Either calftail, deer hair, or elk hair.

HACKLE: Parachute style: color should co-ordinate with body color such as gray body color — badger, grizzly, and brown or grizzly hackle. With cream body color — cream or badger hackle, etc.

THREAD: Black or light cream monocord.

1. Select medium brown elk hair. Make sure that all strands are even. Measure for size as shown above.

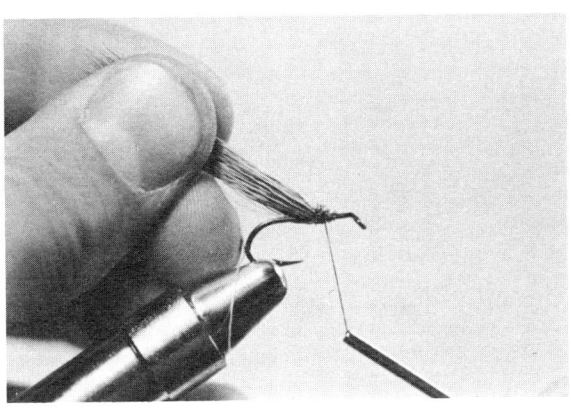

2. Tie base of hair to hook shank.

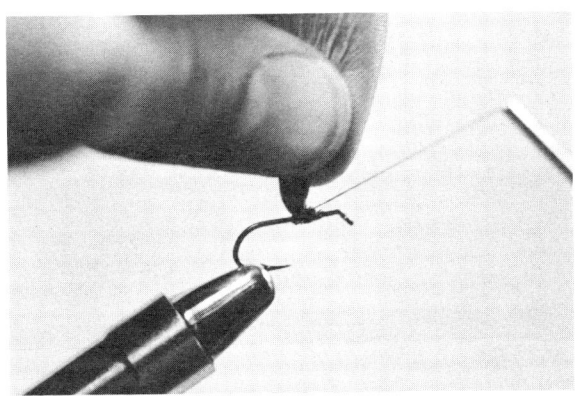

3. Wrap behind elk hair in circular fashion clockwise.

4. Tie in half-hitch behind wing.

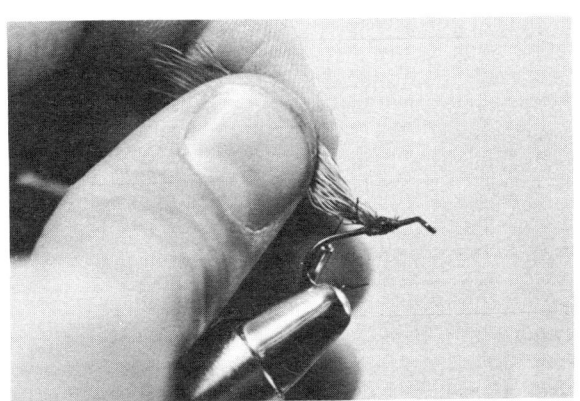

5. Wrap up body using thumb and finger to hold hair upward.

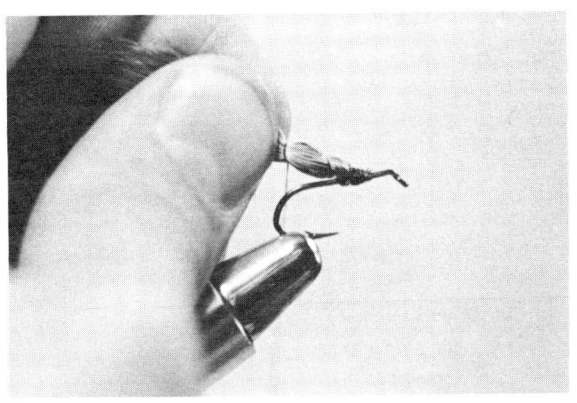

6. Continue to wrap body moving toward tail as if you were ribbing the hair.

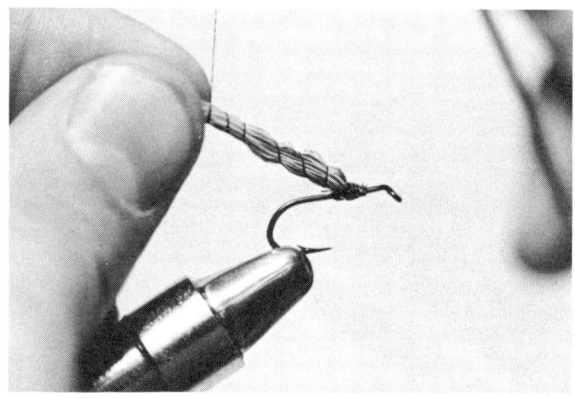

7. Thread ribbing hair in this picture.

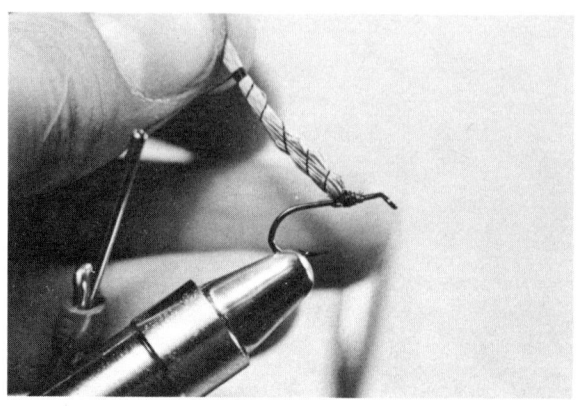

8. Wrap tightly around end of hair forming tail.

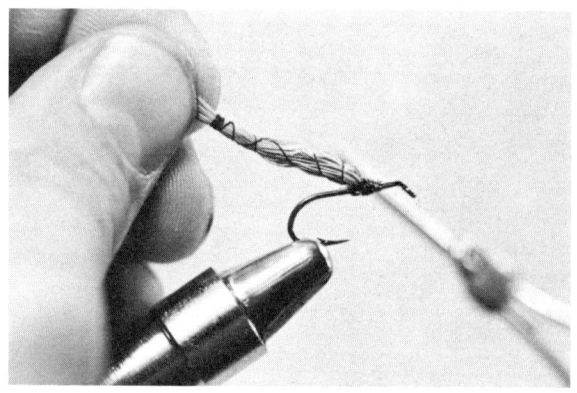

9. Wrap forward criscrossing previous ribbed thread.

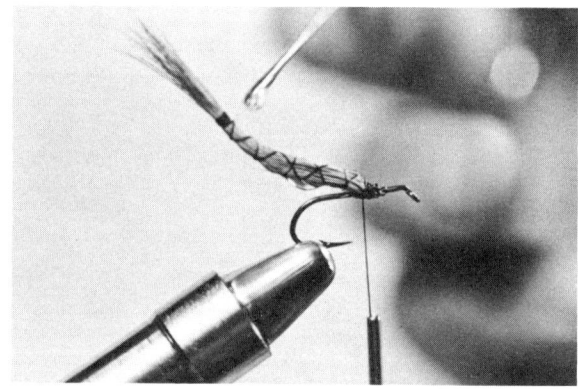

10. Continue to wrap until you get back to the base of the hook. Thoroughly cement the complete tail and body.

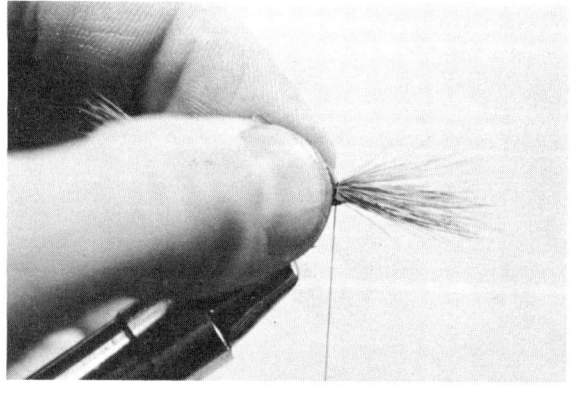

11. Tie on some medium brown elk hair. Tie forward over eye.

12. Trim base of hair.

13. Release hair and wrap behind hair toward body.

14. Wrap clockwise up wing as shown above.

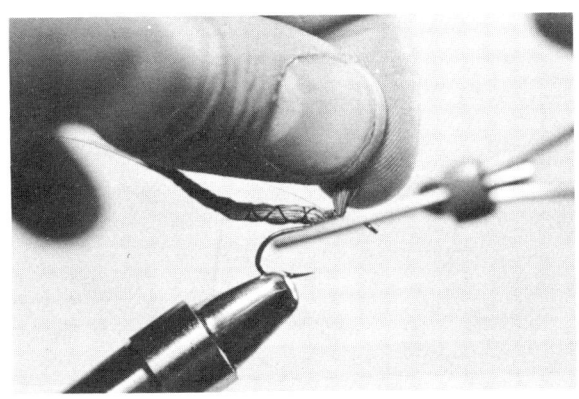

15. This picture shows gripping of wing between wraps.

16. Tie on two brown or other color saddle hackle or wide spade hackle. Make sure that vein of hackle is tied up to base of thread. Hackle should have dull side facing downward parallel to desk.

17. Attach hackle pliers, after one wrap has been made parachute style around wing base.

18. Continue to wrap hackle up toward base of thread and back down. You can use scissor points to remove any hackle that has become tied down.

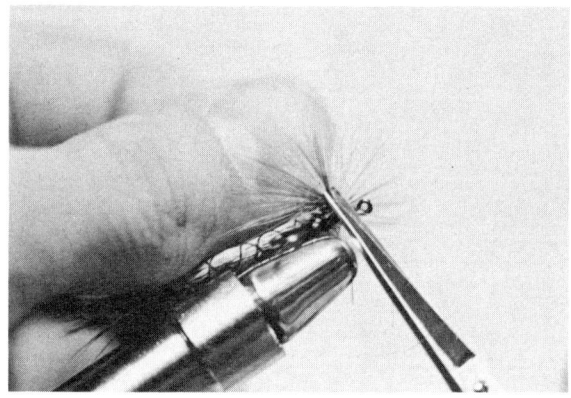

19. Tie on hackle, whip finish and laquer. Trim beneath fly for any protruding hair.

Finished Fly

Special Hair Streamers

Step by Step Instructions

MUDDLER MINNOW

In my opinion the Muddler Minnow is beyond all doubt the greatest fly ever tied. It was first developed in Canada by Don Gapen and later tied and popularized by Dan Bailey of Livingston, Montana. Since then, many versions of the Muddler Minnow have been tied throughout the world. In large sizes the Muddler represents one of the trouts' favorite foods, the sculpin minnow. There are as many different types of Muddler styles as there are varieties of sculpins. I know that if I were limited to one fly for fishing in the West, I would choose the Muddler Minnow because it performs so well in many different conditions. It can represent a grasshopper or a large Stone fly when fished dry. On a size 12 or 14 hook it can suggest a cricket or any number of other insects.

I like to cast the Muddler tight against a grassy or brush-laden bank. I fish it upstream letting it swing down with the current beneath the logs and bank. I then raise and lower the tip of my rod giving it a pumping action. It also can be cast straight downstream into a big hole with the same sort of pumping action. You also can use a careful strip at the same time you pump the rod giving it a little dart action. This movement mimics a struggling minnow very closely.

Brown trout are especially vulnerable to this fly and they have been known to charge out of an undercut bank to hit the fly like a freight train. Sometimes they will careen end over and through the water trying to throw the fabled Muddler. There is something about the way that a fish hits the Muddler that excites me more than any other type of fishing. There is no hesitation on the part of the fish as they strike and you can usually see the fish as they attack a Muddler.

I particularly like to use a floating line to fish a Muddler three or four inches under the surface where I can keep my eye on it. Tying it slightly weighted will help it bore a little deeper and is sometimes very effective. When floating down a river in a rubber raft, I don't think there is another wet fly that can touch a Muddler. It can be fished in and out of little fish-holding pockets of water with greater facility than most other flies. When you are floating a river, cast this fly upstream, then let the movement of the boat and the current swing the fly against the bank. Many people fish it downstream thereby diminishing its proper action. Sculpin minnows do not often swim upstream against a heavy current. Therefore casting the Muddler downstream and retrieving it against the current isn't the most effective way of fishing this fly in Western waters. The exception to this practice would be in deep, quieter holes or where the current is light. In that case a cast which is quartered downstream and stripped back can be just what the doctor ordered. There are many different ways of fishing the Muddler and each person will develop a way that works best for him.

Another good method to fish a Muddler is to put it right on the bottom by using a sinking line. This is extremely effective in rivers such as the Missouri and Yellowstone where the current is heavy and deep and the large fish lie on the bottom.

One further method to employ while fishing from a boat is to use a sinking tip line. A sinking tip line enables you to put a fly a little deeper than usual and yet is an easier line to pick up off the water than a regular sinking line when you are ready to cast again.

I have had good luck with a Muddler on the undercut small, deep, grassy creeks, such as Dell Creek in Montana, Flat Creek in Wyoming, and some stretches of Silver Creek in Idaho. I crawl on my hands and knees to get up to the deep holes and make a cast across the stream to the opposite bank, laying the fly on the grass. Then I pull it gently off the grass letting it hit the water. I let it float a short distance before swinging it beneath the undercut banks then stripping it back to the main current. Hopefully, at that time a large dark shadow will cut directly out of the bank and attempt to remove the Muddler Minnow from my line.

Where the rivers are very clear and slow-moving, it is important to use a light leader, even though it will be harder to cast the Muddler Minnow with one. When fishing in a larger, heavier river, the Muddler should be attached to a short heavily butted leader (seven and one-half feet is a good length). Such a leader will turn over better when you are fishing a big fly like a Muddler (which is not an easy fly to cast in any circumstance).

You will be surprised at some of the places where the Muddler will work. A few years ago, my friend and fellow fishing companion, Curt Gowdy, and I were fishing one of the Wyoming spring creeks. This particular creek is known for its many large trout. It is the sort of creek that one would look at and think "dry fly only".

We used Muddlers on 6X tippet with results unbelievable! We broke off many just because our tippet was so light yet they wouldn't touch a heavier leader. 10 trout over 2 lbs. were caught and released over a 3 hour period. That's results!

MATERIALS: Dennis Muddler Minnow

HOOK: 3665A Mustad.

SIZES: 1/0 to 12.

TAIL: Brown mottled turkey quill.

BODY: Yellow floss.

RIBBING: Tightly ribbed with medium gold flat tinsel.

UNDERWING: Fox squirrel tail.

UPPERWING: Mottled brown turkey quill, matched and tied wet style.

HEAD AND HACKLE: Clipped bullet shaped deer hair gray or light brown in color.

MUDDLER MINNOW – BAILEY STYLE

As Created By Dan Bailey's Fly Shop

THREAD:	White or gray Nymo thread or any heavy rod wrapping thread.
HOOK:	Mustad 9672 or 79580.
SIZES:	1/0 to 14.
TAIL:	Laquered brown mottled turkey quill.
BODY:	Medium gold tinsel (flat).
UNDERWING:	Brown calf tail.
UPPERWING:	Two matched brown mottled turkey quill.
HACKLE OR HEAD:	Clipped brown body deer hair; trim as per above picture.

MUDDLER MINNOW – DRY STYLE

THREAD:	Black or yellow Nymo thread.
HOOK:	Mustad 9672 or 79580.
SIZES:	8 to 14.
TAIL:	Brown mottled turkey quill.
BODY:	Yellow polypropolene yarn.
UNDERWING:	White calftail.
UPPERWING:	Two mottled brown turkey quills matched and tied curve up.
HEAD OR HACKLE:	Clipped deer hair; trimmed flat under head as per above picture.

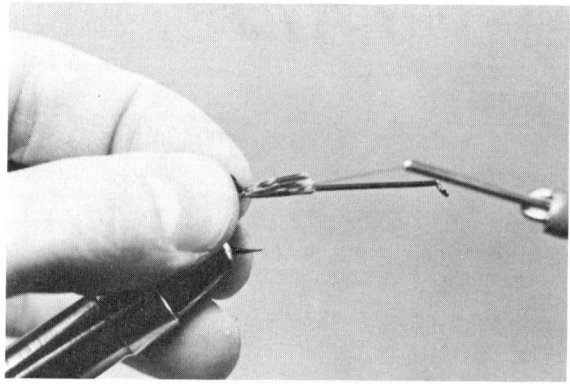

1. Trim one small piece of mottled brown turkey quill. Lay it on end of hook directly above the barb of the hook.

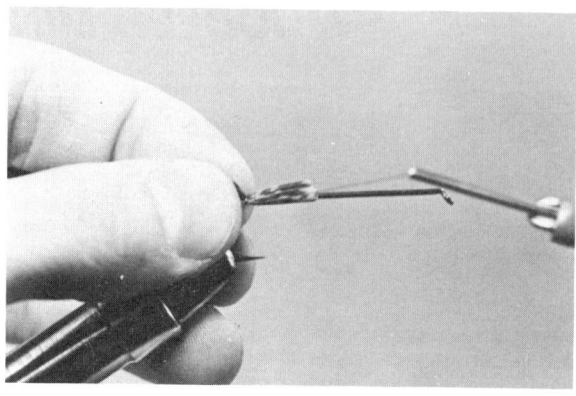

2. Tie down with thumb and forefinger. As you are tying down, push them forward giving a curve to the feather.

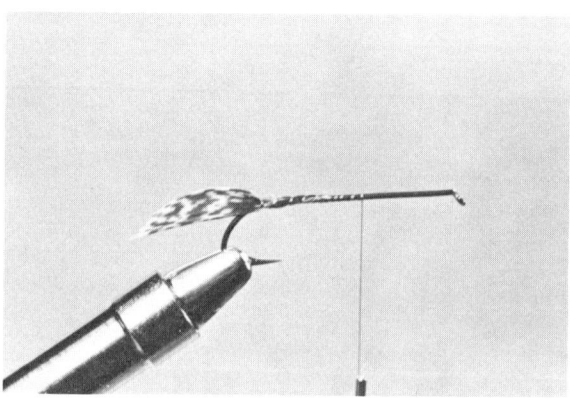

3. Feather should have a nice, even curve as shown. A touch of laquer on quill is good here.

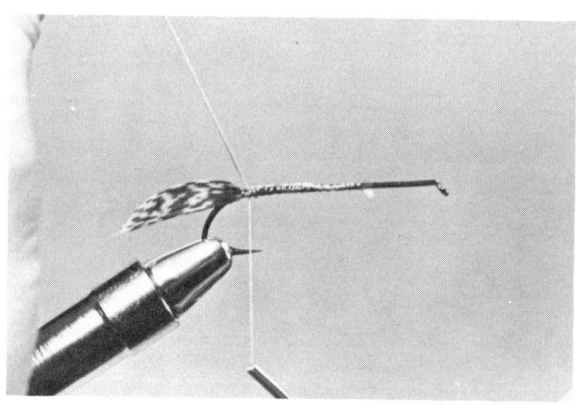

4. Tie in a piece of four-strand yellow floss. Notice that end of floss is wrapped along shank approximately two-thirds down body and tied directly back to tail.

5. Tie on flat gold tinsel, size depends on size of hook. Average size 12 is best. Tie it the same as floss was tied in.

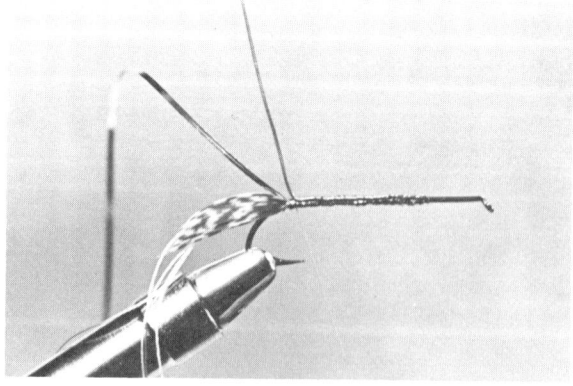

6. Tie on a piece of lead. Again, start wrapping it down where floss and tinsel are attached, tying it into the tail. It should meet tinsel and floss.

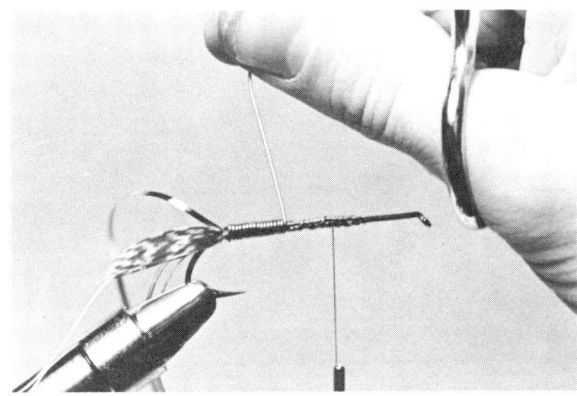

7. Wrap lead forward very tightly.

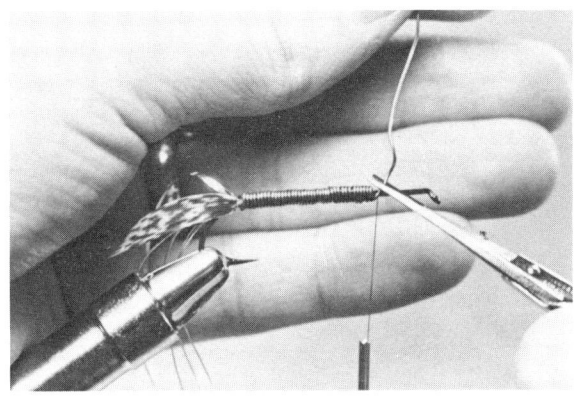

8. Trim lead and stop where floss, tinsel and lead were begun. It is approximately two-thirds to three-quarters of the way down the hook.

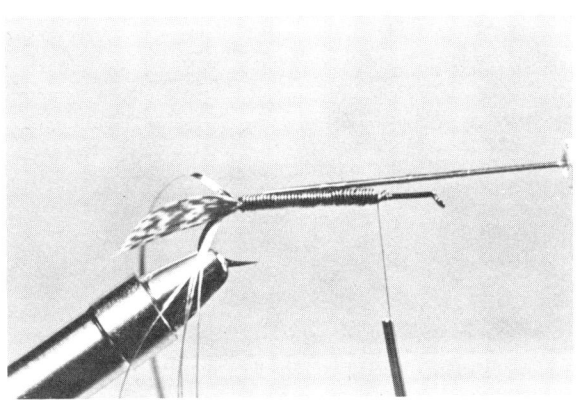

9. Laquer lead thoroughly.

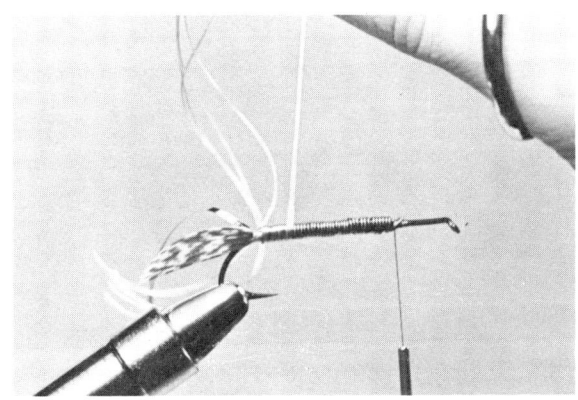

10. Wrap floss forward covering lead, making a nice, smooth, even body.

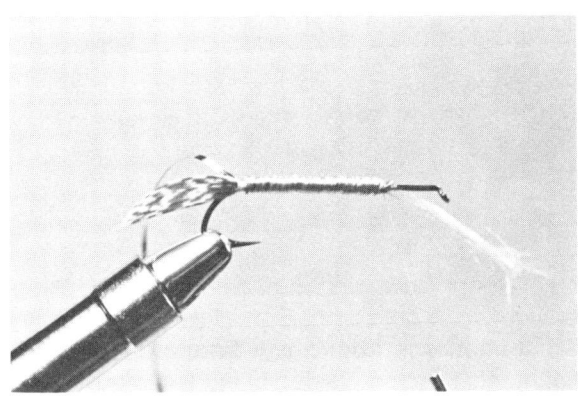

11. Tie off gold floss. At this point laquer may be applied.

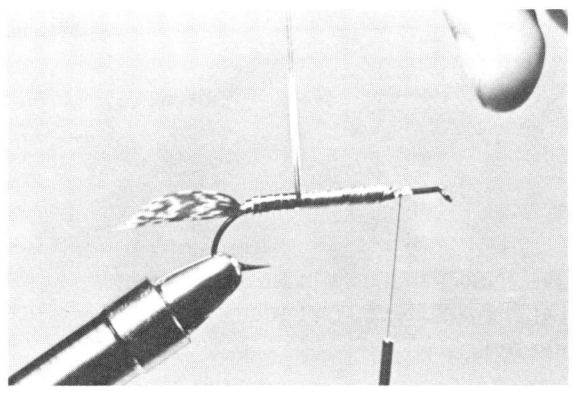

12. Wrap tinsel forward covering floss. Tinsel should be nice and even.

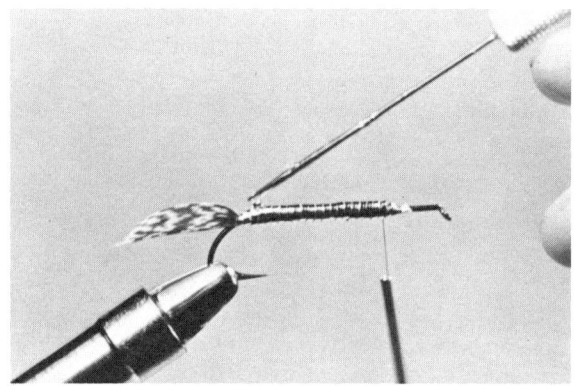

13. Laquer tinsel thoroughly.

14. Tie in either fox-squirrel tail or any other hair previously mentioned for underwing. Make sure that underwing does not exceed the length of the turkey quill tail.

15. Select a nice mottled brown turkey quill. Either a left or a right. With scissor points, measure and trim a wing from both sides of quill.

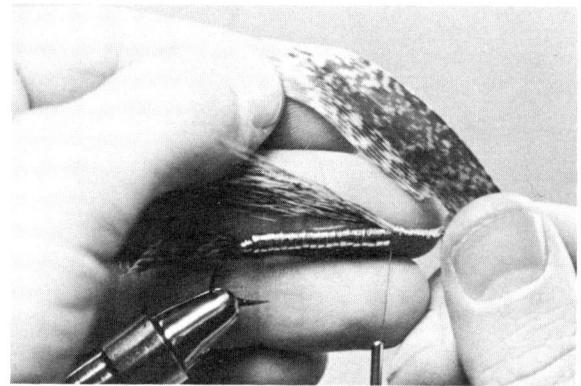

16. Meld both light sides of quill together forming a single wing.

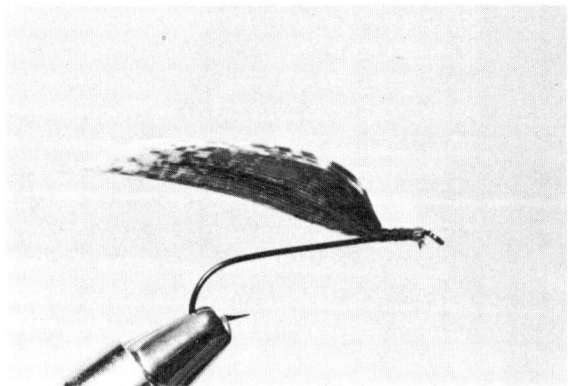

17. Notice that the wing is a single melded wing. On this picture you can see how the curve is up, the wing is full.

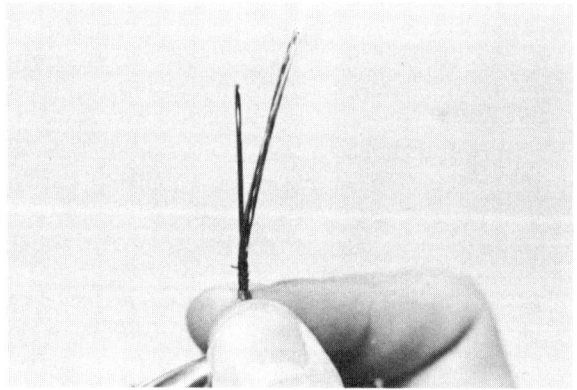

18. Notice how wing is curved. This is looking straight down onto hook. Some take one quill from a right and one from a left. I prefer to use quill segments from both sides of the same quill. This will give a little hook to the wing as shown. This renders more action to the fly when going through the water. I have made tests on this and have proved conclusively that this is a much better wing. It also makes turkey quills go twice as far.

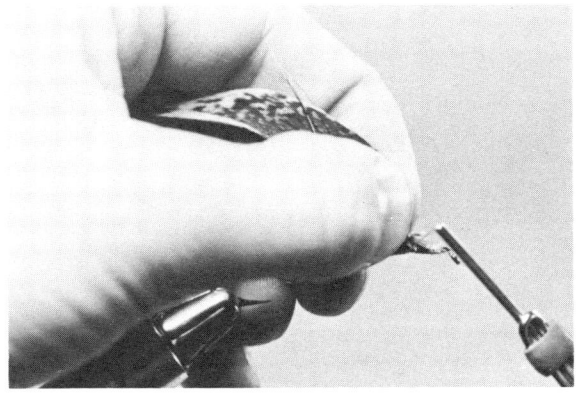

19. Tie on turkey quills with thumb and finger pushing forward as shown above tying it right on top of the squirrel tail underwing. Wrap tightly.

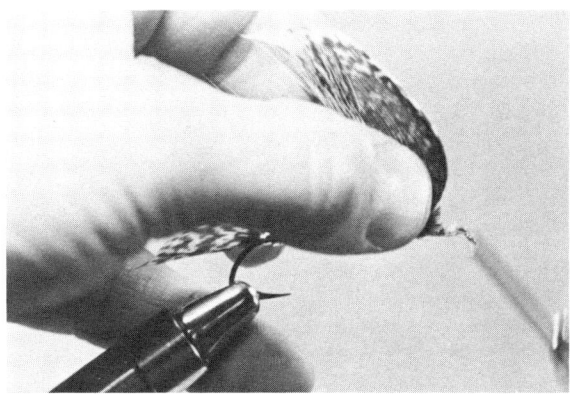

20. As you are wrapping, the thumb and finger are pulling the quill forward. This will give a nice bent curve that was evident in the previous steps.

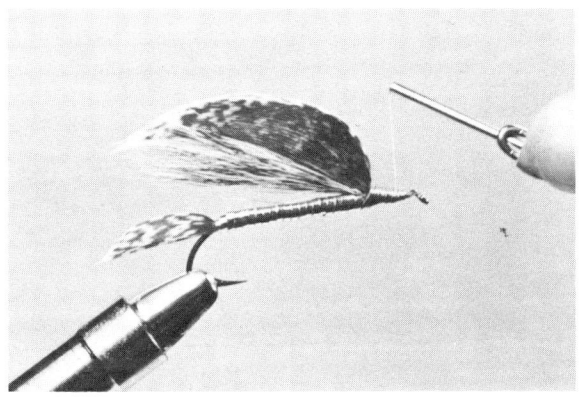

21. Make a smooth, even head, a good thread base on which to wrap the deer hair. Notice curve of wing.

22. Laquer thread base and bring thread up against wing.

23. With thumb and two fingers lay some coarse gray deer hair directly against the side closest toward you. Thread and bobbin are ready.

24. With thread make one wrap over and pull down tightly.

25. Wrap another wrap pulling again tighter.

26. Make the tightest pull on the third wrap and if necessary make another wrap. Make sure that the hair does not twist and is tied securely to head.

27. Take an equal amount of deer hair as was taken the first time and using thumb and forefinger put it on the opposite side of the quill in the same position as you did the first group of hair.

28. Make one tight wrap.

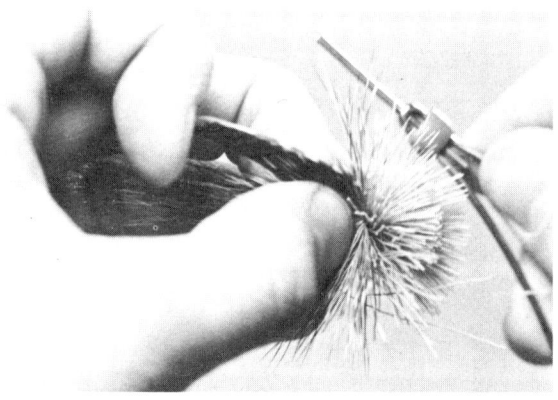

29. Again make another tighter wrap.

30. Make the tightest wrap.

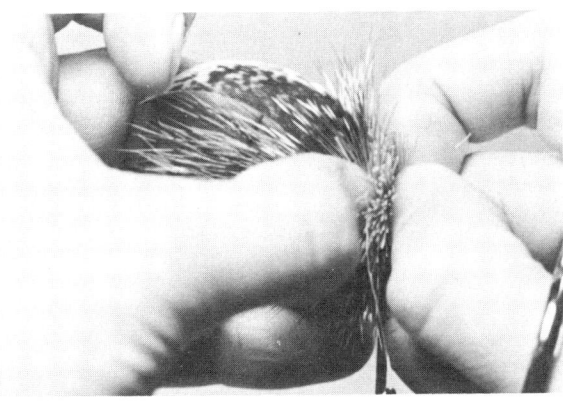

31. Wrap tying thread to the eye of hook and with thumb and forefinger of both hands push together making sure that deer hair is firm and tight.

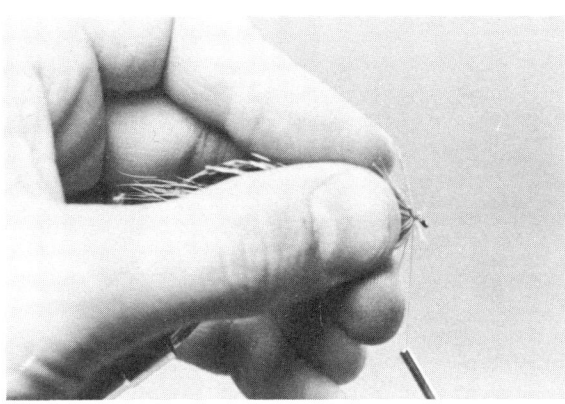

32. Pull back on deer hair and wrap a thread head. Whip finish and laquer.

33. Trim around deer hair until a smooth tapered head is made as shown above. Heads may vary in size and shape depending on the waters fished.

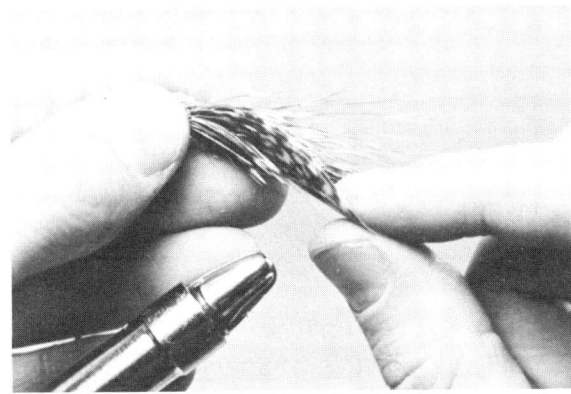

34. Notice the curve in wing when looking down directly on the Muddler Minnow.

35. Notice how head has been trimmed. Some of the deer hair tips are left as for a hackle collar and the rest is trimmed in the bullet-shaped head. Notice on the under side of the head it is trimmed flat and there is more hair on top of hook than below it. I feel that this is the best proportion for this fly.

MISSOULIAN SPOOK

This fly is one of the many variations of the Muddler Minnow. As a matter of fact because of its light color it is sometimes called a white or albino Muddler. The Missoulian Spook was first tied by Vince Hamlin who just happens to be the creator of "Alley Oop". The Spook was named after one of the characters of his comic strip.

It is a popular pattern among those who fish the large streams and rivers of Montana. It is particularly effective when used for large rainbows. Tie in sizes four through ten.

Not only does it look like a pale Muddler and is tied like a Muddler, but it is fished like one and works like one!

MATERIALS: Missoulian Spook

HOOK: Mustad 3665-A, 9672 or 79580.

SIZES: 1/0 to 14.

TAIL: Light mottled turkey quill.

BODY: Butt of red wool, white wool or floss, silver or gold flat tinsel rubbing.

UNDERWING: White calftail.

WING: Light mottled turkey quill.

HEAD: White deer hair clipped.

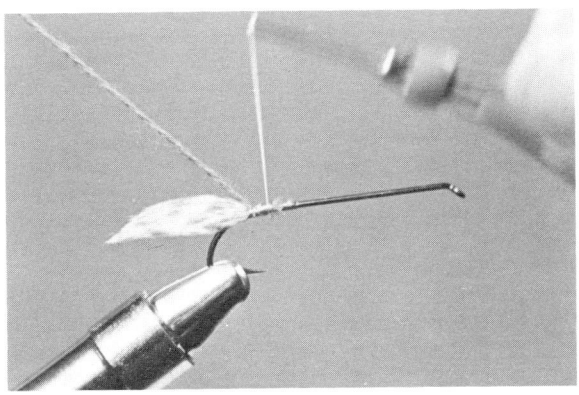

1. Tie in one light turkey quill curved down forming tail. Tie in double strand of red wool.

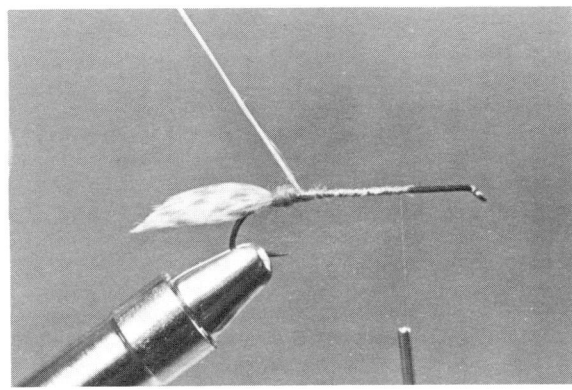

2. Wrap wool forward and tie off forming a butt or egg sac. Tie in a four-strand piece of white floss.

3. Tie on either silver or gold tinsel.

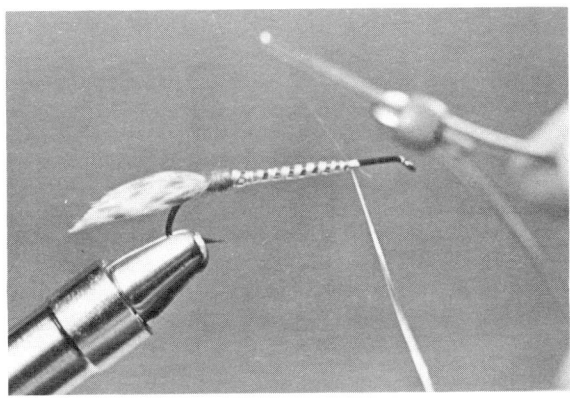

4. Wrap floss forward, tie off. Spiral forward tinsel ribbing.

5. Tie in white calftail tightly to shank of thread.

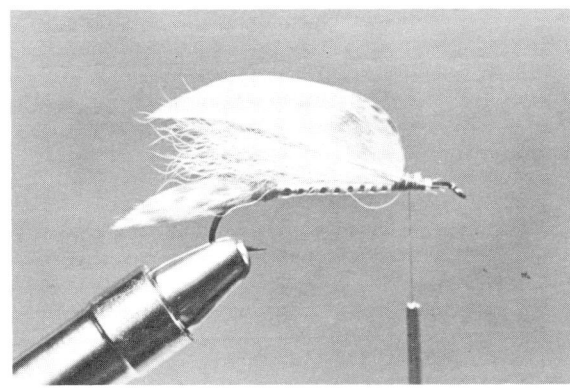

6. Tie on white turkey wing. This can be taken from a mottled turkey that is a light white or creamy color.

7. Tie a bunch of white deer hair on both sides of hook. Refer to Muddler Minnow on page 153 for further instruction on how to tie muddler head.

8. After both groups of hair have been tied in, the thread should be whip finished and laquered and the deer hair head should be trimmed and formed, as shown in next photo. This shows the completed Missoulian Spook. Notice how head is trimmed.

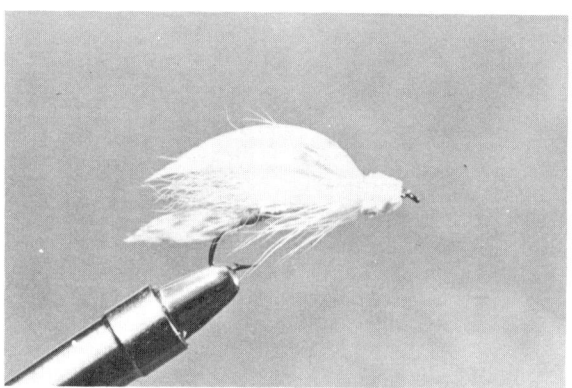

Finished Fly

MARIBOU MUDDLER

In my opinion the Maribou Muddler is one of the greatest brown trout flies ever invented. The soft breathing action of the maribou feather together with the minnow-like appearance of the fly constitutes one of the all-time great combinations. Designed by Dan Bailey and since improved by others, this Muddler will snap up every salt or fresh water fish that will hit a surface plug. I have even tried these flies on striped bass with great success.

The Maribou Muddler is tied in several styles; however, I am describing a mylar body style which I feel is one of the most deadly bodies known to the fly tyer today. This fly should almost always be weighted to counter-balance the light Maribou feather. It can be slightly or heavily weighted depending on the water you intend to fish. I particularly enjoy fishing the Maribou Muddler in heavy, brushy streams where the browns hide. Either from a boat or from the bank. I like to drift the fly down into the hole and then, with long strips on the retreive, pump the rod to give the fly the breathing action that allures trout so well. The pumping action employs the full value of the Maribou feather which gives the fly its advantage over the standard Muddler Minnor. The largest trout that I have ever hooked was fooled by a number two yellow Maribou Muddler.

MATERIALS: Maribou Muddler

HOOK: 9672, 9671, 3665A, or 79580.

SIZES: 1/0 to 12

BODY: Silver or gold tinsel; or silver or gold sparkle chennille (tinsel chennille) or mylar tubing in either silver or gold.

HEAD: Clipped deer hair.

UNDERWING: None (or light and brown calftail or fox squirrel tail).

UPPERWING: Maribou plume feathers — either white, brown, black, yellow, olive, or any other combination of colors that is suitable.

HEAD: Clipped deer hair.

TAIL: Either red neck hackle or none.

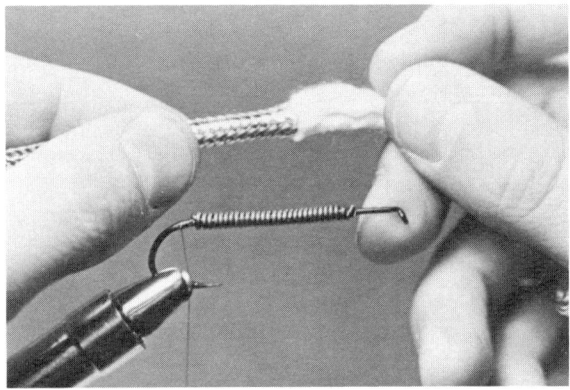

1. Wrap on medium lead leaving room at bend of hook. Wrap the red at that point. Remove cotton fiber of mylar tubing.

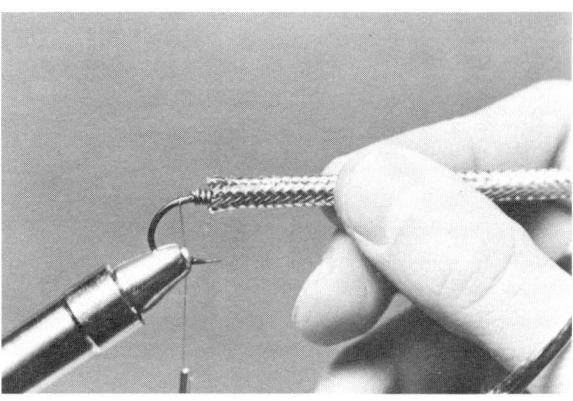

2. Put tubing through fly at eye and push backward.

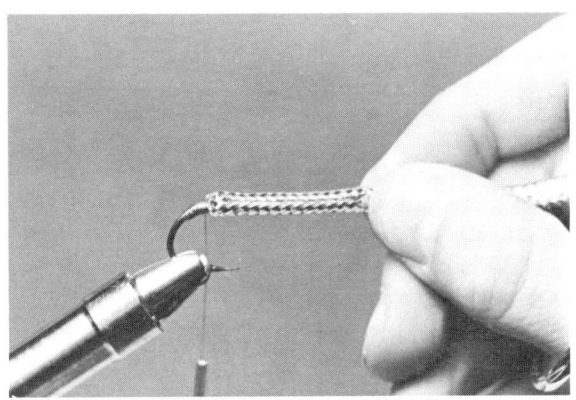

3. Tie down mylar with red wrapping thread neat and even.

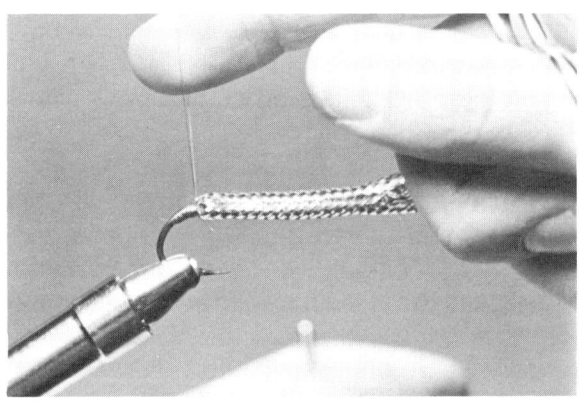

4. Wrap a half-hitch or whip finish by hand.

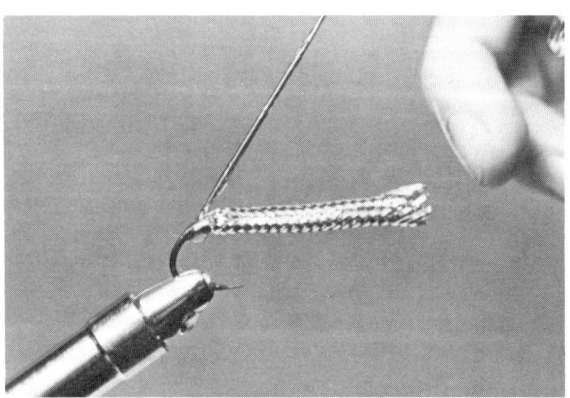

5. Laquer end thoroughly.

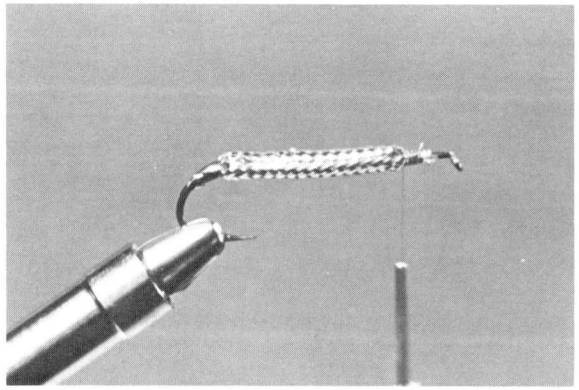

6. Tie thread down and pull forward tying it down. Make sure that it is stretched enough to be tight.

7. Tie on a plume of white maribou tied tightly. Trim off excess.

8. Laquer thread. Notice that there is a firm base of thread before tying on head.

9. Wrap hair on both sides of hook as shown on Muddler Minnow. Make sure thread is tight.

10. Trim head again as shown previously in Muddler Minnow instructions.

Finished Fly

SPUDDLER

First created by Dan Bailey and Red Monical of Livingston, Montana, the Spuddler combines the attraction — versaticity of the Spruce Fly with the allure of the Muddler. This deadly sculpin imitation is considered one of the hottest flies in the many rivers of Montana, where it is tied in sizes 2 through 10. When floating the mighty Missouri, it is a great fly to flip into the back eddies and up against the brush banks. Fish it heavily weighted and drop it under the grassy and willow stream banks, then jerk it backward with a quick retrieve (or you can just allow it to swing naturally under the bank). It also teases trout out of heavy, deep pools if you use a sinking line to let it bump the bottom.

My own experience with the Spuddler has been on the Green River in western Wyoming, where I find that it is a good producer on both browns and rainbows. Fishing it in the morning at the shallow tail waters of a pool tricks large brown trout feeding on rock sculpin. Keeping it slightly dry and then pulling it under the surface with short, quick jerks is a very effective method.

I tie this fly a little differently from the original designed by Bailey. I am including both patterns, mine and Bailey's, so that you can catch twice as many fish!

MATERIALS: Spuddler — *Dennis version*

HOOK: 9672, 9671, or 79580.

BODY: Cream wool.

UNDERWING: Fox squirrel tail (or none).

UPPERWING: Grizzly or variegated hackle, tied flat to the hook with one curvature going left, the other going right.

HEAD:	Antelope hair trimmed flat.
TAIL:	Brown calftail.
THREAD:	Nymo, cream or light brown.
MATERIALS:	Spuddler — *Bailey version*
HOOK:	9672 or 79580
BODY:	Dubbed wool or cream spun fur or wool.
UNDERWING:	Brown calftail tied standard or dyed brown.
UPPERWING:	Plymouth Rock neck hackles dyed brown.
HEAD:	Antelope hair, reddish brown spun on and trimmed.
THREAD:	Monocord, cream, black, or brown.

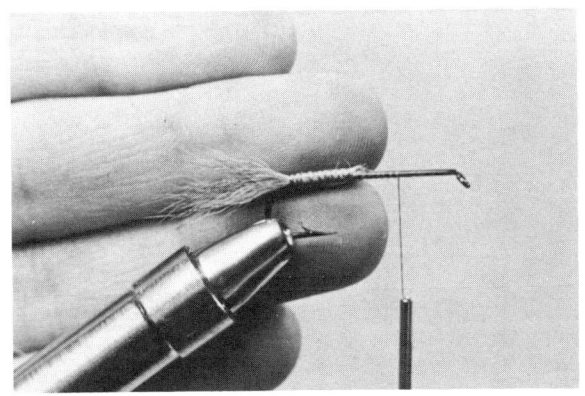

1. Tie on brown calftail to form tail.

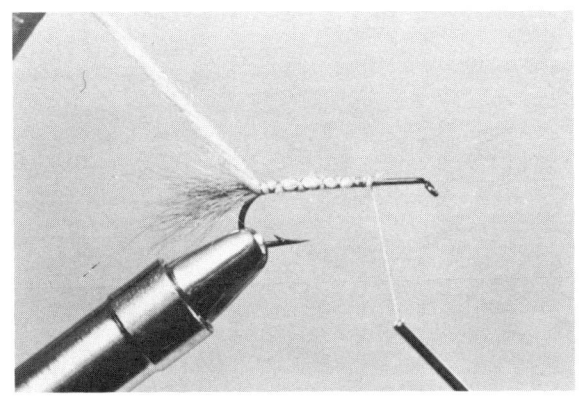

2. Either dub or tie on creamish wool.

3. Wrap creamish wool forward to form a taper.

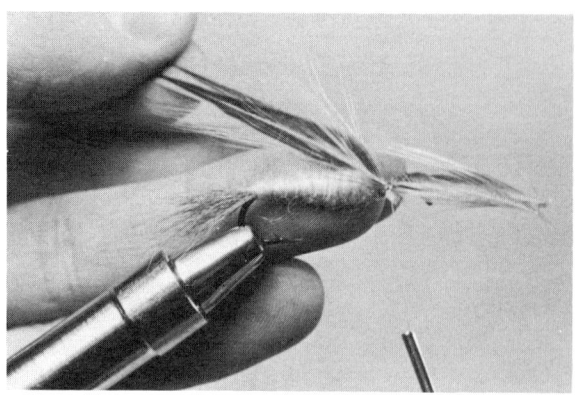

4. Tie on two either badger or variegated or ginger variant or brown dyed grizzly hackle, dark sides facing.

5. Pull hackles wide so they spread out.

6. Tie on two bunches of reddish brown antelope hair as shown previously in Muddler instructions.

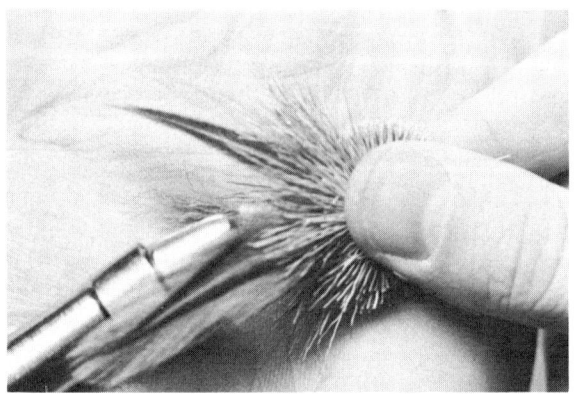

7. After tying off and whip finishing head, use thumb and forefinger to spread out head.

8. From eye of hook cut at a 45° angle. Repeat this on other side. Trim on top and on bottom.

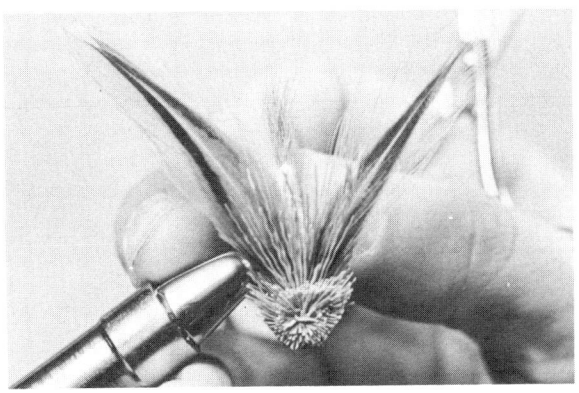

9. Form by trimming a triangle shaped head that will be flat on bottom and top.

Finished Fly

Nymphs

Step by Step Instructions

MONTANA NYMPH

In the Idaho — Montana — Wyoming area of the West this fly is known as the number one nymph, the trout killer! It always produces. It is basically a stone fly imitation but can be used to represent other nymphs. Its several variations can be either weighted or non-weighted. The larger sizes of Montana Nymphs are effective in the large, deep rivers of the western U.S. Small sizes, such as 12 and 14, function well on small springs, and spring fed ponds. I have found that beaver ponds, which may have good populations of large trout, are great places for this fly. On the heavy and fast Snake River, I have had good success with a heavily weighted number 6 Montana Nymph, reaching down to the deep holes. I have discovered that this pattern in sizes 10 and 12 in smaller spring creeks using a dead drift will catch trout that I never dreamed were there.

Fly fishing for trout in ponds and lakes is becoming quite popular. This nymph performs very well in small lakes for me. The best method to fish with the fly in slow or still water is to use short jerks when retreiving it. In faster moving water I have noticed that it is best to let the nymph sink and swing around, which drops it deep into the hole, and then to retreive it with large strips. Most of the time, the fish will hit the fly on its swing while the current is moving it. If you have never tried the Montana Nymph, I think that you will be pleasantly surprised at its results.

MATERIALS: Montana Nymph

TAIL: Black hackle tips or brown hackle tips.

BODY: Black chennile.

THORAX: Orange, yellow, or insect green chennile.

HACKLE: Black or brown hackle.

CASE: Black chennile.

THREAD: Red, black or yellow, (I prefer red).

HOOKS: Mustad 9671, 9672, or 3906B.

SIZES: 6, 8, 10, 12, 14.

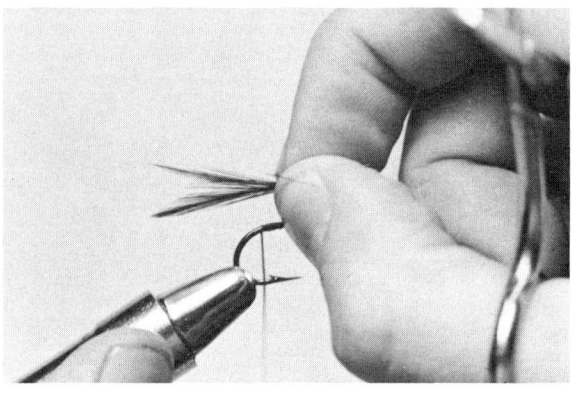

1. Attach hook to vise. Wrap thread back to end of barb. Select two black hackle tips. Have hackle tips inside curve facing or darker sides of hackle facing each other — forming V.

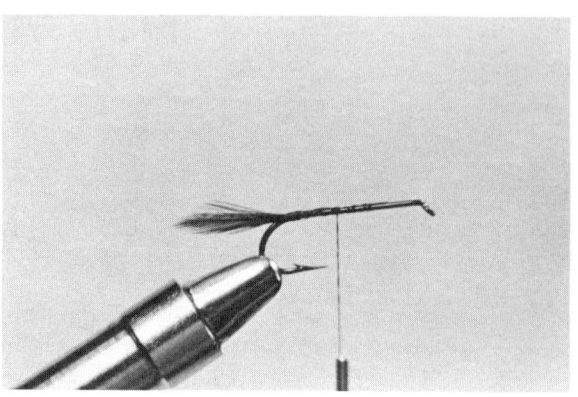

2. Tie tail on. Tail should be divided in V formation at end of hook.

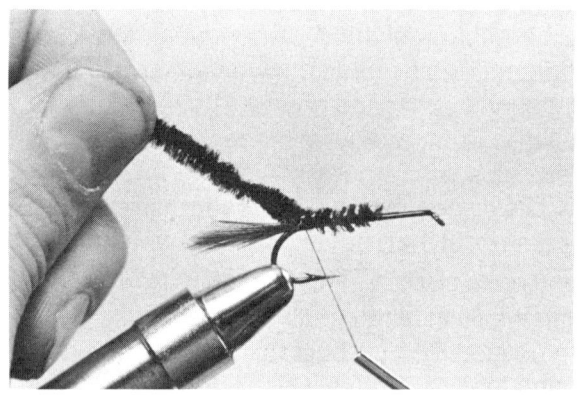

3. Tie on medium black chennile. Secure tightly. Wrap thread forward half-way to eye of hook.

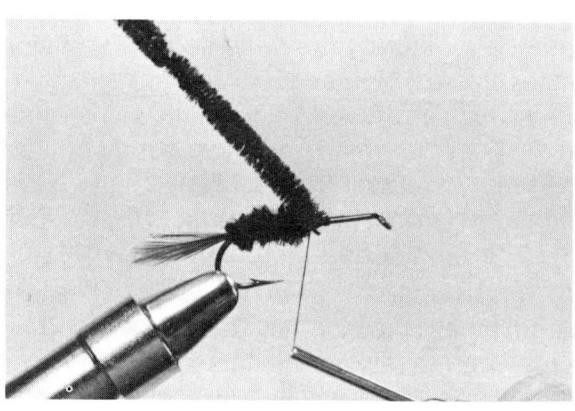

4. Wrap chennile forward ½ length of hook and secure with thread. Do not cut, leave hanging.

5. Tie on medium yellow chennile on first ½ of hook, tying back to meet black chennile.

6. Tie in either brown, furnace, or black hackle with curve of feather facing forward, so when wrapped the hackle will fold back.

7. Wrap yellow chennile forward leaving room for head. Tie off, and trim.

8. Wrap hackle at least three wraps and tie off at head.

9. Pull the remaining piece of black chennile back over the yellow chennile or thorax.

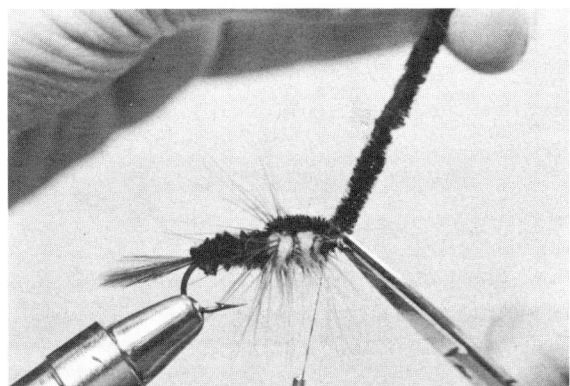

10. Tie and trim off black chennile forming case. Whip finish and cement.

Finished Fly

STONE FLY NYMPH

The stone fly is probably the most common nymph in most western waters. Because there is such a great variety of stone fly nymphs in the West, I suggest that you tie a stone fly pattern which imitates the nymphs in the area you intend to fish. In the fly pattern dictionary in the back of this manual there are several different patterns that are worth a try. The stone fly usually comes in two basic colors — either gray or brown — with many different shades or variations of these colors. The most predominant color in the Montana- Idaho- Wyoming section of the West is a dark brown.

The pattern illustrated in the pictures is one which was shown to me by Phil Wright formerly of Aspen, Colorado, now of Wise River, Montana. I have made some basic modifications of the original pattern using more available materials.

According to Phil this was an offshoot of a stone fly pattern by the master nymph tier and authority, Ernest Schwiebert. I have used this pattern all over the West and found it to be very effective. Phil claimed that if this fly were correctly fished that it would definitely be the most effective nymph wherever dark brown stone flies hatched. It is a time-consuming fly to tie and one that you won't want to lose very often.

I have found the fly to be most effective when cast directly across from you into a heavy current letting it drift down into the hole with slight twitches given to the line. After the fly makes its swing, strip it back with long smooth strokes. Generally the fish will take the fly on its first dead drift into the hole. When the current swings the nymph you will feel the fish strike it.

Most of my experience with this fly has been on the large rivers such as the Madison, Yellowstone, Snake, and Green Rivers where stone flies are most predominant. I have not used it in any lakes or small springs, but some of my fellow fishermen have told me that these flies tie in small sizes and are very good in small spring creeks. I definitely would tie this fly weighted, and I believe it produces best with sinking tip line such as the High D Wet Tip Fly line. I think that the fly is most effective when cast and drifted directly to the bottom, worked through the bottom on a swing then immediately jerked back and recast to a different position. A sinking tip line better accommodates this type of casting than conventional sinking lines. I have found that a 9 foot, heavy butt-leader, either 2x or 3x, is the best complement for this fly.

MATERIALS:	Stone Fly Nymph
THREAD:	Black monocord.
HOOK:	Mustad 9671 or 9672.
SIZES:	4, 6, 8, 10.
TAIL:	Moose body hair.
BODY:	Dark brown wool with a small strand of gray or dark cream wool.
RIBBING:	Stripped peacock herl.
THORAX:	Dark brown chennile.
HACKLE:	Dyed brown grizzly.
CASE:	Moose body hair.
FEELERS:	Moose body hair.

1. Tie on a bunch of dark brown or black moose hair with butt ending ½ way up shank of hook. Secure tightly with thread.

2. Divide tail in two equal parts, tying from one side to the other forming an X pattern, thus dividing tail.

3. Strip two peacock quills.

4. Tie peacock quills to body.

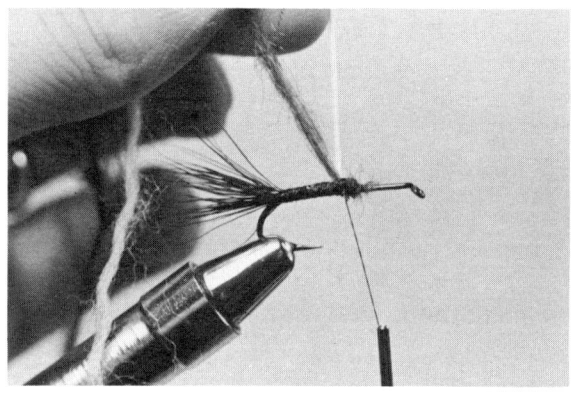

5. Tie one strand of cream wool to a large strand of medium brown angora or wool.

6. Twist both strands of yarn together till they form one single strand.

7. Wrap yarn forward forming body. Be careful to taper body correctly.

8. Wrap both stripped peacock quills forward ribbing tapered body.

9. Tie off peacock quills. Notice proportion and body taper.

10. Tie on a medium bunch of dark moose hair. Tie very securely.

11. Tie in medium brown chennile.

12. Tie in one or two, depending on thickness, dyed brown grizzly hackle.

13. Laquer thorax liberally.

14. Wrap brown chennile forming thick thorax.

15. Wrap dyed brown grizzly hackle forward. Three to four wraps is sufficient. Tie off hackle.

16. Wrap thread back from eye toward moose hair.

17. Trim top hackle over thorax. Use thumb to guide scissors.

18. Pull moose hair forward forming case. Wrap thread over moose hair in middle of thorax, tying it down tightly.

19. Thread securely ties down first part of case.

20. Wrap forward and tie down remaining moose hair, forming full thorax. Divide remaining moose made at wing, X-ing at same pattern as the tail was.

21. Trim bottom hackle. Notice divided front antennae.

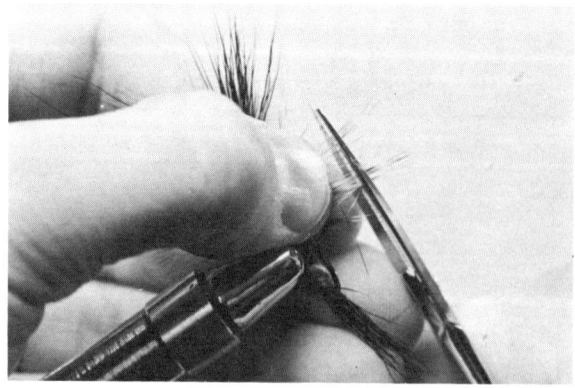

22. Trim side hackle leaving approximately ¼" from body.

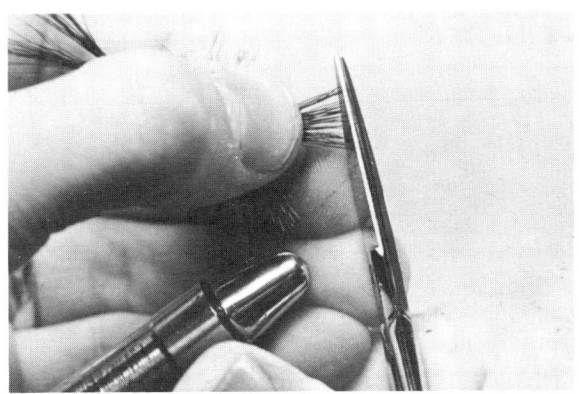

23. Trim antennae forward.

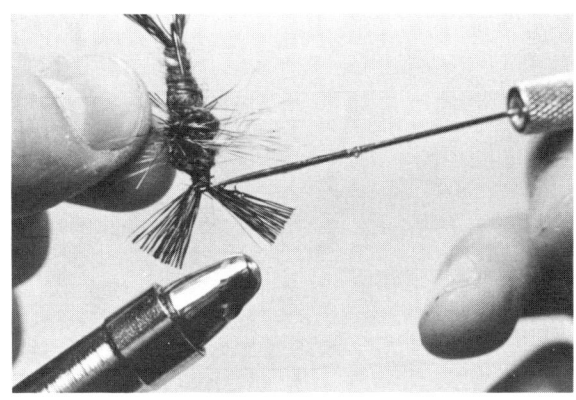

24. Laquer antennae, and notice proportion of antennae to main body.

25. Laquer case and tail liberally. Also laquer ribbed tapered body.

Finished Fly

MAY FLY NYMPH

There are many variations of mayflies, which are important in the diet of Western trout. I have presented the standard May Fly Nymph pattern, but I will suggest some modifications which can increase the versatility of this basic tie. The type of mayflies in your region would dictate the proper color for flies fished in that area. For the Rocky Mountain West, a selection of nymphs in gray, cream, brown and off-yellow should be sufficient to match most local mayflies. There are several other nymphs which can also imitate the mayfly nymphs to a "T." As your proficiency as a tyer progresses, you will learn these patterns and should make good use of them.

An important thing to remember when fishing the Mayfly Nymph is that it is usually most effective in a dead drift. This, of course is the hardest method for fishing any nymph. Some people describe it as if fishing when completely blind. Many times the only hint of a strike is a slight swirl on the water, the flash of a fish or just a hunch that the trout has taken your fly. I have found that using an orange or white fly line is helpful in keeping an eye on a dead-drift nymph. Following the line out to the very end and then judging the normal leader length, — say — 9 feet, — and keeping your eye on the general area where the fly should be is usually the most reliable method. The nymph will then end its dead drift arcing through the current downstream. When the fly is directly downstream from you, strip in and cast once more.

MATERIALS:	Light May Fly Nymph
THREAD:	Cream herb howard pre-waxed
HOOK:	3906B or 9671 or 7957B
SIZES:	8 to 16.
TAIL:	Wood duck barred breast feather or dyed imitation wood duck mallard breast feathers.
BODY:	Tapered cream fur dubbing, can be fox, coyote, otter, or any other cream fur.
THORAX:	Cream dubbing fur.
CASE:	Wood duck barred breast feather fibers pulled over thorax, can be imitation wood duck.
HACKLE:	Cream neck hackle tied beard-style.

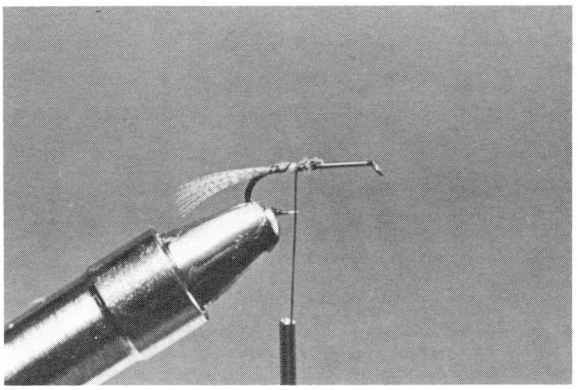

1. Tie several strands of wood duck or dyed wood duck mallard breast on for tail. Tail may vary from ½ length of hook to ¼ length of hook (as per tyer's preference).

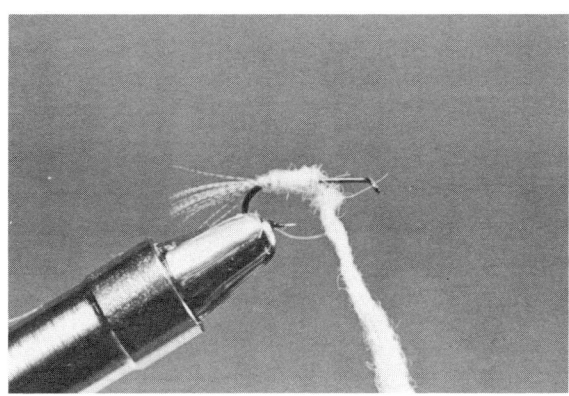

2. Dub on cream dubbing, either red fox fur, coyote, or similar cream dubbing. Dub on as shown by previous dubbing method.

3. Finish dubbing and taper dubbing from tail to front, 2/3 of way down hook.

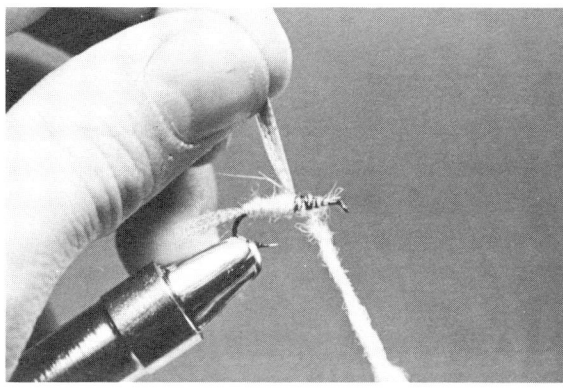

4. Tie in one wood duck breast or dyed mallard wood duck breast then add cream fur dubbed to thread.

5. Wrap dubbed cream fur forward forming thorax.

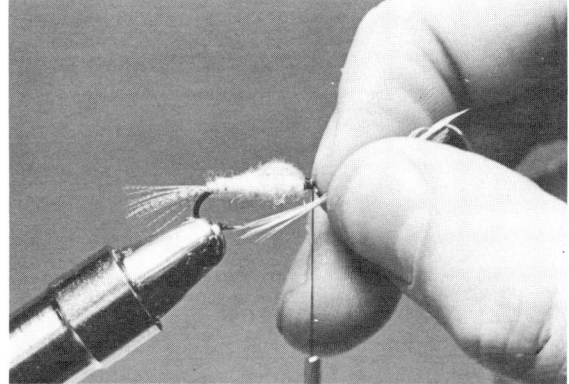

6. Pull mallard breast forward over thorax forming case. Tie down securely, then pull several fibers from a soft cream neck hackle or hen hackle. Judge size first before tying.

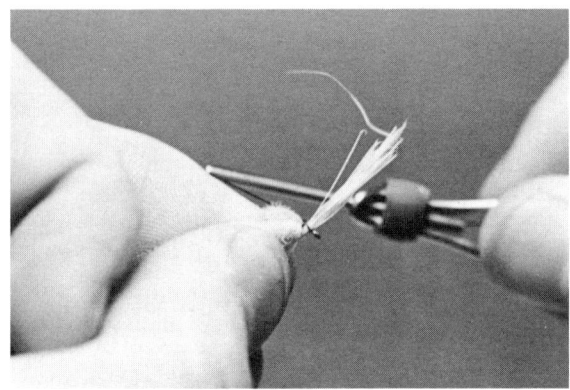

7. Tie beard hackle directly underneath the body as shown. Trim whip finish and laquer your mayfly nymph.

Finished Fly

MARCH BROWN NYMPH

This nymph is a well-known one anywhere and can be purchased in almost any fly shop throughout the U.S. The method of tying this fly varies from region to region. This pattern is generally approved by trout anywhere in the West. Most of my experience with the March Brown has been confined to spring creeks and small spring-fed rivers . . . usually slow-flowing ones with lots of moss and many different insect hatches. I like the nymph fished on a dead drift with no action at all. I usually tie it in sizes 10 and 12. It is also an excellent imitation when small brown mayflies are hatching. Try fishing it two or three inches below the surface. It is just an all-round good nymph to dig out when you are wondering what to tie on.

MATERIALS: March Brown Nymph

THREAD: Herb Howard pre-waxed black or black monocord.

HOOK: 9671 or 3906B

SIZES: 8 to 16

TAIL: Brown hackle.

BODY: Brown floss.

RIBBING: Stripped peacock eye.

THORAX: Peacock herl, two or three strands.

HACKLE: Soft brown neck hackle.

CASE: Turkey quill fiber.

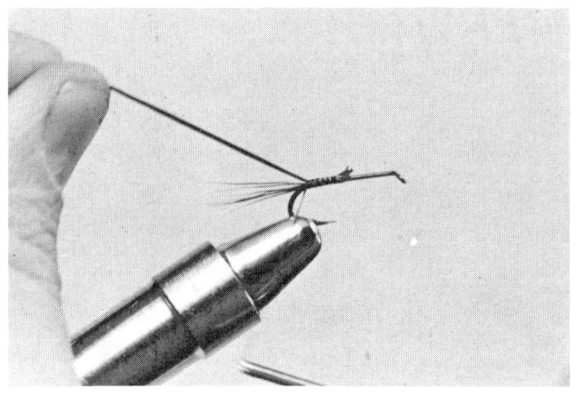

1. Tie in five or six strands of moose hair, preferably dark brown or black for tail. Also tie in four strand brown floss.

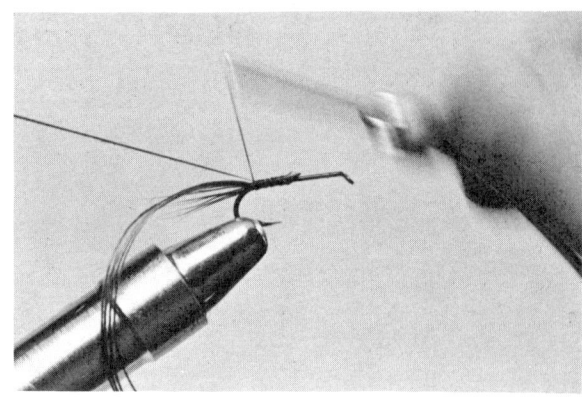

2. Add one stripped peacock quill. Tie it carefully so as not to cut fiber.

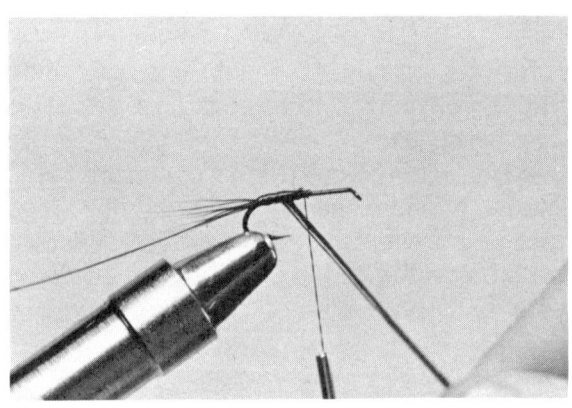

3. Wrap floss forward, tapering it from tail to front. Stop approximately ½ way down fly.

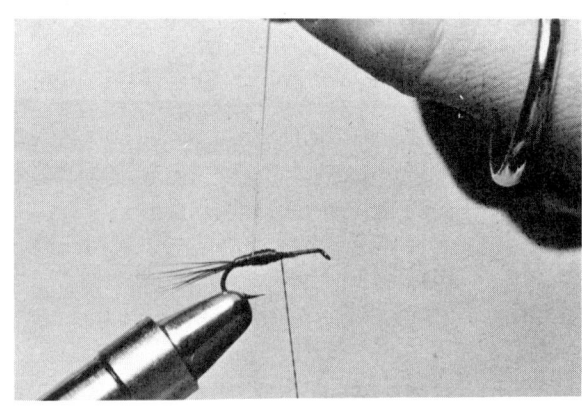

4. Spiral stripped peacock herl forward ribbing floss. Notice taper on body. Tie off peacock quill.

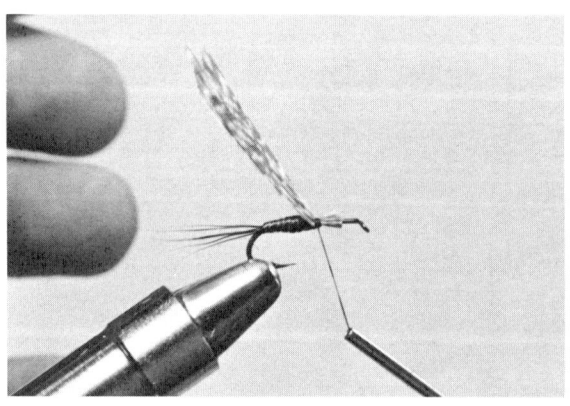

5. Tie on strip of mottled brown turkey quill.

6. Tie on three to four strands of peacock herl.

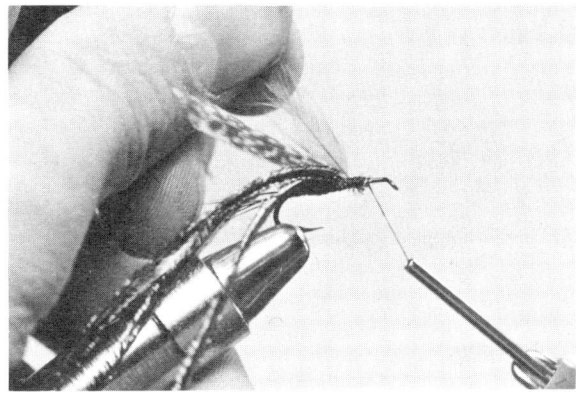

7. Tie on one soft brown neck hackle, medium color.

8. Wrap peacock herl forward forming thorax.

9. Wrap brown hackle forward usually three of four wraps is sufficient.

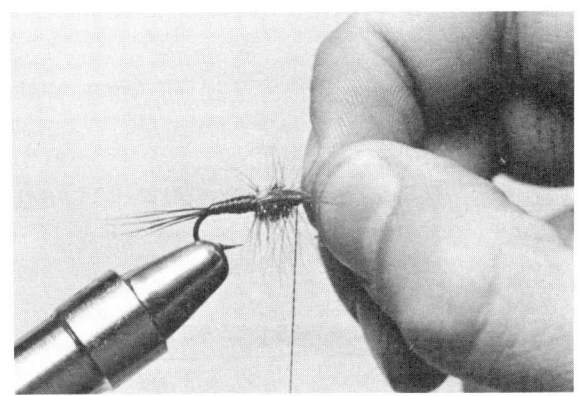

10. Pull turkey quill forward forming a case.

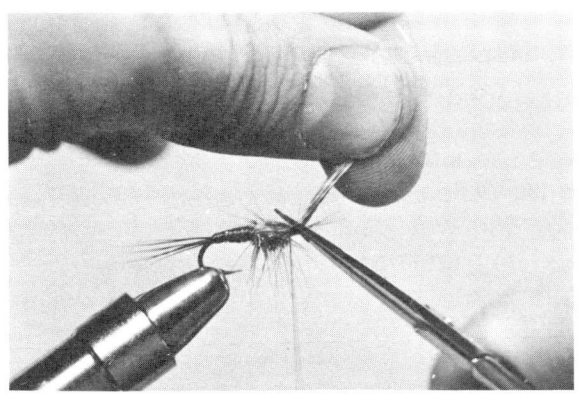

11. Tie off turkey quill and trim. Whip finish head and laquer.

Finished Fly

TELLICO NYMPH

This nymph claims popularity all over the West, because it is suggestive of many different kinds of nymphs and even some of the beetles found at high altitudes. In fact, it is a fair copy of several terrestial insects that hatch around the lakes above 7,000 feet. A great favorite of the late Buz Buszek, and often employed by him for fishing high-mountain lakes, it demands the attention of all avid nymph fishermen. Tied either unweighted or weighted, it floats in the surface film or penetrates to the bottom.

My experience has proved it to be a good heavy nymph. I find it most productive in the high mountain lakes or in the spring-type rivers such as the Firehole and the Meadow section of the Madison River through Yellowstone Park. I would recommend it as one of the best nymphs for fishing in Yellowstone Park. But it doesn't seem to be as productive in swifter rivers, such as the Snake, lower Madison, and Big Hole. Many of my friends use the Tellico Nymph to catch high-mountain brook trout and also for the famed California golden trout.

Here in Wyoming, where the world's record golden trout was caught, there are many lakes above 9,000 feet which hold these flashy treasures. They seem to be most vulnerable to small nymphs such as the Tellico, and to dry flies such as small black gnats. I would have to say that it is one of the best golden trout nymphs that I have ever discovered.

I think that it attracts most trout when fished on a dead drift with very little movement. Sometimes, the line on a dead drift slightly gives it a little action in the surface film and really fools them. I try to tie this fly with the softest and most absorbent wet fly hackle I can find. I thus highly recommend hen hackle for use on this nymph. If you are planning summertime pack trips, don't forget to include a few small Tellico Nymphs in your box.

MATERIALS:	Tellico Nymph
THREAD:	Small sizes: Black Herb Howard waxed thread. Large sizes: Black monocord.
HOOK:	Mustad 3906 or 7957B Mustad.
SIZES:	8 through 16.
TAIL:	Usually none, or fibers from a mallard flank feather.
BODY:	Yellow floss or wool, ribbed with a single strand of peacock herl.
CASE:	Four to five strands of peacock herl tied over the back.
HACKLE:	Brown hen hackle.

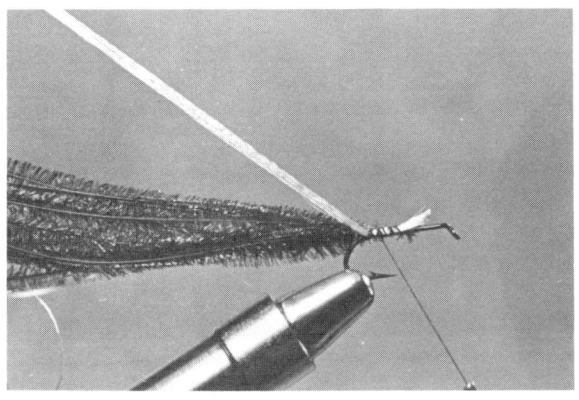

1. Tie on four strand yellow floss or two strand yellow wool. Should be medium yellow wool or bright yellow floss, not gold. Also tie on four to six strands of thick peacock herl.

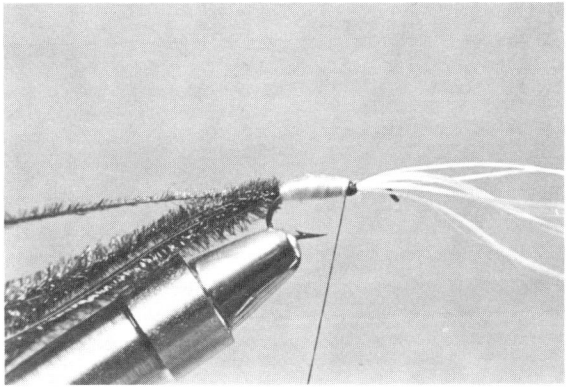

2. Wrap floss forward forming thick body.

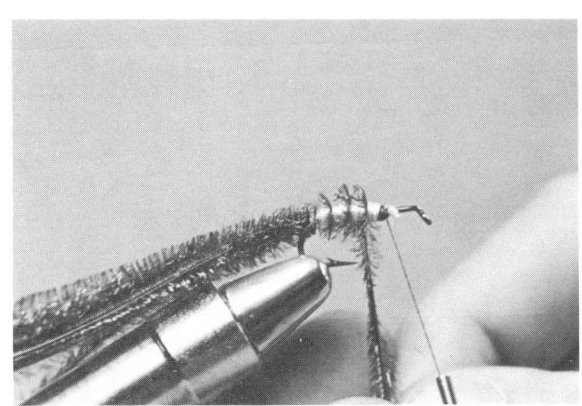

3. Wrap one strand of peacock herl forward, ribbing floss body.

4. Pull remaining peacock herl forward over body forming case.

5. Tie off peacock herl and trim. Note proportions.

6. Tie on and wrap one soft brown neck or hen hackle. Should be medium brown or furnace color. Tie off head, whip finish and laquer.

Finished Fly

FRESH WATER SHRIMP

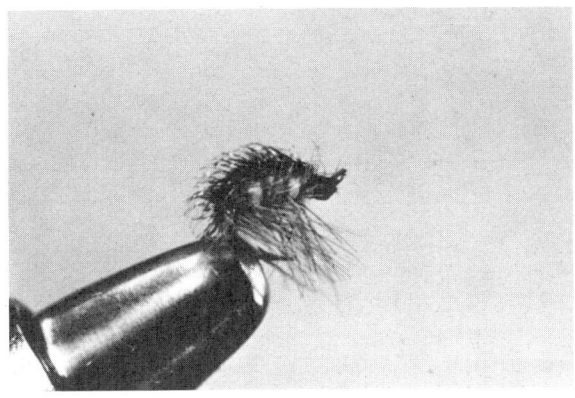

No doubt you have heard of the fresh water shrimp-laden lakes scattered throughout the West. The growth-rate of the trout in these lakes is certainly phenomenal. A prime example is Henry's Lake in Idaho, where brook trout reach weights of eight to ten pounds and rainbows weighing eight to twenty pounds have been caught. There is a definite accelerated growth pattern in these lakes. According to biologists the reasons is that fresh water shrimp inhabit these lakes in such great numbers and their nutritional value to trout is higher than most other food sources.

There have been many imitations of the fresh water shrimp but I will show you one of the popular standard ties. (I suggest you try some others such as the Fiddler's Lake Nymph, Henry's Lake Nymph, Devil Bug and Roberts Woven Shrimp.) Most people tie the following shrimp pattern in small sizes, 14, 16, and 18, although other imitations can be tied on larger sizes, 8, 10, and 12.

Most of the fresh water shrimp are confined to lakes and spring-fed ponds. Although they may catch fish in rivers the exact imitations are mostly found in lakes and it is there that they are most effective.

Most of my luck while using this fly has come about by casting to cruising fish, letting the nymph lie for few seconds, then moving it in a steady slow strip, approximately six to eight inches per strip. Do this very, very slowly. Tie several shrimp patterns and visit some shrimp water at your first opportunity. It's an experience you owe to yourself.

MATERIALS: Fresh Water Shrimp

THREAD: Herb Howard pre-waxed — black, yellow or orange.

BODY: Pink wool or floss; yellow and orange; or light green.

HACKLE: Trimmed brown neck hackle.

CASE: Two or three strands of peacock herl.

HOOK: Mustad 9253 or any short shank, up eye hook.

SIZES: 10 to 20.

1. Tie on single strand of pink wool. On top of wool tie down two or three strands of peacock herl.

2. Tie in one brown neck hackle the same place wool and herl were tied in. Light side should be facing eye. tie in securely.

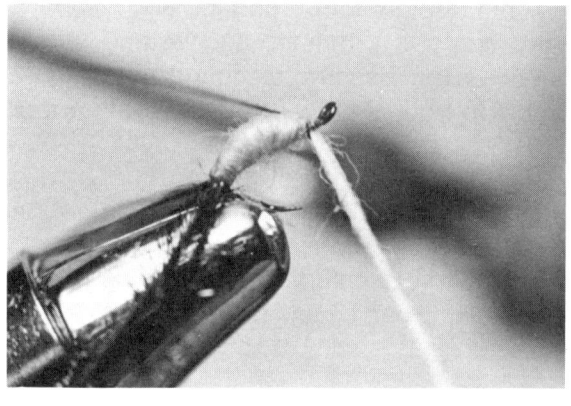

3. Wrap pink wool over shank of hook and shape as illustrated.

4. Wrap brown hackle Palmerstyle.

5. Trim hackle on top and on sides of fly. Leave only bottom hackle sticking out.

6. Pull peacock herl forward and tie at eye.

7. Make sure peacock herl is tied securely and laced tightly along body. Wrap and whip finish.

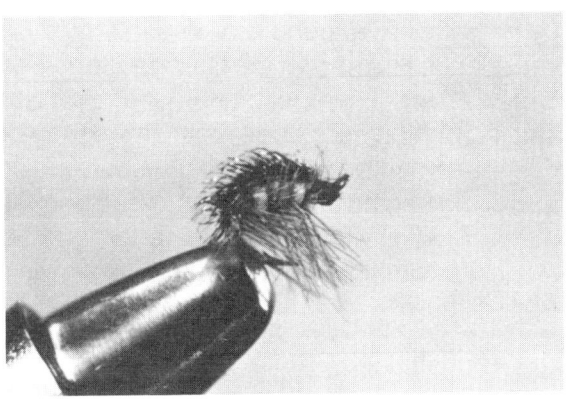

Finished Fly

GRANDE STONE FLY

This nymph pattern, popular throughout the U.S., is effective anywhere there is a gray stone fly hatch. I have found that it works best when weighted and fished deep on the bottom. My experience has shown the Grande Stone Fly to be especially effective on the rainbow trout of the Green River. There is a boulder-strewn section of the Green River where deep pockets are located behind each huge rock. There may be as many as twenty or thirty boulders in a section of river one hundred yards wide. A fisherman can easily wade this stretch of water with a good shot at casting behind the boulders. These pockets, whose depths vary from four to eight feet, provide handy feeding stations for some large rainbow and an occasional brown. The newly-hatched stone flies get sucked in the vacuum of swirling current behind the rocks, then end up in the quiet eddies there.

I find that the Grande Stone Fly performs best if you throw it above the rock and allow it to be sucked into the calm water. Let the fly drift naturally in the current, keeping slack out of the line. Sometime try casting the fly directly upstream, let it drop on the rock, and slide into the water. I hope that you will find a corner in your box for the Grande Stone Fly, as I think it is an important addition to anyone's collection.

MATERIALS: Grande Stone Fly

THREAD: Black monocord

HOOK: 9671 or 9672

SIZES: 4 to 12

TAIL: Two stripped brown hackle veins.

BODY: Gray spun angora fur or gray dubbed muskrat.

RIBBING: Medium gold flat tinsel.

THORAX: Spun gray fur.

CASE: Brown mottled turkey quill.

HACKLE: Furnace saddle or medium brown neck hackle.

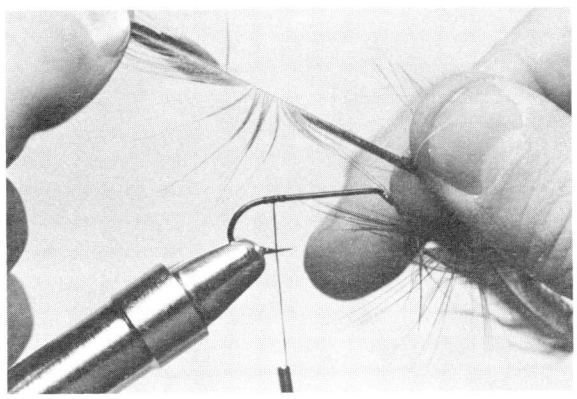

1. Strip two brown hackles, of fibers, leaving only vein.

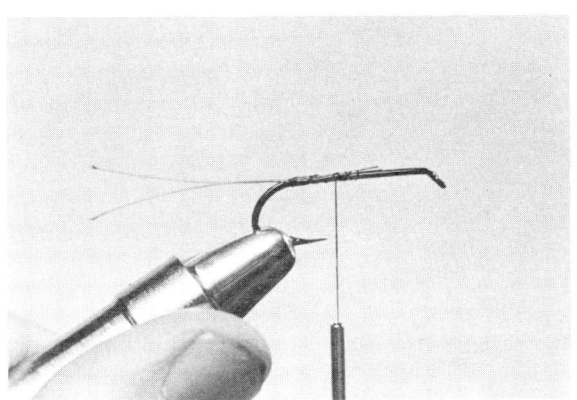

2. Tie both hackle veins on forming divided tail.

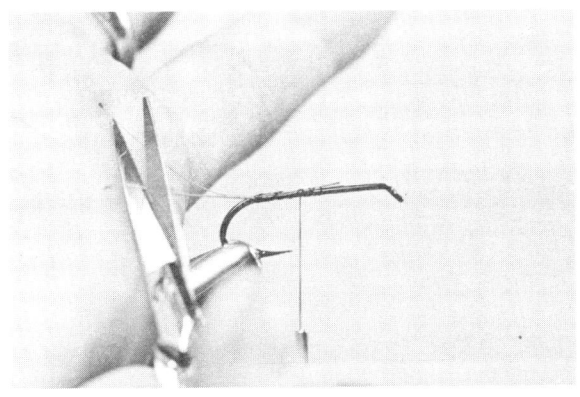

3. Trim both hackle veins to size. Approximately 1/3 of hook shank.

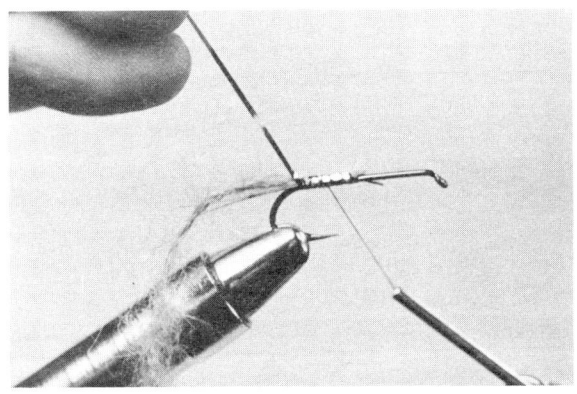

4. Tie on spun gray angora fur and #14 medium flat gold tinsel. Tie both securely. Wrap thread forward.

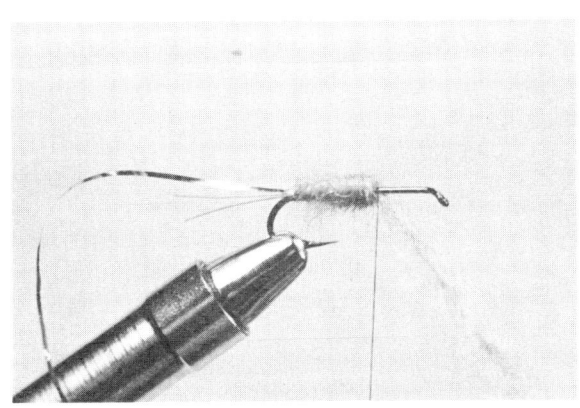

5. Wrap angora fur and taper. Tie off.

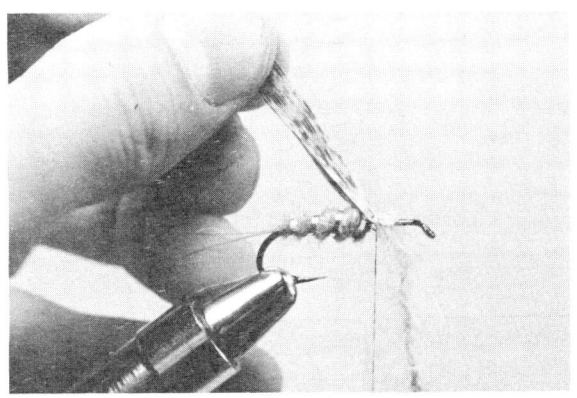

6. Wrap tinsel forward ribbing gray angora fur body. Tie in section of turkey quill at the end of body.

7. Tie in a soft brown neck hackle curvature facing forward.

8. Wrap angora fur forward to form thorax. Wrap hackle forward and tie off.

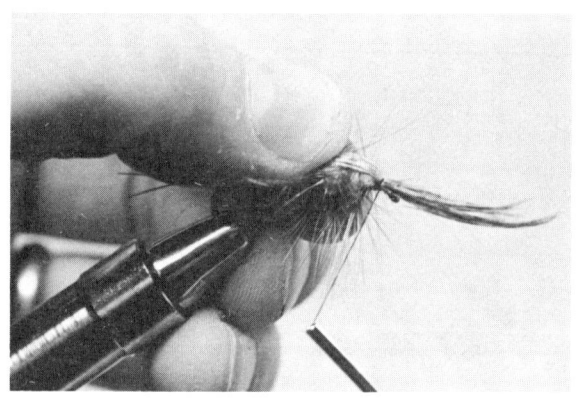

9. Pull turkey forward forming case.

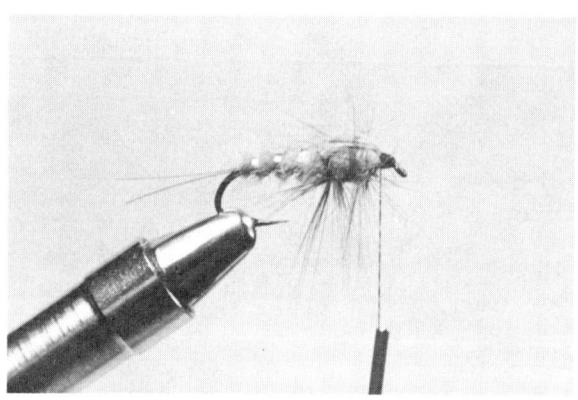

10. Tie off case, form head.

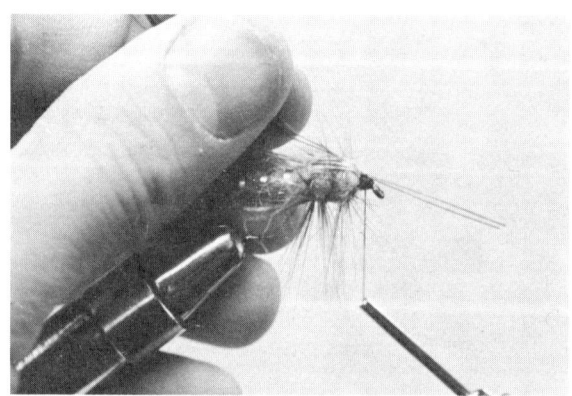

11. Tie on two stripped brown hackle veins to form antennae.

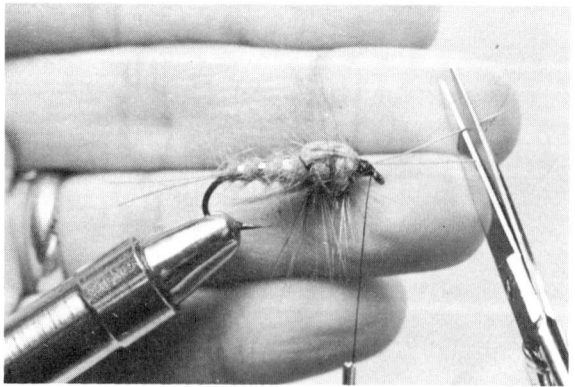

12. Trim hackle veins to form antennae.

MOSQUITO LARVA

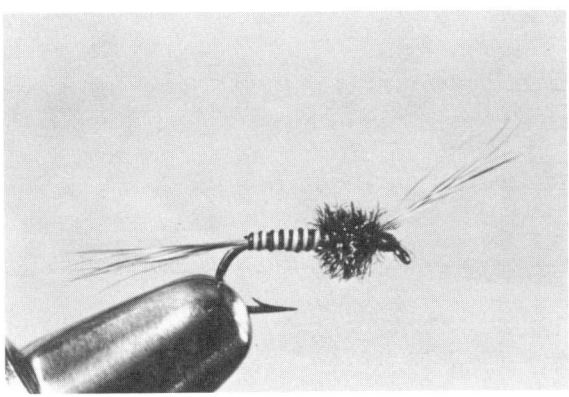

This particular little nymph, which dwells in almost every section of the country, is a widespread trout food. It flourishes mainly in spring creeks or ponds where there is a marsh or bog nearby. These larvae live in the surface film usually an inch to three inches. I suggest presenting the mosquito larva with a floating line and fishing it as you would a dry fly. Let it ride at a dead drift with an occasional slight twitch to the line. It can be tied numerous different ways, but I have selected this particular pattern as one of the most alluring I have ever found. Eastern fish also find it "mouth-watering," and I suggest tying it in small sizes for them.

MATERIALS: Mosquito Larva

HOOK: 94840, 7947B, or 3906, sizes 16, 18, and 20.

BODY: One light, one dark moose mane.

HEAD: Two strands of peacock herl.

ANTENNAE: Grizzly hackle fibers.

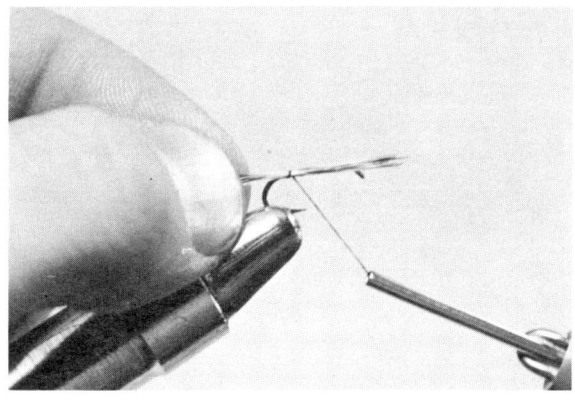

1. Tie in several fibers of grizzly hackle. Tail should be approximately the length of the shank.

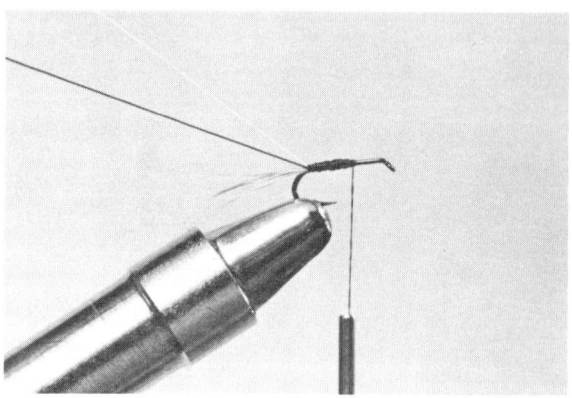

2. Tie in one dark strand of moose mane and one light strand of moose mane. Lay a thread base as shown above.

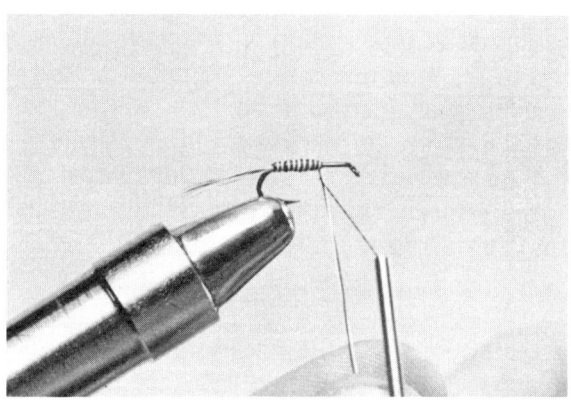

3. Wrap both light and dark mane forward forming quill body as shown above. Be sure to watch proportions.

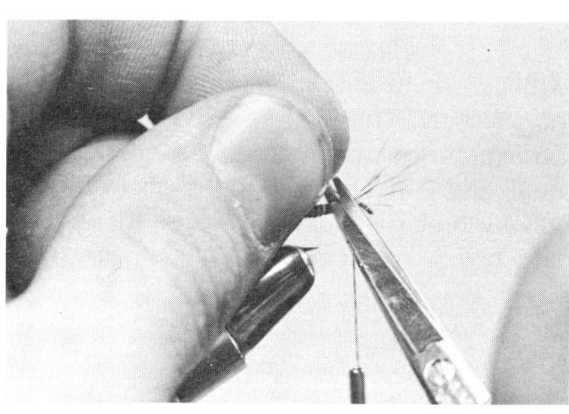

4. Tie in several strands of grizzly hackle fibers forward as if to tie a tail.

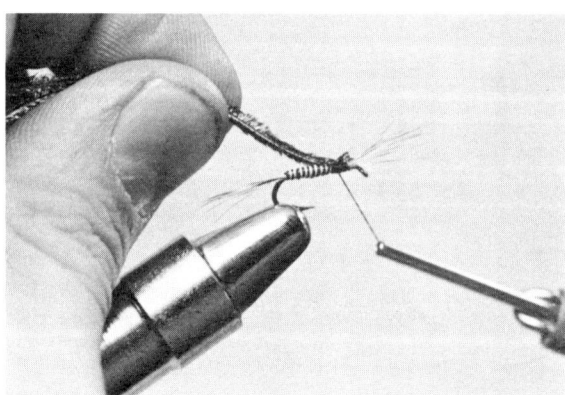

5. Tie in two strands of peacock herl next to quill body.

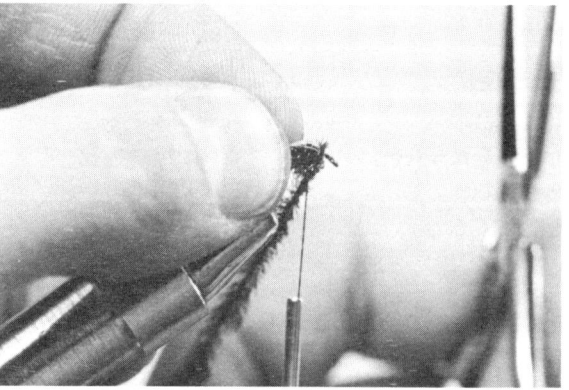

6. Wrap peacock forward with one wrap going in front of grizzly hackle fiber. Notice how hackle fibers are pulled back.

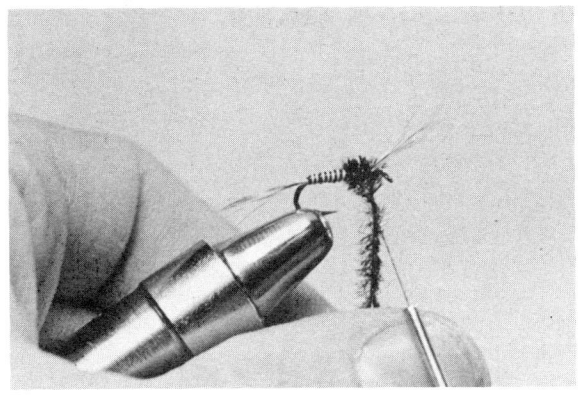

7. Tie off, whip finish, cement head and quill body.

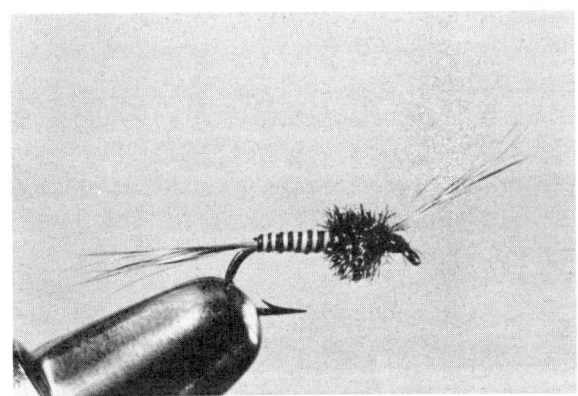

Finished Fly

MUSKRAT NYMPH

I consider the Muskrat Nymph the basic western nymph. This little nymph is probably used by more people than any other nymph in the Rockies. Some people call it the gray nymph, others call it a caddis nymph. This pattern imitates the caddis case that is found in proliferation in most all the waters in the West. There is probably not a stream, lake, river, pond, or spring where this fly at one time or another will not work. It is a very simple fly to tie and a good one to practice your dubbing on, paying special attention to producing a good body taper. I recommend that you use a light pre-waxed thread such as Herb Howard pre-waxed. This fine, light thread has amazing strength and will always be a good one to remember when you are tying dubbed body flies.

I am particularly fond of the Muskrat Nymph for brown trout. There are several springs which feed the New Fork River that are favorites of mine. The heavy brush in this area makes casting very difficult. It's a boggy area and one can step into deep muskrat holes and almost disappear. There are small brook trout in these springs but my targets are the large browns which come up out of the New Fork to feed there. I suspect that they are there to feed on the small brook trout, but I'm close-minded enough to belive that they are there to feed on my Muskrat Nymph!

I use this nymph more than any other in these waters where caddis cases abound. I like to fish these springs on a cloudy or a rainy day, when it is much easier to stalk the large browns. As you are walking in the goo or mush you can see the large browns cruising and their wakes go back and forth throughout the spring looking for feed. I use a floating line with a ten foot leader having a number 8 Muskrat Nymph attached to its 6X tippet. I like to watch for the wakes of the trout and throw it approximately ten feet in front of them, letting the fly sink. Sometimes I weight the Muskrat just slightly. I let it just sit there and wait for action. Often those brownies will swim right up to where the wet fly landed and turn and go in the opposite direction. I feel that it is important to cast the fly some distance from the wary trout. I have had my best luck by keeping the fly at least ten feet away and imparting no movement to it. In these springs the fish have amazing eyesight and notice almost anything that drops in.

I have had good luck in spring fed ponds which have been planted with brook trout. Here, I use a sinking line, let the nymph sink to the bottom, and strip in the fly very slowly, bumping the bottom for large brook trout. You should experiment with the different ways of using Muskrat Nymphs tied in several different sizes.

MATERIALS: Muskrat Nymph

THREAD: Herb Howard black pre-waxed thread.

HOOK: Mustad 3906, or 7957B or 3906B.

TAIL: None

BODY: Dubbed gray muskrat with guard hairs left in.

HACKLE: Two black ostrich herls tied near the front of the hook.

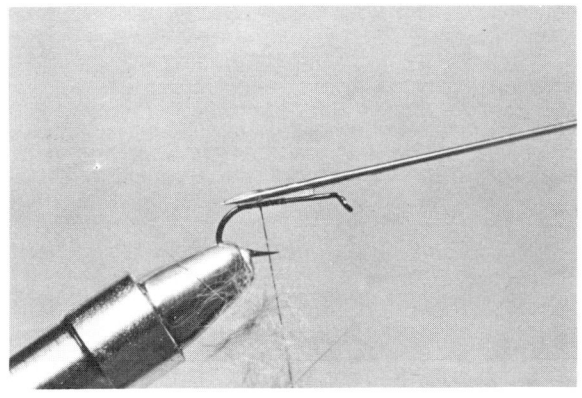

1. Wrap down Herb Howard wrapping thread forming a thread base on hook. Drop head cement on hook and start dubbing muskrat fur guard hairs included.

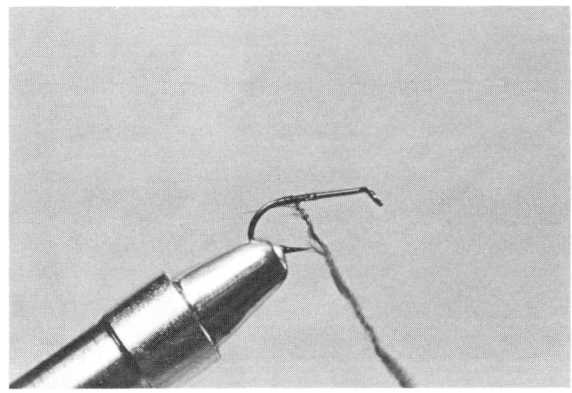

2. Dub fur tightly before wrapping.

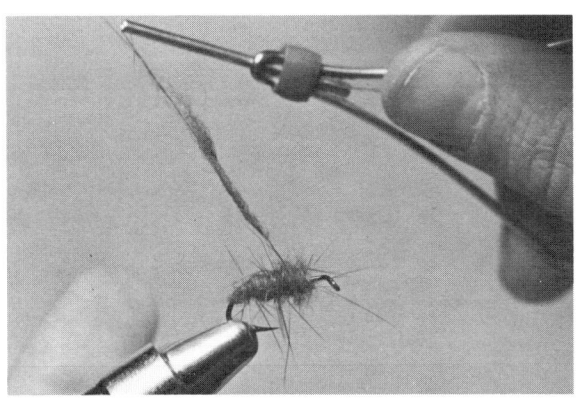

3. Wrap on muskrat fur with guard hairs projecting from body. Be sure to taper body. It is necessary to add more dubbing fur as you work, to make the body thick and nice.

4. Body is tapered and shaped with guard hairs protruding. Notice room between body and eye.

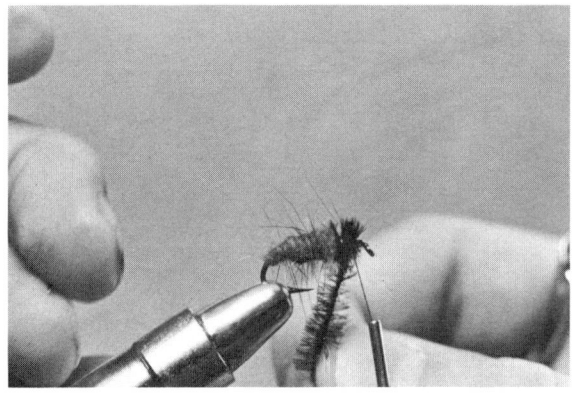

5. Tie on two strands of black ostrich herl and wrap forward making full head.

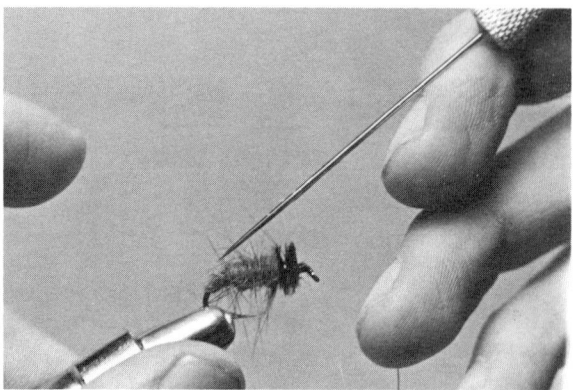

6. Tie off ostrich and whip finish head. Use bodkin to pick out more guard hairs.

Finished Fly

GOLD RIBBED HAIR'S EAR

For all you Colorado, or Colorado-bound fishermen here it is! A nymph that works best in your waters. My sources for this information are the famous fly fishermen of Aspen, Colorado, Chuck Fothergill, Phil Wright, and Jack Cole.

I was first told of the importance of the Gold Ribbed Hare's Ear to the Colorado fisherman about three years ago when I became acquainted with the well-known restaurant entrepreneur of Aspen, Jack Cole. Besides sharing a rabid interest in gourmet food, Jack and I both also enjoy fly fishing. That's just what we did one October morning which was so cold that even a self-respecting moose would not be out and around.

I took Jack to one of my favorite springs and we proceeded to fish it carefully with my standard killers. The only problem was that on this particular day, my standard killers were not killing! In fact, they embarassed me. We had had good luck on the Snake River with Muddlers, large dry flies, but now the situation had changed. We were looking at five or six two to six lb. trout which were cruising (but not feeding) in the clear spring stream. It was tough, but we were not about to give up. We tried all the flies that I normally would use with Jack silently taking my advice. Finally he stopped and suggested that I look in his box. Well, I did, but the only flies in the box he handed me were about six dozen Hare's Ears, from size six to size eighteen in weighted and unweighted versions. He looked at me and offered, "Pick any one you like, they're all good."

I tied on the luscious fly and promised to show him that there really were trout in the spring. The fly hit the water, sank about two feet, and — BAM! A hit! We were in luck.

I fished the nymph the rest of the day and found it to be a fine one for the Jackson Hole springs. Jack then revealed the story about how the fly produces bigger and better fish for him in the Colorado waters than any other pattern. I had heard about the fly from other Colorado fishermen but had never tried it. I now heartily recommend this one to anyone fishing the West. In Colorado it is as popular as the Humpy is in Jackson Hole, Wyoming. Almost every store in Colorado sells this little gem, and all the fly tying classed in Colorado have at least one class entirely devoted to tying the Gold Ribbed Hare's Ear. One secret I am told, is that you must tie the fly in the ugliest, fuzziest, furriest manner possible. According to my friend Jack this is the only way it looks juicy enough to work — the uglier the better.

MATERIALS: Gold Ribbed Hare's Ear

THREAD: Tan Herb Howard prewaxed thread.

HOOK: Mustad 3906 or Mustad 3906B.

SIZES: 6 to 18.

TAIL: Guard hair fibers from English Hare's Ear. (Some fur can be in the fibers).

BODY: Spun dubbed fur (including small guard hairs) from English hare's ear.

RIBBING: Gold fine wire.

CASE: Thicker and heavier dubbed hare's ear fur.

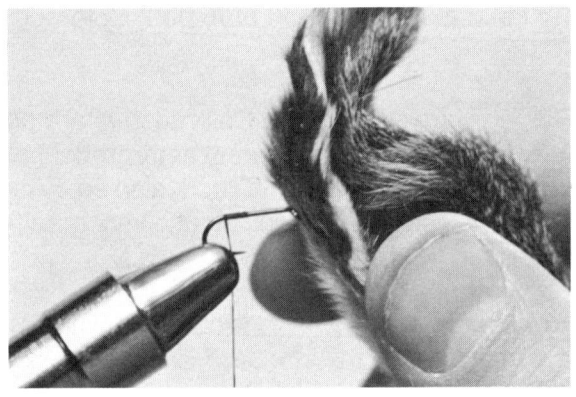

1. Secure hook in vise and wrap thread on hook. (Above is English Hare's ear).

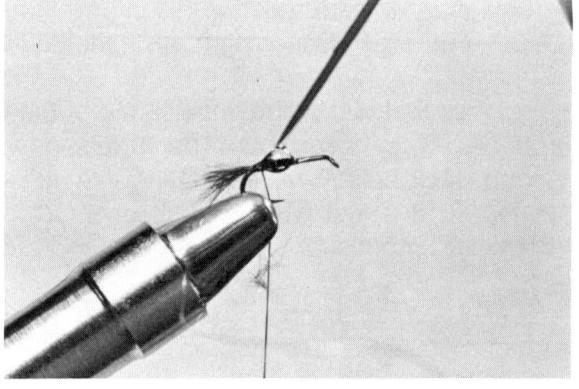

2. Tie in guard hair from hare's ear to form tail. Laquer thread with light head cement.

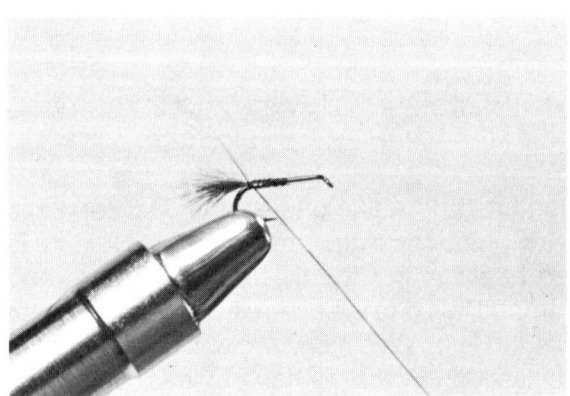

3. Tie in gold wire tightly.

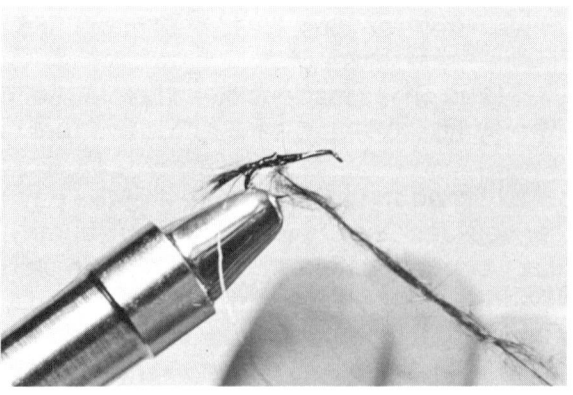

4. Spin dubbing fur including guard hairs from hare's ear on pre-waxed thread. Spin very tightly.

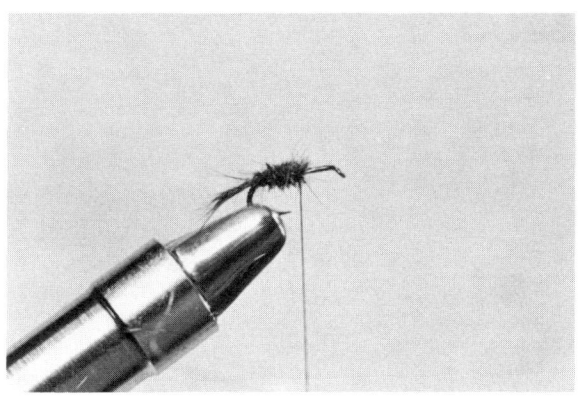

5. Wrap spun hare's ear fur forward tapering it. Stop half way down hook.

6. Wrap gold wire through dubbing and tie off at the end of body.

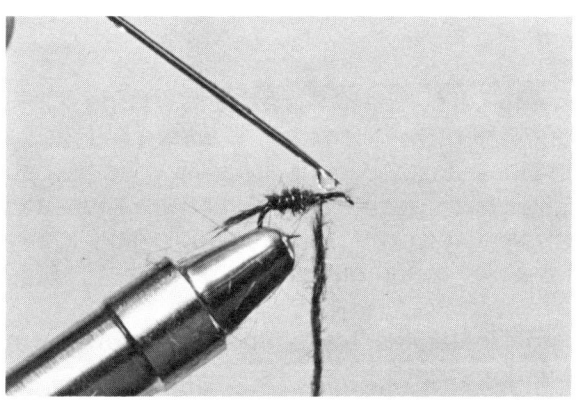

7. Dub on more hare's ear fur including guard hairs enough to form a large thorax.

8. Wrap dubbed fur to form large thorax. Whip finish and laquer.

Finished Fly

FLEDERMAUS

The Fledermaus or bat fly is a popular western nymph. It can be tied in extremely large sizes, 2, 4 and 6 and can imitate a small bat or mouse that might have fallen into the water. It is also a good late evening and night fly in many of the lakes in Monatana and Idaho. It can represent a bat, its namesake, at that time of the evening. On small sizes it is a good caddis nymph imitation, and generally has widespread use on lakes. Of all the nymphs used in our country I would have to say that the Fledermaus would be right near the top for an all-round effective nymph.

It is very simply tied and should be weighted in most instances. I recommend that you tie it in different shades of gray and cream, then fish it in various ways to test its effectiveness.

One good way to fish the Fledermaus is to use a shooting head to cast the nymph out as far as possible, let it sink slightly and then retrieve it with long strips, two to three feet in length, very slowly. Be patient. Fish it *slow,* then a little slower. It works. This is an important fly, and without a doubt should be included in your Western collection.

MATERIALS: Fledermaus

THREAD: Black Herb Howard pre-waxed.

HOOK: Mustad 3906 or 3906B

SIZES: 1/0 to 14.

BODY: Dubbed muskrat fur with guard hairs included.

HACKLE: None

WING: Gray squirrel tail.

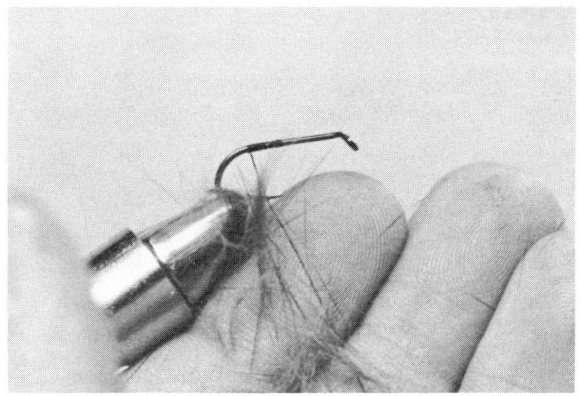

1. Wrap base of Herb Howard thread. Laquer may be applied to secure dubbing fur. Add dubbing fur to waxed thread. Spin tightly.

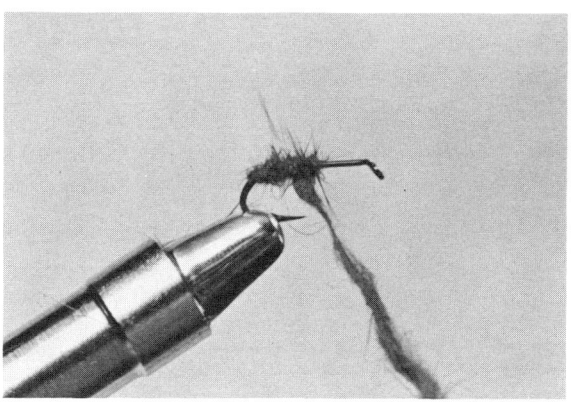

2. Wrap dubbing fur forward. It may be necessary to twist fur as you wrap. This causes fur to wrap tighter.

3. Dubbing fur should be tapered and made very bulky as shown above.

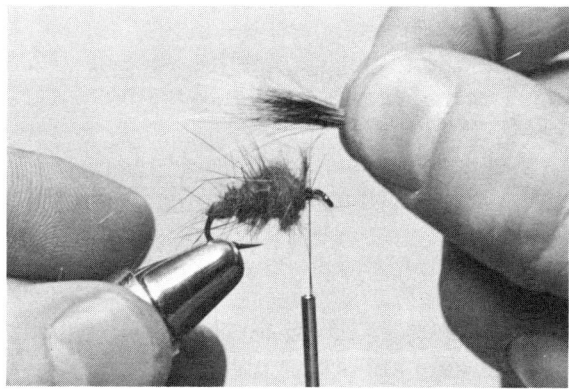

4. Trim off a medium amount of gray squirrel tail. Estimate length of squirrel tail so it will slightly exceed length of body.

5. Tie on squirrel tail tightly. A touch of laquer here is good.

6. Tie off gray squirrel tail and whip finish. Bodkin may be used to pick out more fur making a buggy looking body.

DARK CADDIS

The Dark Caddis is one of my favorite nymphs. When I was a youngster I was strictly a dry and wet fly fisherman, as I had not been introduced to the great world of nymph fishing. I stumbled across a copy of FAMILY CIRCLE GUIDE TO TROUT FLIES, now known as NOLL'S GUIDE TO TROUT FLIES, a small, beautifully colored paperback book. As I was looking over the book, I noticed an interesting pattern named, Dark Caddis nymph. I thought to myself that this would be a good fly to tie up and keep in my box.

Some time later I was fishing the Snake River in Wyoming when a friend of mine caught a nice 14 inch cutthroat on a dry fly. Fishing had been slow that day, so were anxious to look at the fish to see if there were any clues as to what had been its food. Upon close examination we found the trout's mouth full of nymphs which looked very much like the Dark Caddis that I had tied.

I quickly reached into my box and hurriedly tied on a Dark Caddis nymph. I rushed downstream about one hundred yards where a small spring had entered the river. I knew that there was a big fish there that I had been trying to catch for several months. I laid the fly out upstream and let it drift down with creek's current right into the main river where the junction formed a large hole. The fly had no sooner floated fifteen feet than BAM! I had the big fellow on. I estimated that he would weigh at least five or six lbs. For 30 or 40 seconds I was in Angler's Heaven . . . and then my leader and the fish parted company. In my haste I had not properly tied the fly to the leader. Instead of using an improved cinch knot, I had hurriedly tied a plain cinch knot. The beautiful new Dark Caddis ended up in the Cutthroat's mouth. From then on I remembered two things: I kept plenty of Dark Caddis Nymphs in my box and learned to tie improved cinch knots!

MATERIALS: Dark Caddis

THREAD: Herb Howard prewaxed thread, black or cream.

HOOKS: Mustad 7957B or 3906.

SIZES: 6 to 18.

BODY: Muskrat hair dubbed with guard hairs removed.

WINGS: Badger hackle tips.

HEAD: Peacock Herl.

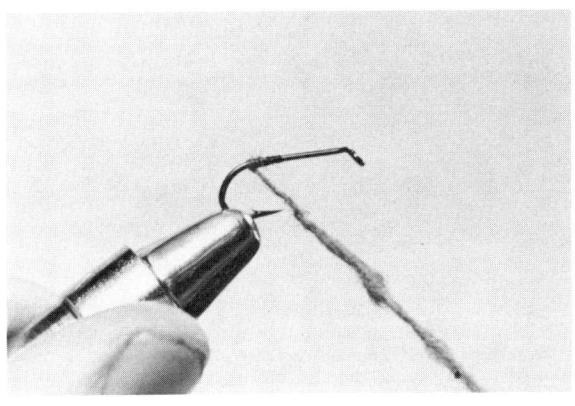

1. Tie on Herb Howard wrapping thread. Attach gray medium muskrat fur to Herb Howard thread and spin tightly.

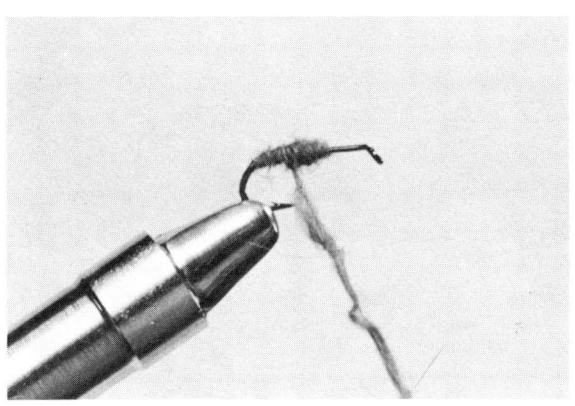

2. Wrap dubbed muskrat fur forward tapering body.

3. Continue to taper leaving guard hairs in fur.

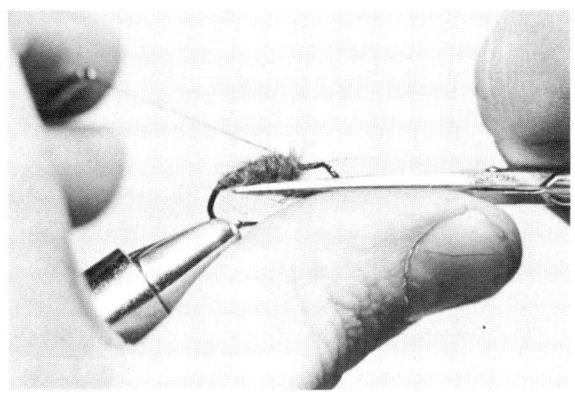

4. Trim guard hairs using thumb as guide for scissors.

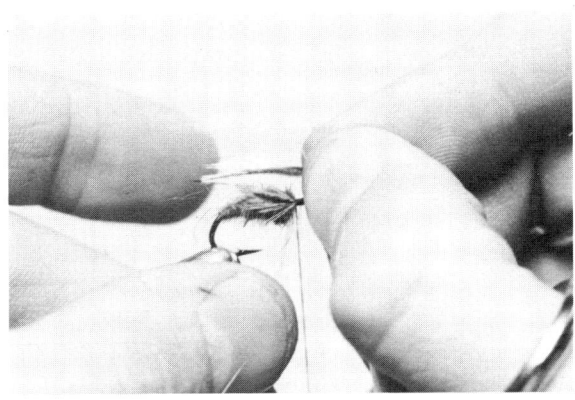

5. Select two badger hackle tips.

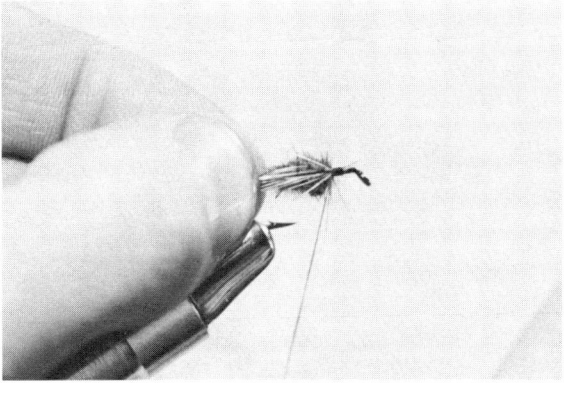

6. Attach badger hackle tips along side of nymph, on one side one on the other.

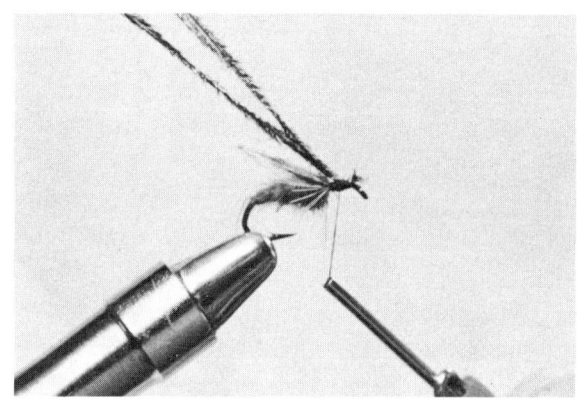

7. Attach two strands of peacock herl.

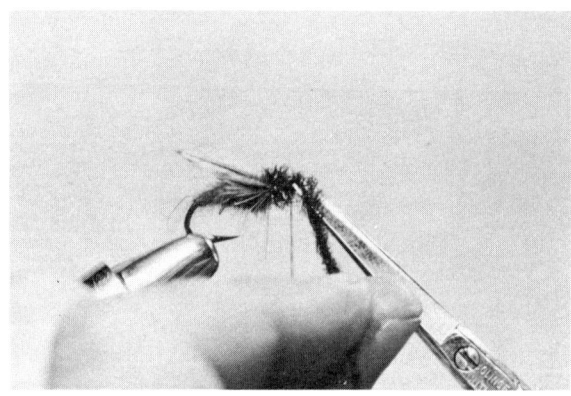

8. Wrap peacock herl forward forming head. Trim, whip finish and laquer.

Finished Fly

ZUG BUG

This little nymph sounds like something right out of Africa — a wild name, for a wild fly. It has to be one of the best slow-water nymphs ever invented. It is a peacock herl fly with a simplicity that may fool you. It seems to be very good in springs and beaver ponds. Here in Jackson Hole there are many different beaver ponds which formerly hosted brook trout which had been planted there. Nowadays, most of these ponds are populated by our native cutthroat trout with an occasional scattering of brookies.

A long-time friend, and fellow guide, Bob Carmichael, Jr., first introduced the Zug Bug to me. We both were fond of fishing Blacktail Ponds in Jackson Hole. At this time nymphs were not nearly as popular as dry flies, wet flies, and streamers in our area. In fact very little was known about them. Bob had made some fishing trips outside of Jackson Hole and had picked up some of these fantastic little nymphs.

He kept urging me to try some, but I was still an emphatic dry fly fan and it was hard to get me to use any wet fly other than a Blue Dun Squirrel Tail. Bob liked to fish his nymphs on a silk line, ungreased. He had what was basically an early prototype of a slow-sinking line, which acted a lot like our modern sinking tip lines.

Bob was an expert at fishing beaver ponds and especially the Blacktail ponds which are only a mile from where he lived. The ponds were famous for large cutthroat which would resist anything. When someone really bragged on his fishing talents, all one had to do was escort him to the Blacktail ponds and the truth would come out in a hurry. Bob always declared, by gosh, there was a six lb. plus cutthroat in those ponds and he was going to get it. We had always known of the large trout in the beaver ponds because ten to fifteen years prior to this time fish up to eight pounds were taken quite consistently. But now fishing pressure had made the pond even harder to fish.

One day while I was fooling around Bob's tackle shop swapping lies with the other fishing guides, Bob strolled in with a huge cutthroat trout. Casting a smile in my direction, he announced that this fish had been caught on a Zug Bug. "Suffer, you dry fly boys, suffer," was the expression written all over his face.

Immediately, I purchased two dozen of his Zug Bugs and tore off to the Blacktail Ponds. Unfortunately as an inexperienced nymph fisherman, I did not have any luck. That was fifteen years ago and times have changed. I have now learned a great deal of the ways of nymph fishing. I always have the Zug Bug around when I head for the beaver ponds and small springs. I have found that I too could pull in a few large ones with this tricky little nymph. I believe that it is an important fly for everyone to learn to tie and keep around. You never know, sometime you may find yourself at the Blacktail Ponds.

MATERIALS: Zug Bug
THREAD: Black Herb Howard pre-waxed, or black monocord.
HOOK: 3906 Mustad, or 9671, or 3906B.
SIZES: 8 to 16.
TAIL: Three peacock sword fibers.
BODY: Several strands of Peacock herl, thickly wrapped.
RIBBING: Small gold oval tinsel.
CASE: Turkey quill.
HACKLE: Brown neck hackle fibers, tied beard style.

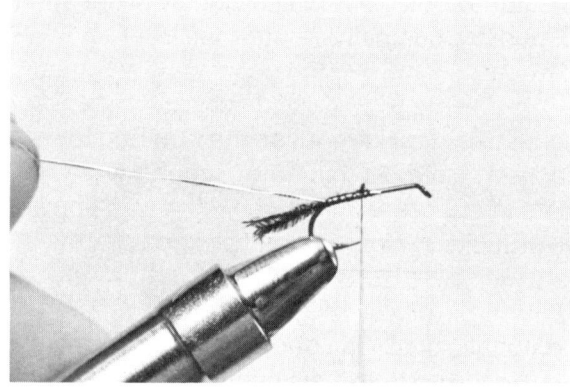

1. Wrap on tying thread with three peacock sword fibers. Tie on #16 gold oval tinsel.

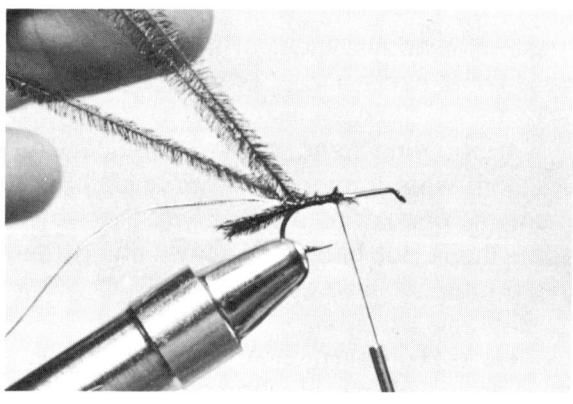

2. Tie two to three strands of heavy thick peacock herl.

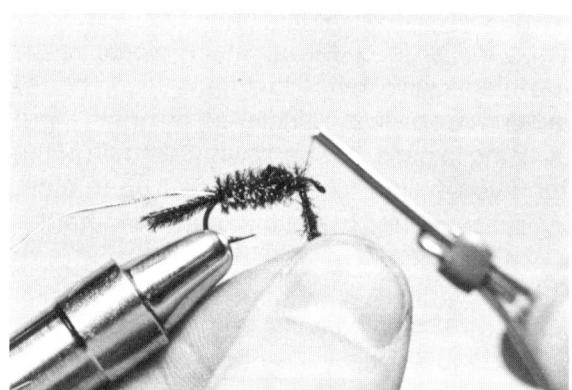

3. Wrap peacock herl forward and tie off.

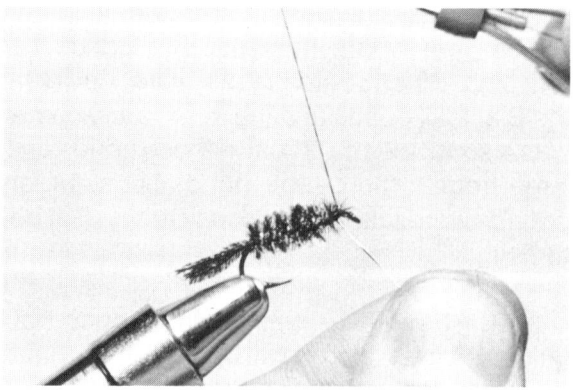

4. Rib body tightly with gold oval tinsel and tie off.

5. Notch one piece of turkey quill.

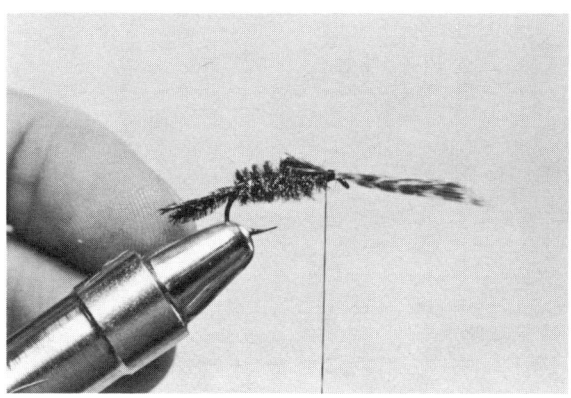

6. Tie turkey quill directly on top, flat onto thorax. Trim excess which extends over eye.

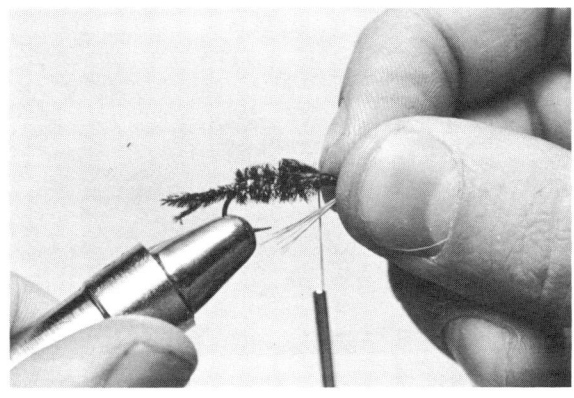

7. Strip several strands of medium brown soft hackle and estimate size.

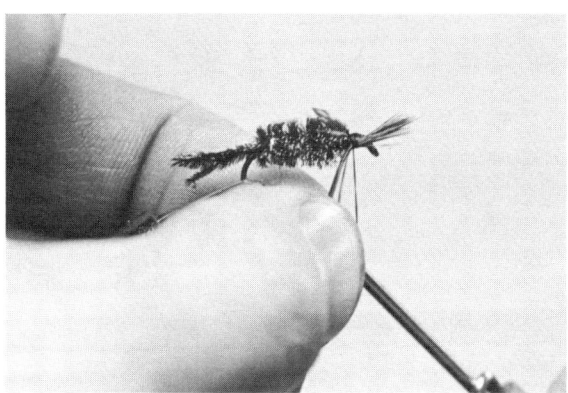

8. Tie on brown hackle directly under body. Make sure that hackle is not tied on either side of fly but is tied directly underneath. Trim, whip finish, and laquer.

Finished Fly

Streamers

Step by Step Instructions

SPRUCE FLY

This useful fly has become a favorite of many fishermen in the West, because it is a real producer for steelhead, trout, salmon, Arctic char, and many other species of fish. Basically a wet fly which has been modified into a streamer, it frequently attracts large trout when others fail. It can be tied in two shades, the Light and the Dark Spruce Fly, and both usually take the most fish when they are used with a sinking tip line (such as Scientific Anglers High D wet tip line). Its long hackle wings give it a "breathing" motion, thus rendering it incredibly lifelike. When viewed from the top side while traveling through the water it represents the swimming action of most minnows.

It is a fatal mistake to tie the Spruce fly with long, narrow, stiff saddle hackle instead of wide, soft neck hackles for the wings. I think that good badger hackle is imperative for this fly. Use a soft wide hackle with good coloration for the wings, but to prevent their folding beneath the hook and around the bend they must be short.

My experience with the Spruce Fly dictates that it should be sunk deep into the hole and retreived by interspersing long strips with short pauses. The Spruce Fly functions well on any river inhabited by a variety of minnows and sculpins. In the smaller sizes it entices small Brook trout, both in ponds and creeks. I regard it as one of the most efficient Brook trout flies I have ever used. This fly is a must for the fly box of any angler who plans to fish in Montana.

MATERIALS: Spruce Fly — Light or Dark

HOOK: Mustad 9672 or Mustad 9671 (For those who like Limerick bend hooks, Mustad 3665A).

SIZES: 4 through 14.

BODY: First portion red floss, ribbed with gold embossed tinsel.

WING: For Light Spruce Fly: 2 Badger soft wide neck hackles with white hackles edges and a deep black bar down the middle of the feather. For Dark Spruce Fly: 2 large, wide, soft furnace neck hackles in a deep brown color with black center strip.

TAIL: Approximately 4 strands of Peacock sword herl.

THORAX: Wrapped thick peacock herl.

THREAD: Black monocord.

HACKLE: For Light Spruce Fly: Soft Badger neck hackles
For Dark Spruce Fly: Soft furnace neck hackles.

HEAD: Black and well laquered.

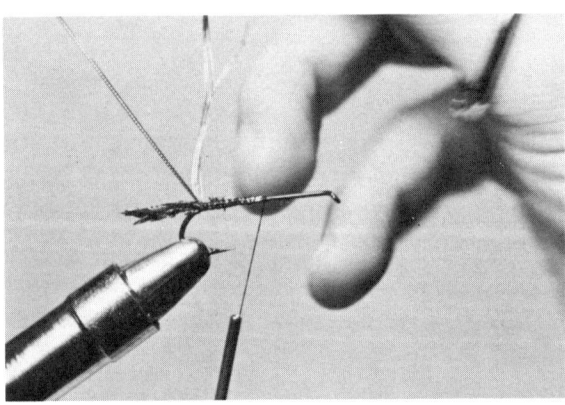

1. Tie on two to three peacock sword herl forming tail. Should be approximately ¼ length of shank. Tie on red floss four strand and #14 gold embossed flat tinsel.

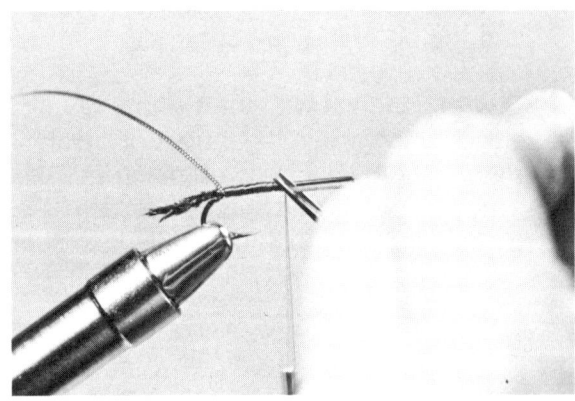

2. Wrap red floss forward approximately ½ way down hook, trim.

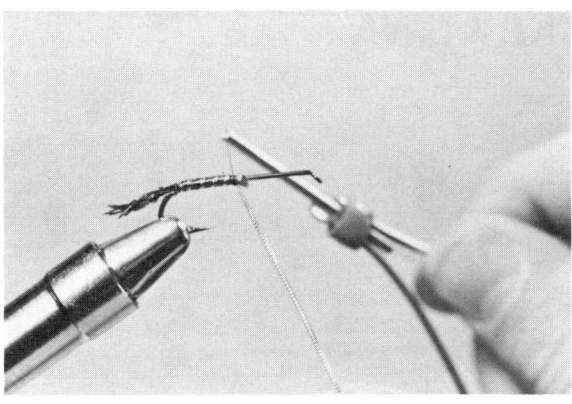

3. Wrap gold embossed tinsel forward ribbing red floss.

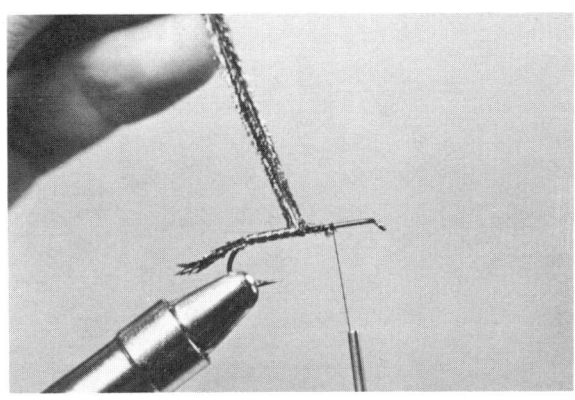

4. Tie on two to three strands of thick peacock herl.

5. Wrap peacock herl forward forming a thick body. Leave plenty of room from body to eye.

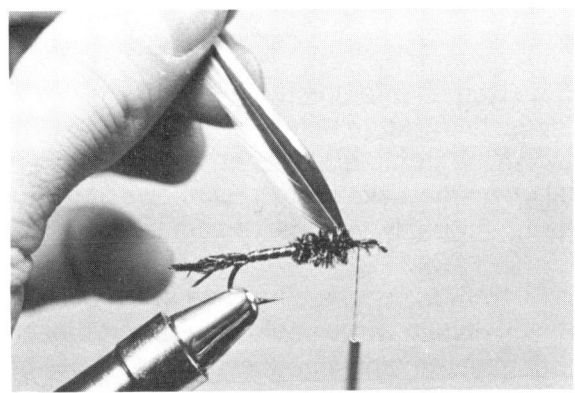

6. Tie on one thick soft badger neck hackle wrapped forward with curvature facing back wrapping hackle forward so fibers lie back over body.

7. Take one wide soft neck hackle from one side of neck and one from other side with the darker or curved side facing each other forming a divided wing as shown above. Whip finish and head cement.

Finished Fly

(MYLAR) MICKEY FINN

Named after the famous drink, this fly, too, is a knockout! The deadly pattern is famed for devastating large rainbow trout. In almost all the Western states, this fly catches the most fish when the standard streamer method is employed. In Henry's Lake of Idaho it reigns as King! It is a killer on the Lake's large Rainbows and Brooks. I endorse it as an especially fine fly for Brook trout; probably the best streamer for Rainbow; as well as a sure shot on Brown trout.

Prior to mylar tubing tyers constructed the standard pattern with embossed silver and oval tinsel ribbing which could not really represent a minnow's body shape. However, several years ago mylar tubing introduced into fly tying an uncannily lifelike image of a minnow body.

Several years ago I was fishing the Wind River in Wyoming with a good friend and truly great woman fisherman, Leona Michelle. We had fished the better portion of the morning without much action. Having drifted the usually successful Muddler Minnow and the Maribou Muddler down through the holes without even a touch, we pulled into one of the best holes on the river planning to give it our best efforts before heading home for the day. Leona, who is one of the most determined fishermen I have ever known, reached into her fly box and pulled out an old chewed-up Mickey Finn. She looked at me and smiled, "What do you think of that one!" I shrugged, "I've never used it here; it's sort of a gaudy thing, but let's give it a go." Before I could say "cutthroat trout" she had hooked a large fish, and after several minutes she had landed a 2½ lb. Rainbow. Then she hooked another large trout with the very next cast. This time she beached a fine Brook trout. I teasingly looked up at her and laughed, "O.K. the next fish has to be a Cutthroat!" She then proceeded to make another cast and let the fly drift deep into the hole bringing it back with short strips, and BANG! Another large trout was on — and, you guessed it — a 2¼ lb. Cutthroat! In all my years of guiding I have never seen this happen: three casts, an three different types of fish. She made several more casts into the hole with no luck, not even a strike. We shoved the boat out and floated down to the next hole. As we were leaving the hole we spotted a log on the far side of the bank. With amazing accuracy she dropped the fly behind the log and out darted a trout taking a swipe at the Mickey Finn. However, her quick reactions were not enough and the trout winged into the bank. She exclaimed to me with a wink, "That must have been the Brown!"

MATERIALS: Mickey Finn

HOOK: Mustad 9672, 9671, 3665A, or 79580.

BODY: Silver mylar tubing.

WING: Dyed yellow bucktail, then dyed red bucktail and another topping of yellow bucktail, giving a three color effect.

TAIL: Wrapped red monocord tying down the mylar tubing.

THREAD: Black and red monocord.

SIZES: 2 through 14.

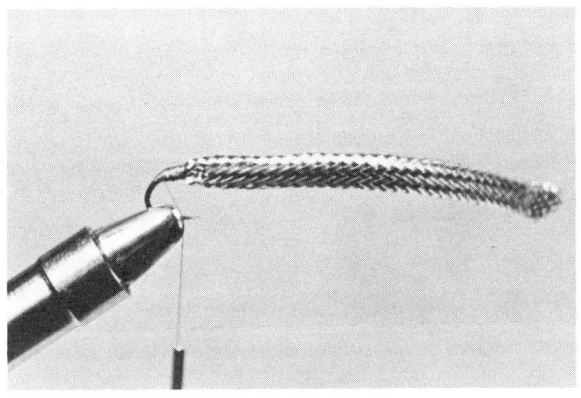

1. Trim one piece of mylar tubing. Remove inner cotton filler. Wrap tying red thread at bend of hook. Stick tubing through eye back to bend of hook and tie down with wrapping thread.

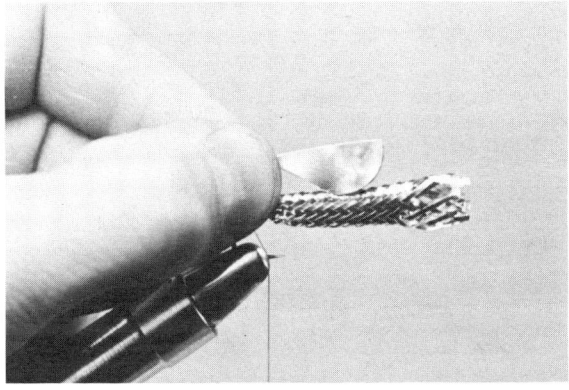

2. Trim one flip top from soda pop or beer can in half as shown in picture.

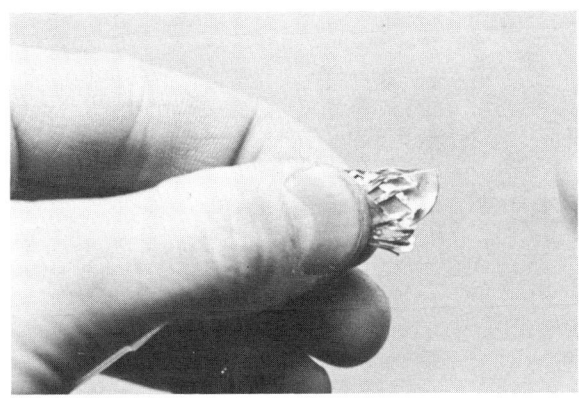

3. Insert flip top can tab in tubing and push toward rear of hook.

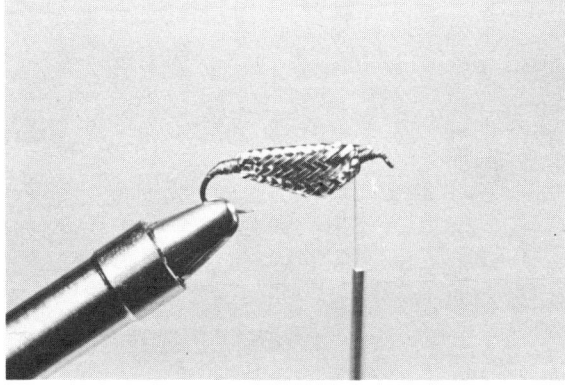

4. Tie end of tubing. Tin tab will form belly of fly and give tubing a rigid flat body.

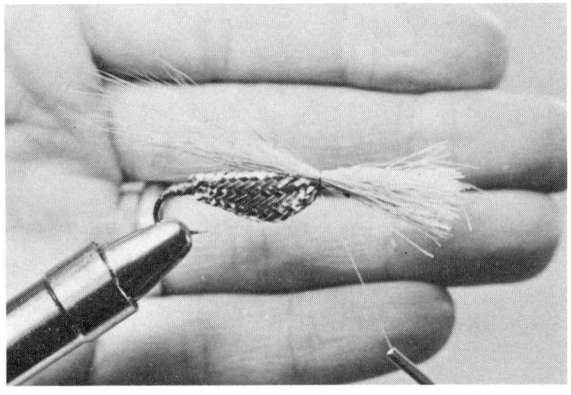

5. Tie down yellow bucktail. Be sure bucktail is not too long or too bulky.

6. Tie in strands of red bucktail.

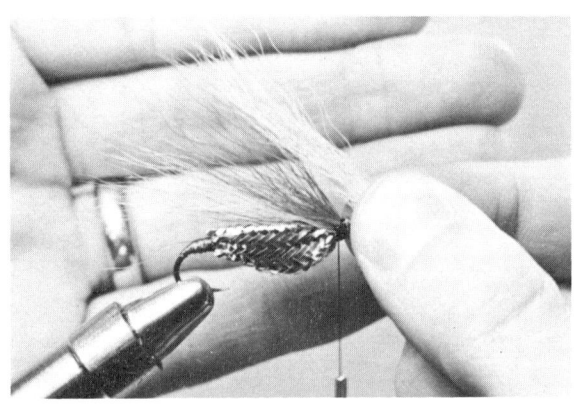

7. Add final yellow bucktail and tie over red. Tie securely and form tapered head. Whip finish and make sure that hair is tied securely.

8. Laquer thread tag securely and laquer mylar tubing and head.

Finished Fly

MARIBOU STREAMER

There are many variations of the Maribou Streamer using several colors of Maribous and different body styles. This fly can catch bass, trout, steehead, salmon, salt water fish and more besides! It is the maribou feather that holds the secret of its appeal. When dry it is fluffy and does not resemble anything fishy, but the moment it hits the water it becomes one of the most lifelike streamer imitations ever invented. When it is stripped through the water, the maribou feathers compress into a streamlined minnow like shape; then at the end of each strip, the feathers fan out to create lifelike breathing action; then the whole process is repeated on the next strip of the retrieve. This motion, as viewed by the trout, is almost identical to that of a live minnow. The "pumping action" as it is called, can be most enticing when it is used to attract the large trout which seem to be extremely vulnerable to this fly. It should be tied and fished weighted because the fly should penetrate deep into the hole and be retrieved with short jerks or long slow pulls which gives it that special "breathing" action. While retrieving this fly, lift your rod tip with the strips or jerks. The pumping action at times drives the trout crazy. This maneuver can be practiced and exercised to perfection with any large streamer.

It is important to tie this fly with good quality maribou, yet the feathers are becoming extremely difficult to obtain. The short feathers do not give the proper action and thus discredits this fly to the practiced eye of the trout. Buying it in small bags usually means only a few good long feathers out of a dozen. Therefore, it is best to purchase maribous in large quantity and then sort out all the plumes that are not satisfactory.

MATERIALS: Maribou Streamer

HOOK: Mustad 9672, 9671, 79580 or 3665A.

SIZES: 2 to 12.

BODY: Can be a tinsel or wool body ribbed with gold tinsel. Also try a mylar tube body, floss body, chennile body, tinsel chennile, or any other water absorbing material. Body color should be appropriate to the maribou color used on the wing.

WING: Can be a solid color (such as white or yellow) or a combination of colors, such as brown, white, and black; green and yellow; red and yellow; or orange and red. Use your own imagination. Also, feathers such as grouse hackle, pheasant tippets or peacock herl can be tied in as a topping on the edge of the fly, making it more attractive as a streamer.

TAIL: None, or can be a variety of materials: trimmed red floss, red hackle fibers, red wool yarn, etc.

HEAD: Can be black, white, red or any other desirable color, but should be monocord.

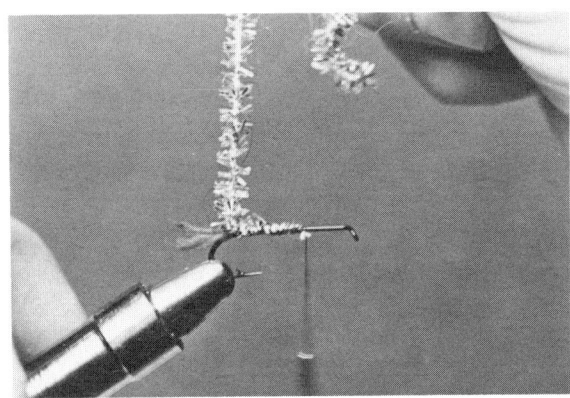

1. First tie on small strand or two of red wool yarn forming tail. Tail should be short, ¼ length of shank. Then tie medium sparkle chennile and wrap thread forward.

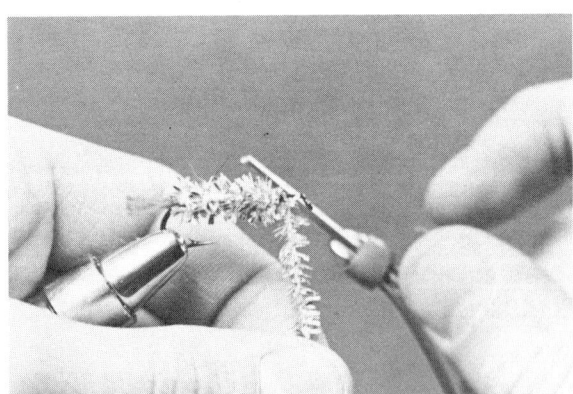

2. Wrap sparkle chennile forward tightly. Push forward with both thumb and forefinger from each hand, making sure that body is tight.

3. Tie on one color of maribou. First maribou feather should be lighter than top one, such as in a red and white streamer, the white should be tied first. Secure maribou tightly with thread.

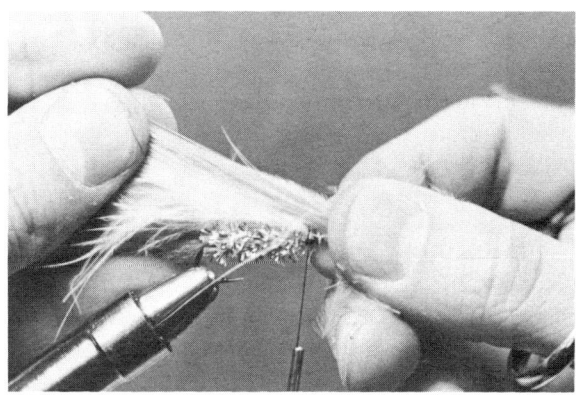

4. Secure darker maribou feather. Tie it down securely. At this point jungle cock eyes or jungle cock hackle, or silver pheasant could be added on side for topping to imitate gills.

5. Whip finish and laquer. Note large bunch of maribou. It is important that you put on more maribou than seems necessary as it loses thickness with water.

Finished Fly

BUCK ROYAL

This fly is a steelhead variation of the standard Royal Coachman Streamer. I have found it very effective in our western rivers when they begin to clear. The water of the crystal clear mountain lakes has a greenish cast during the early summer months which perfectly compliments this fly. This is my favorite streamer variation because the white calftail wing has a translucence that renders it more lifelike than the old bucktails. I tie the Buck Royal slightly weighted for the rivers in our area. I find it a tremendous fly fished from a moving raft, for its light color attracts fish which stay in the cover of deep brushy banks. It is easy for the fisherman to see and easier for the trout to see.

One of the most effective ways to fish the Buck Royal is to troll it slowly in the high altitude lakes of the Rocky Mountains. Years before the spinning rod was invented, Western anglers trolled big wet flies behind small boats using a fly rod and reel, sometimes adding a split shot to sink the flies. This method is not used much now, but it still works. I have seen a slow moving sunken fly swayed along the bottom haul fish out of lakes where spin fishermen swear that flies would never work. The Buck Royal fished this way may be just the ticket to get you out of the summer doldrums this year. Give one a try.

MATERIALS: Buck Royal

HOOK: Mustad 9672, 9671, or 3906B.

SIZES: 2 to 12.

BODY: Peacock herl, red floss.

WING: White calftail.

TAIL: Red hackle fibers.

RIBBING: Medium gold embossed tinsel.

HACKLE: Soft dark brown neck hackles or hen hackles.

HEAD: Black laquered.

THREAD: Black monocord.

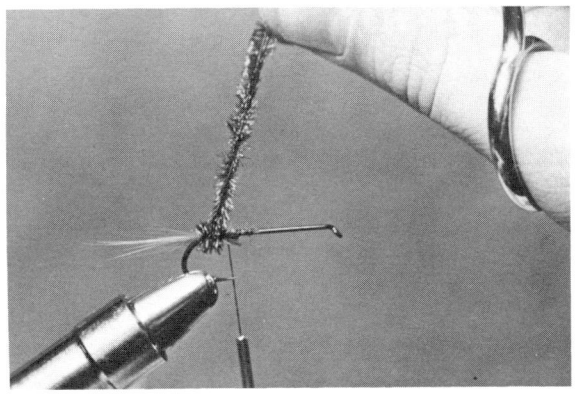

1. Tie tail of red hackle fibers and add two strands of thick peacock herl wrapping a thick tag. Tie off.

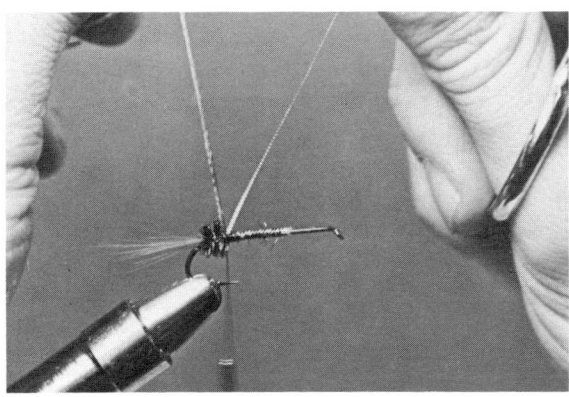

2. Tie red four strand floss and number 14 gold embossed flat tinsel.

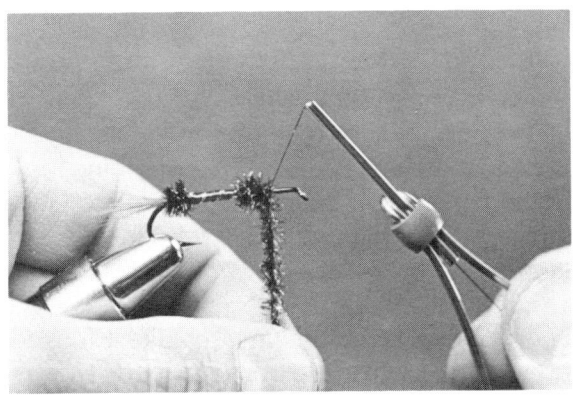

3. Wrap floss forward and rib with gold embossed tinsel. Add second tag of thick peacock herl.

4. Tie in one soft brown reddish or furnace neck or hen hackle wet style.

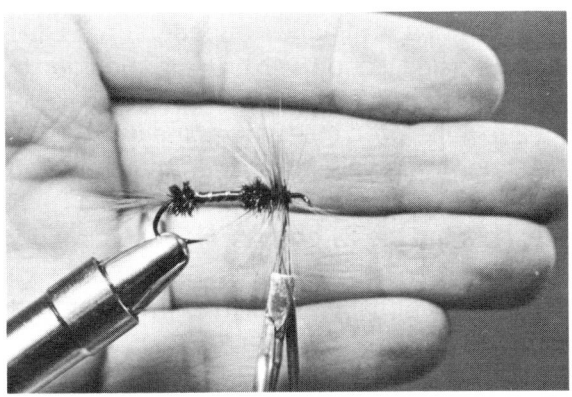

5. Wrap hackle forward. Hackle should lie back over body.

6. Tie on white calftail, making sure that all small fibers have been removed and hair is even in length. Laquer before forming head, then build up head, whip finish and add head cement.

LITTLE RAINBOW TROUT

The trout streamer series was designed by Pennsylvania's Sam Slaymaker II for fishing small Eastern rivers and creeks. His patterns, the Little Brown, Little Rainbow, and Little Brook Trout have become renowned Western flies with little or no modification. For Eastern fishing they are usually tied in sizes 10 or 12, but for the west are tied in sizes 4, 6, and 8. I regard the Little Rainbow pattern as the hottest number in Sam's trout series for alluring brook trout in western mountain lakes. Size 6 is a good bet for this situation.

Soda lake just outside Pinedale, Wyoming is a classic brook and brown trout lake. Blessed with cold, crystal clear water and an abundance of aquatic life on which the trout can feed, it forms a habitat wherein the trout grow to trophy proportions in a phenominally short time. For years, the Fish and Game Commission has collected the eggs from the brookies of this lake because of the great number and excellent condition of the spawners which are found there. This lake is known as one of the most difficult to fish because of its abundant natural food.

In 1969 I was experimenting here with several different patterns and happened on a Little Rainbow in my box. After trying it with a weighted line and sinking it deep with no luck, I decided to try some nymphs close to the surface with a dry line. I worked some of the weed beds off a rocky knoll with no luck. I watched cruising brook trout from 2 to 4 lbs. working through the weeds, but nothing could attract them. I tied on a number 6 Little Rainbow, a little larger than the one I had tried previously. I saw something that seemed to be a lengthy, fat fish swimming at about "11:00" from where I stood. After a couple of quick false casts I placed the fly about 10 feet using a dry line. I gave the Little Rainbow three quick jerks and allowed it to rest. The fish turned, and swam directly toward the fly. I again repeated the jerks and another strip and it smashed the fly almost out of the water. 20 minutes later I had landed a beautiful 4 lb. Brook trout. I released 10 other trout ranging from 1¾ lbs. to 3 lbs. that same afternoon.

I can heartily endorse this fly for streams and rivers where brook and rainbows are found, but, perhaps its greatest quality is the ability to fool the cagey trout in mossy lakes or spring fed Western ponds.

MATERIALS:	Little Rainbow Trout — Western Variation
HOOK:	Mustad 9672, 9671, or 3665A.
SIZES:	2 to 12.
BODY:	Spun white angora fur tapered or white or cream dubbed fur.
WING:	White, red, and green bucktail, with a topping of dark, greenish-brown bucktail.
TAIL:	Either red hackle fibers, or clipped red floss.
RIBBING:	Silver oval tinsel, small or medium.
HACKLE:	Pink calftail tied down.
THREAD:	Black monocord.

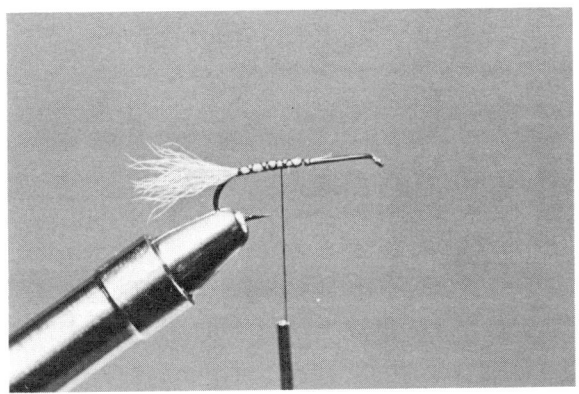

1. Tie in pink calftail.

2. Tie on medium flat gold tinsel and dub on the thread a white or creamish fur fox, otter, coyote, angora or any light fur.

3. Wrap fur forward forming body and rib with gold tinsel.

4. Select some white bucktail and measure for length. Length of hair should not exceed length of tail. Tie down white hair. Add a touch of laquer.

5. Tie in a light bunch of red bucktail. Laquer and trim.

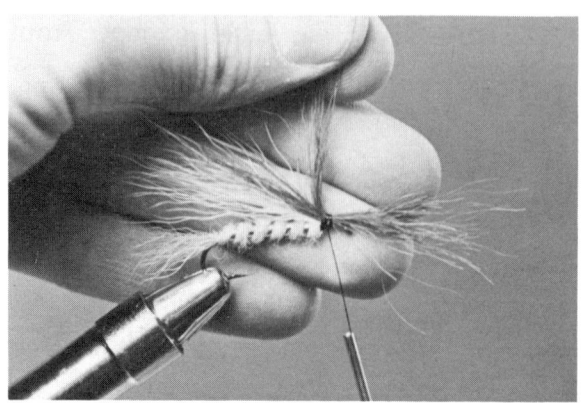

6. Tie in a light green bunch of bucktail.

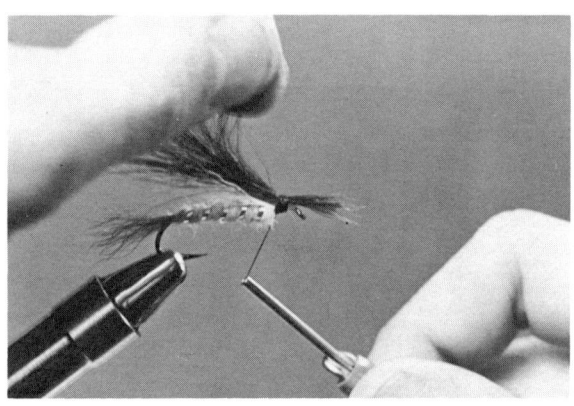

7. Top with dark green bucktail.

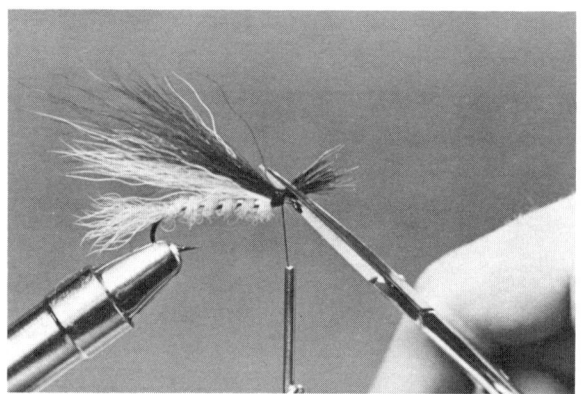

8. Trim form head, whip finish and laquer.

Finished Fly

RED ANT STREAMER

The Red Ant Streamer, first tied in the early 30's is a super California steelhead pattern converted into a trout fly. It is a beautiful work of art besides being a great trout fly. Many of the California steelhead fishermen have tried it on large rainbow and brown trout and pulled them by the dozens during slack steelhead seasons. I learned this pattern a number of years ago when some fine steelhead fishermen asked me to try it in the Rocky Mountain area. I experimented with the fly in various sizes and hook styles and came up with this modified pattern, which I tied in small streamer sizes, mostly 12 and 14. I used them on one particular lake which is sometimes literally covered by newly hatched flying ants. These ants grow up to 1 inch long with very long wings. On a windy day or a stormy day they are washed into the water and are a favorite of the greedy cutthroat trout which inhabit this lake. I cast Red Ants either from the shore or from a boat around the many fallen logs, and work them back slowly or just let them sit giving them an occasional slight twitch, a procedure that has proven deadly.

Four years ago a friend and I caught and released 26 fish from ¾ lb. up to 3½ lbs. — all caught with the Red Ant Streamer. I have used it in larger sizes in the heavy rivers with some success. However, it seems to snare more trout in the many lakes of the western U.S. For larger lakes I recommend sizes 4 and 6, fished by the same method as any other streamer.

MATERIALS: Red Ant Streamer

HOOK: Mustad 9672, 3665A, (for large sizes). Mustad 3906B, 3906 (for smaller sizes, 10 through 14).

SIZES: 2 through 8.

BUTT: 3 strands of peacock herl.

WING: Brown bucktail divided.

TAIL: None

BODY: Red Floss with gold wire.

HACKLE: Soft brown neck hackle.

THREAD: Black monocord.

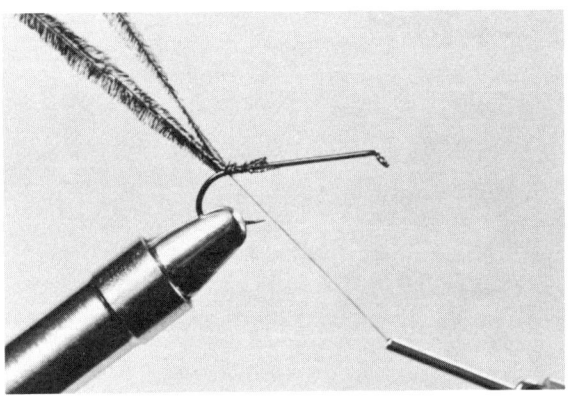

1. Tie two to three strands of peacock herl on hook.

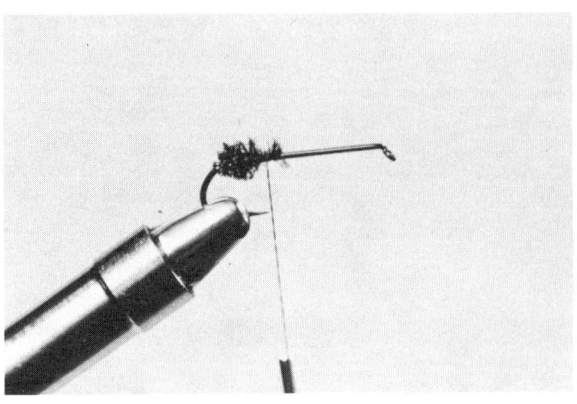

2. Wrap peacock herl forming tag or butt.

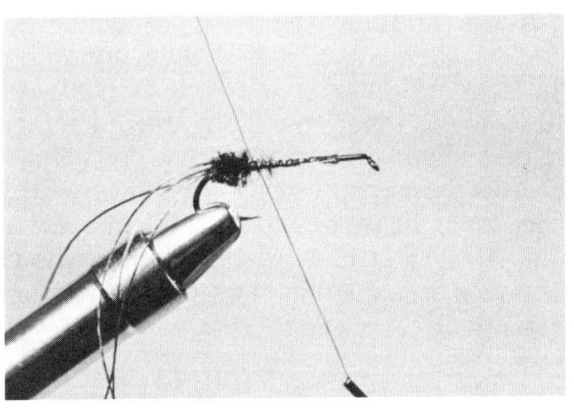

3. Wrap four strands red floss and a strand of gold wire.

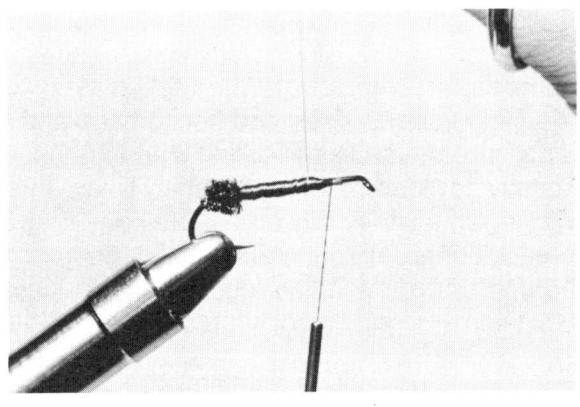

4. Wrap floss forward leaving room to tie on wing then rib floss with gold wire.

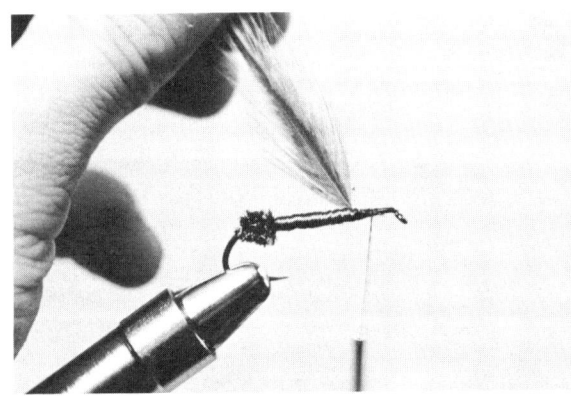

5. Tie on medium brown neck hackle wet fly style.

6. Wrap hackle forward. Hackle should lie back over body of hook.

7. Tie on brown bucktail.

8. Trim butt end of bucktail add head cement.

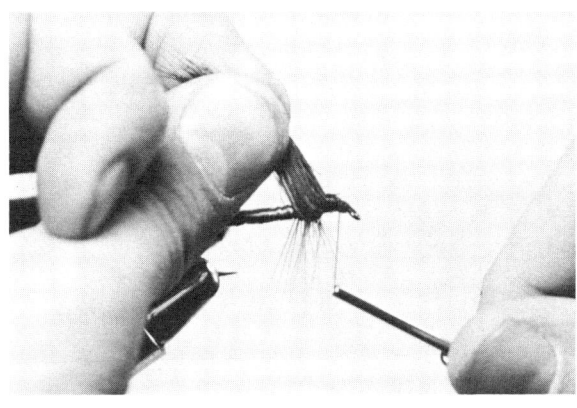

9. Tie down bucktail forming head.

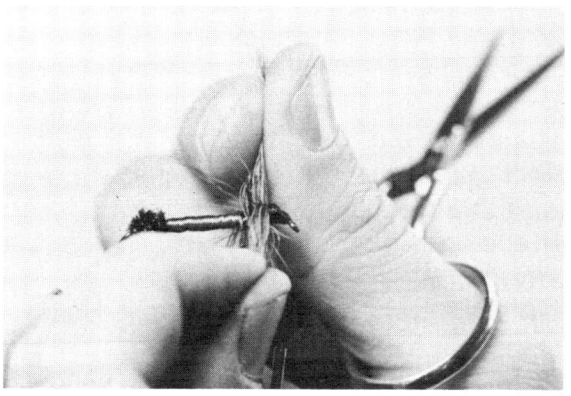

10. Divide bucktail with thumb and finger.

11. Wrap thread between divided bucktail wings, separating them. Wrap off at head, whip finish, and laquer.

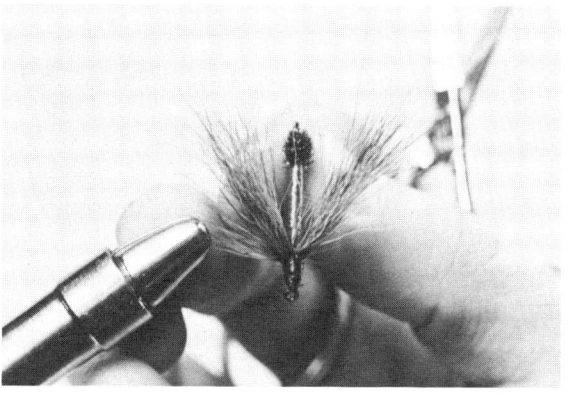

12. Wings should be divided in above manner.

SILVER HILTON

    The Royal Coachman is to trout flies what the Silver Hilton is to steelhead patterns. This famous steelhead fly, which was developed along the Pacific coastline is a remarkable trout streamer. No one really knows why this fly works because it doesn't resemble anything alive. But, by happenstance one day, a vacationing California steelhead fisherman had absolutely no luck fishing the Snake River and decided to try a Silver Hilton in a size 8. Over my violent protest he tied it on and proved me wrong after he steered in 6 beautiful Snake River Cutthroats, ranging from 1½ lbs. to 2½ lbs. We were fishing where a spring meets the Snake River. He kept tossing the fly up into the spring and letting it drift right into the heavy current of the Snake. When it hit the river current it would be dragged so rapidly that the fish sometimes swam behind the fly making violent passes at it with no luck. He would again pitch the fly up the spring and let the current bounce it through the surging water. He teased the fish by raising and lowering the rod tip which imparted an impulsive action to the fly. The more he pumped the harder the fish would strike, until he had caught all the trout he could handle. After this amazing display he calmly walked over to me and confessed that many fishermen in California toss the appetizing Silver Hilton to trout who gobble it up time and again.

MATERIALS: Silver Hilton

THREAD: Black monocord

HOOK: Mustad 9671, 9672 or 3906B

SIZES: 2 to 14

TAIL: Mallard breast fibers

BODY: Black chennile

RIBBING: Medium silver oval tinsel

WING: Wide grizzly neck hackle

HACKLE: Soft grizzly neck hackle

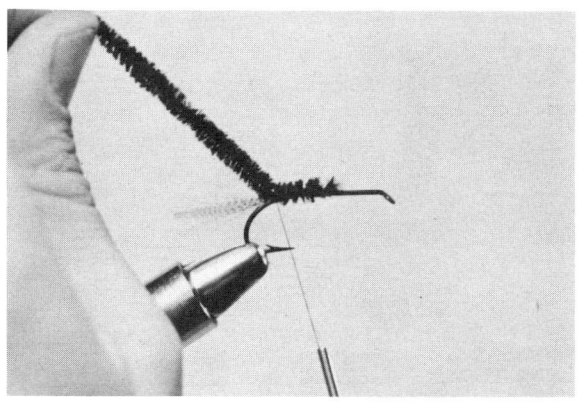

1. Tie on several fibers of mallard breast feather. Tie on medium black chennile securely.

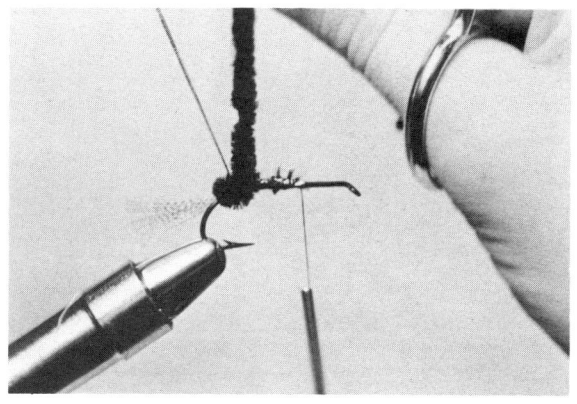

2. Tie on medium oval tinsel and wrap black chennile one wrap behind tinsel.

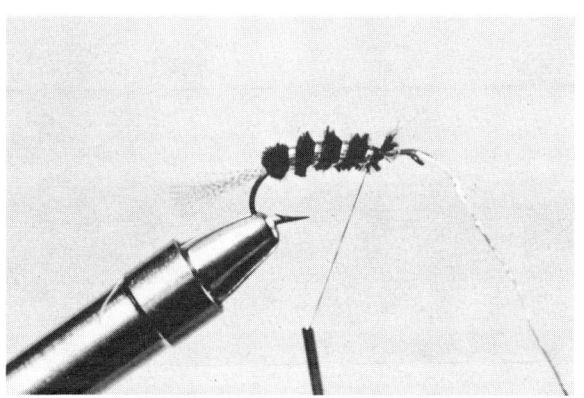

3. Wrap chennile forward forming body and rib with oval tinsel.

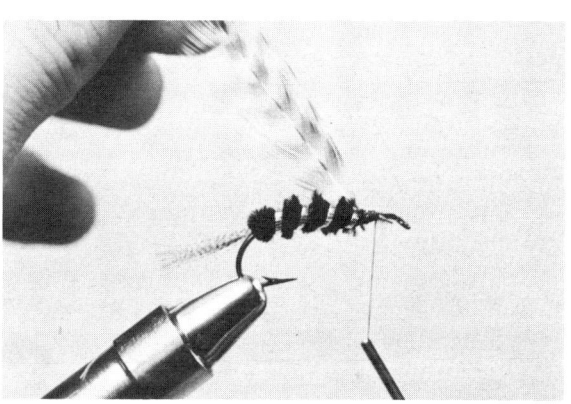

4. Tie in one soft grizzly neck hackle.

5. Wrap neck hackle forward, so the hackle slopes back over body.

6. Take one grizzly neck hackle facing it with another grizzly hackle with curve in forming a divided wing.

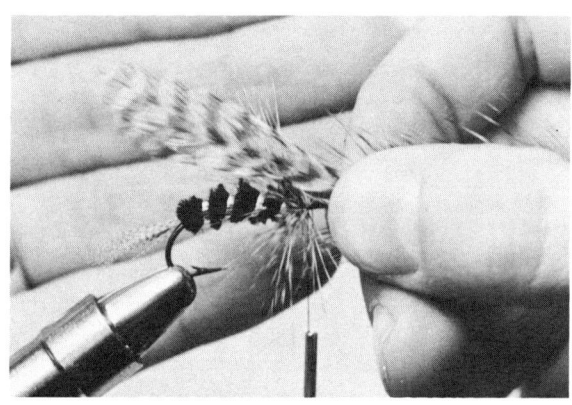
7. Take divided wing between thumb and finger and measure.

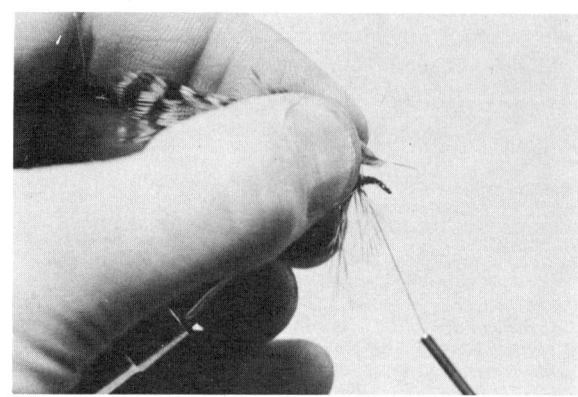
8. Strip fibers from wing and tie down. Whip finish and laquer.

Finished Fly

BLACK GHOST

This is a popular eastern streamer pattern which has been modified for use in the West. The guides for the rivers in Montana tell me that this is one streamer which is a must for anyone who plans to fish that area. I tie it differently from the eastern pattern, by weighting it slightly and fishing it in basically the same manner as all western streamers. The Black Ghost is probably the most deadly on large brown trout, and is a fine pattern for fishing late in the evening or at night.

MATERIALS: Black Ghost

THREAD: Black monocord.

HOOK: Mustad 3906B, 3665A, 9672

SIZES: 2 through 10.

TAIL: Yellow hackle fibers.

BODY: Black chennile.

RIBBING: Silver oval tinsel, medium.

WING: White calftail or white bucktail.

HACKLE: Soft, black neck hackle.

1. Tie several strands of yellow bucktail for a tail and medium black chennile.

2. Tie in medium oval tinsel.

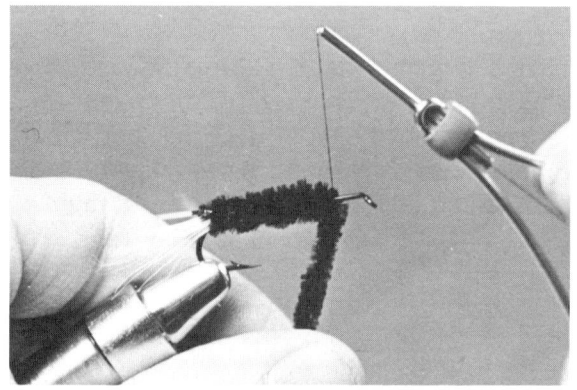

3. Wrap black chennile forward leaving plenty of room for wing.

4. Wrap oval tinsel forward ribbing body.

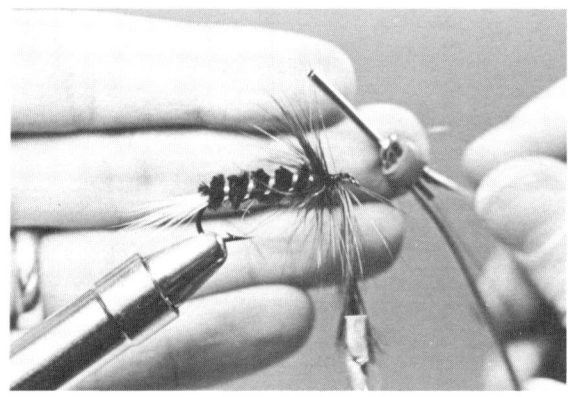

5. Tie on black soft neck hackle and wrap forward. Hackle should lie back over body.

6. Tie on securely white calftail or impala. IMPORTANT: Be sure that all small strands of calftail have been removed and only long strands remain in wing. It is good to laquer at this point before finishing head. After laquering build up head, whip finish, and add final laquering.

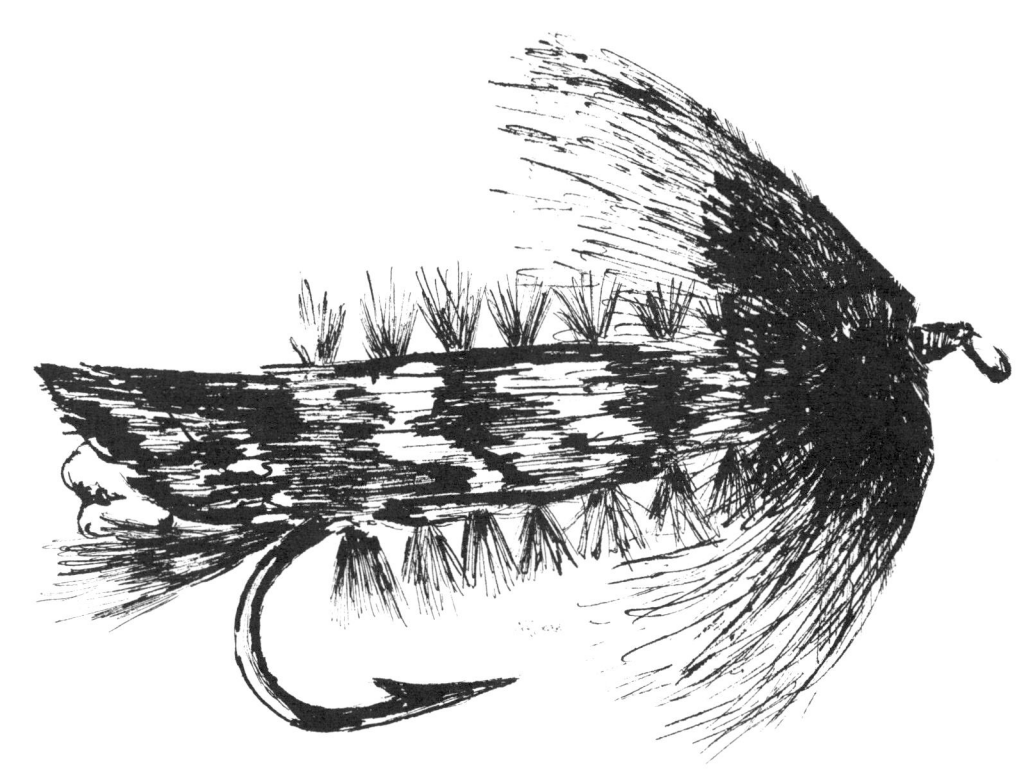

Wet Flies

Step by Step Instructions

WOOLY WORM

There is probably not a fly tier in the U.S. who has not heard of the Wooly Worm. It is a fly that every fisherman should have for fishing in the numerous streams of the west. It is tied in various lengths; it can be weighted or unweighted; colors can be black, orange, yellow, red, green, and you name it! Many variations have sprung up, such as Dan Bailey's Duck Lake Wooly Worm and the Brown Bomber, but it remains basically the same fly. Its chennile body and soft, webby hackle make it a buggy imitation of both terrestials and aquatic nymph life.

Jack Anderson, the fly fisherman and Superintendant of Yellowstone Park, rates the black Wooly Worm as Yellowstone's best all-around fly. In Yellowstone Park it is not uncommon to see a fisherman using three-inch Wooly Worms in places like Lewis Lake to bring in 2 to 3 lb. brown trout. Size eight black Wooly Worms with gray hackle have probably caught more fish than any other flies in Yellowstone Lake. There are many people who fish with only that pattern and consistently catch 1½ to 2 lb. cutthroat in this lake. Heavily weighted Wooly Worms are extremely popular on the famous Madison River. Pat Barnes, renowned West Yellowstone guide, rates the Wooly Worm as one of his all-time favorite patterns.

Many newer patterns have usurped the limelight from the Wooly Worm. Flies such as the Muddler Minnow, Maribou Muddler, Spuddler, Whitlock Sculpin, and Montana Nymph have stolen its glory. I only wish I had a dollar for every fish that was caught on a Wooly Worm prior to the development of those newer patterns.

The secret of the Wooly Worm lies in correctly tying both the body and the hackle. The body should be thick, good quality chennile, and the fly can be weighted, depending on the area to be fished. Next the hackle should be soft, and of the proper size. With the shortages in the feather market today, it is hard to find long, soft Wooly Worm hackle of good quality. It is almost as hard as finding a AA grizzly neck.

My favorite Wooly Worms have black, yellow, peacock green or dark brown bodies with either grizzly, brown, badger, or black hackles. For tails I prefer either red wool yarn which has been doubled to form a small loop, or red hackle fibers.

Fishing a Wooly Worm is a matter of personal preference. Many people float it on a dead drift just like a nymph, others fish it as a streamer retreiving it by various methods. Some even fish the Wooly Worm dry. I don't think that there is any one best method since each situation could call for a different way of presenting the fly.

MATERIALS:	Wooly Worm
THREAD:	Black, red, or yellow monocord, depending on color of body. I prefer wrapping all my weighted Wooly Worms with red thread to distinguish them from the non-weighted ones.
HOOK:	Mustad 9672, 9671 or 79850.
SIZES:	2 to 14.
TAIL:	Red or yellow hackle fibers, wool, or clipped floss.
BODY:	Black chennile is the most popular, followed by yellow, dark green, brown, gray white, green, etc.
RIBBING:	Sometimes the fly will have a small gold or silver embossed rib wound on prior to wrapping the hackle. It is only an option.
HACKLE:	Black, brown, grizzly, or badger hackle.

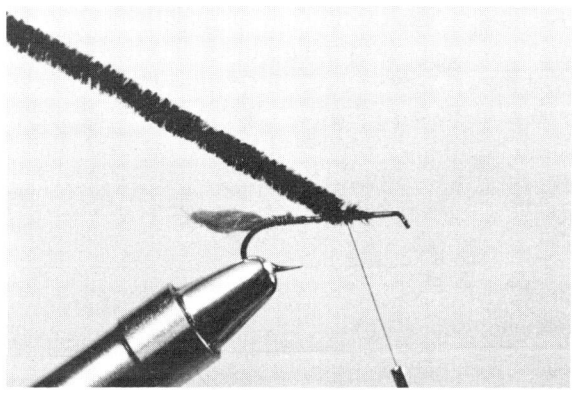

1. Tie on a double or triple strand of red wool or several fibers of red hackle. Then wrap on medium black chennile. Tie in very tightly.

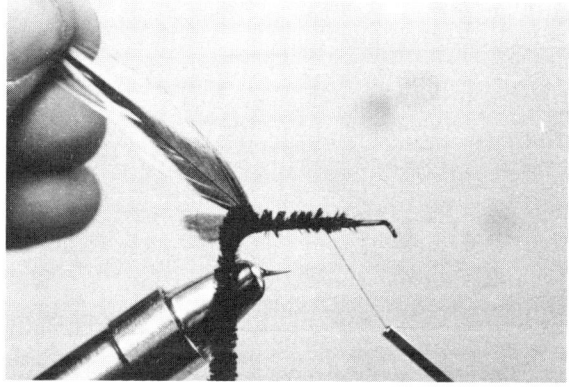

2. Tie in either a badger, grizzly, brown, black or other selected color hackle. Hackle should be long, at least three times the length of the shank. Tie it with hackle facing forward. Darker side of hackle should face you.

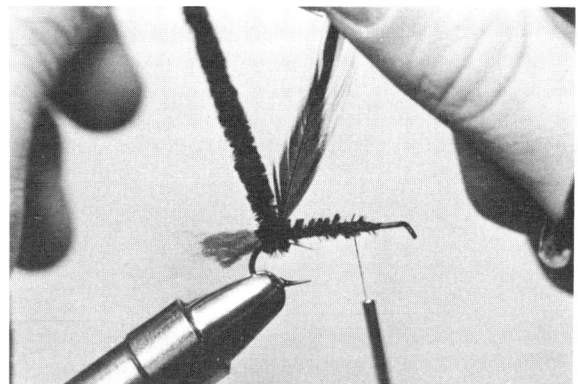

3. One wrap of chennile around back of hackle.

4. Wrap chennile forward making sure that it is wrapped tightly. Push forward with thumb and fingers of both hands making body tight.

5. Wrap hackle forward on evenly.

6. Tie hackle off, wrap head, whip finish, laquer.

Finished Fly

BLUE DUN WESTERN-STYLE

This wet fly is a western version of the standard Blue Dun pattern. I consider it to be the best brook trout fly I have ever found. I have fished many beaver ponds and small spring-fed creeks, and I have yet to find a better under-water fly . . . nymphs, streamers, or otherwise. It is usually tied in sizes eight to fourteen and should be fished three to four inches beneath the surface. I have fished it on occasions deep with a wet line, but usually I use the fly in shallow water.

For me it is most effectively used with a long slow retreive or a short, jerky retrieve. I have had some luck dead-drifting it in springs. While fishing ponds and springs, I have caught some large brown trout on this fly. The pattern was handed down to me from my father, who always told me that anytime you were among the brook trout to certainly try the Blue Dun. To this day it is still his favorite wet fly.

MATERIALS:	Blue Dun
THREAD:	Black monocord.
HOOK:	Mustad 7957B or 3906.
SIZES:	8 to 14.
TAIL:	A reddish brown hackle or fibers from the reddish feathers from a golden pheasant.
BODY:	Gray wool yarn or dubbed muskrat fur.
RIBBING:	Gold embossed tinsel medium.
WING:	Gray squirrel tail.
HACKLE:	A medium blue dun hen hackle or soft neck hackle.
HEAD:	Black

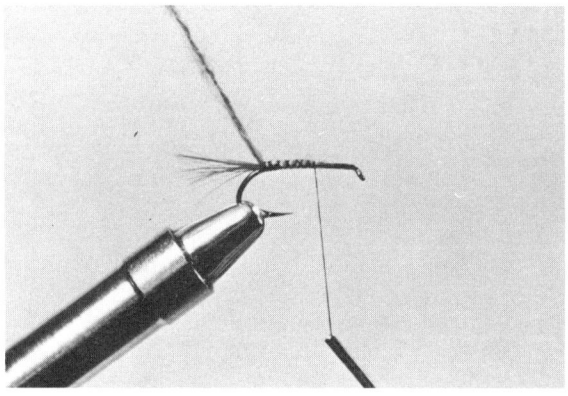

1. Tie on thread, reddish brown neck hackle fibers or a bright red breast feather from a golden pheasant. Then tie on a strand of spun angora fur. Tie securely.

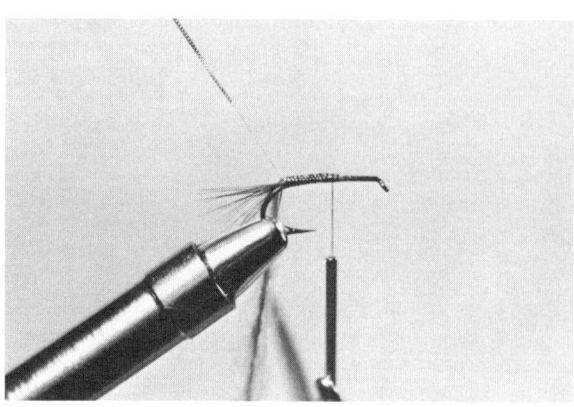

2. Tie in #14 gold flat embossed tinsel.

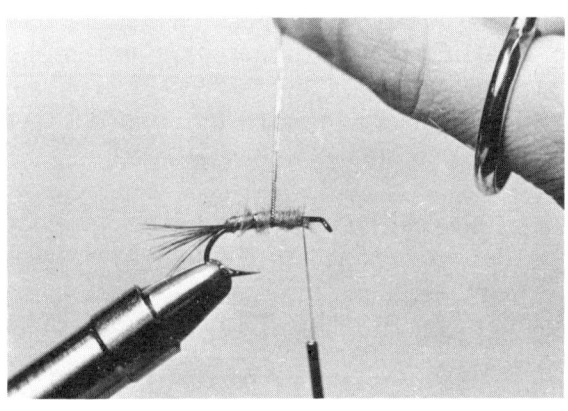

3. Wrap angora fur forward forming body then rib with tinsel.

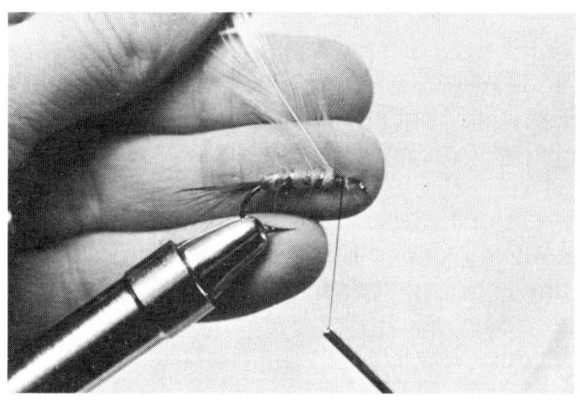

4. Tie on a medium blue dun soft neck or hen hackle.

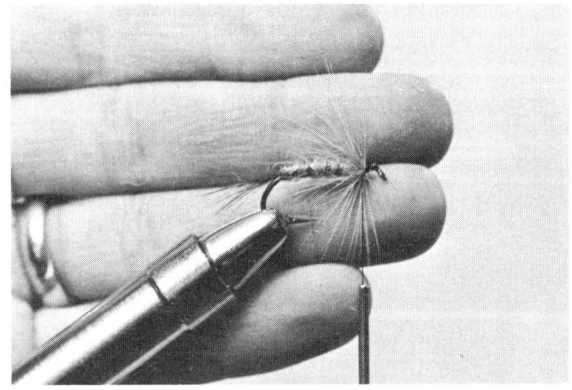

5. Wrap hackle forward three to four times so hackle fibers lie back softly over body.

6. Tie on gray squirrel tail. Length of squirrel tail should not exceed length of tail. Trim, whip finish, and head cement.

RIO GRANDE KING

If you are ever checked by a game warden in Colorado you may be fined if you do not have a Rio Grande King in your box. It is almost a state tradition in Colorado to fish with one of these. I myself, have never had much faith in this white-winged fly, but I find it hard to argue with its many adherents who have had great success with it. For many people, trust in this fly rivals their faith in the Almighty. There are some fishermen who will not fish with anything else, and they become even hostile when you suggest that it might not work in your area. Throughout Idaho, Montana, Utah, California, Colorado, Washington, Oregon, and Arizona the name Rio Grande King is well known and revered. In almost every tackle shop in these areas there are Rio Grande Kings for sale. The wet fly version is the most popular style of this pattern.

My experience with this fly is limited, but its avid followers tell me it is best fished in fast, turbulent water in the same manner as you would fish any wet fly or streamer. I have even been asked (by one of its ardent admirers) to tie some of these in sizes two and four for lake fishing. The fly can be tied several ways, but the one here is the standard approved version. I might note that calftail can be used to replace the duck quill wing.

MATERIALS: Rio Grande King

THREAD: Black monocord.

HOOK: Mustad 7957B, 3906, or 3906B.

SIZES: For large streams and lakes: 2 through 8. For small streams 10 through 16.

TAIL: Golden pheasant tippets.

BODY: Black chennile.

WING: White duck quills or white calftail.

HACKLE: Brown neck hackle, medium shade.

HEAD: Black

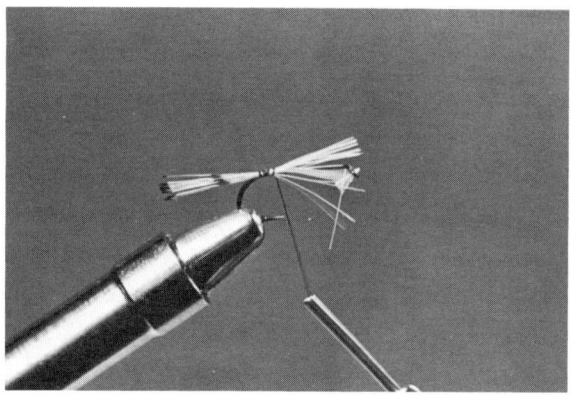

1. Tie in several fibers of golden pheasant tippet.

2. One medium black chennile tied tightly to shank.

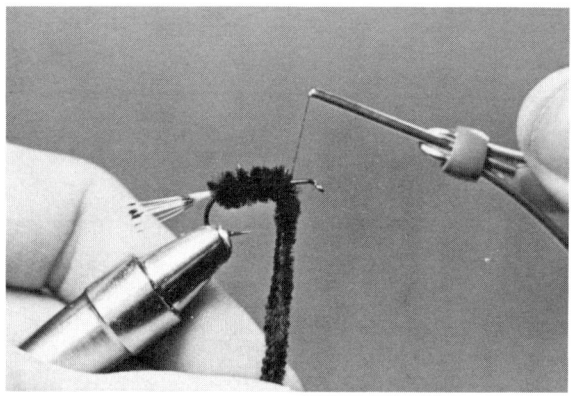

3. Wrap chennile forward forming body. Notice proportions.

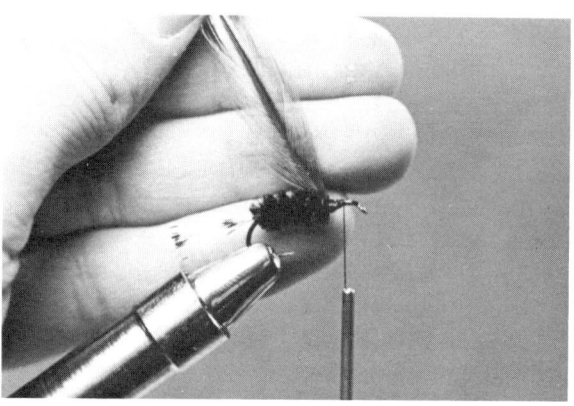

4. Tie in one soft, medium brown furnace neck hackle wet style.

5. Wrap neck hackle forward. Trim out any stray fibers after tying on.

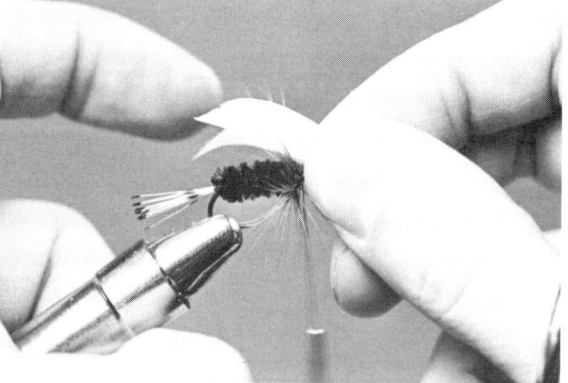

6. Select two white matching duck quills. Quills can be either melded together, which means the inside curves facing or they can be put with outside curves facing forming a divided wing. (Shown here is a divided wing.)

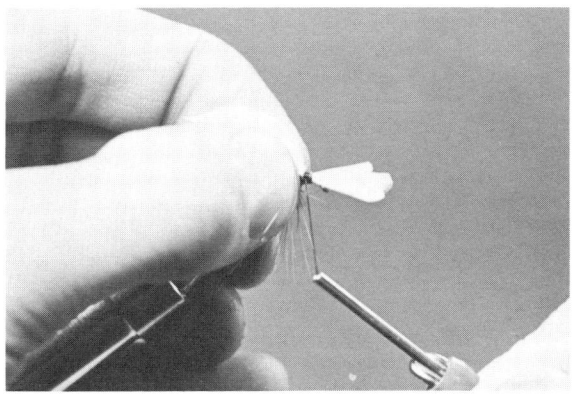

7. Tie in duck quill wing pushing slightly up with thumb and finger when tying down.

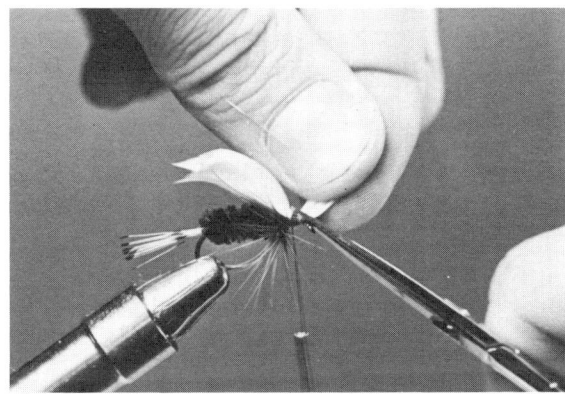

8. Trim off butt end of white duck wing, make smooth even head and whip finish, then laquer.

Finished Fly

CAREY SPECIAL

The Carey Special is a renowned pattern in the Northwest and has a popularity that grows every year. It is becoming widely known throughout the whole U.S. It was first designed by Colonel Tom Carey and was later improved on by other local fly tiers. Originally it was tied to resemble sedge flies, then it was tied in darker colors to suggest dragon fly and damsel fly nymphs. With its different variations it has become a pattern that can represent many types of aquatic nymph life.

It is considered one of the top lake wets in existence today. The lakes of Oregon and Washington in the coastal areas have fish which respond to it with gusto.

The fly is tied with ring-neck pheasant hackle which is a very soft, breathing feather. I have been told that it thus works best when retrieved with long steady strokes. It can be weighted and fished deep, or it can be fished close to the surface. I suggest that you become well acquainted with the water you intend to fish in order to determine the depth at which you want to use this fly.

MATERIALS: Carey Special

THREAD: Black monocord.

HOOK: Mustad 3906B, 9672 Mustad.

SIZES: 2 to 10.
TAIL: None, or several ring neck pheasant breast hackle fibers — greenish and blueish in color.

RIBBING: Gold or silver embossed tinsel (medium) optional.

HACKLE: Ring neck pheasant flank hackle.

HEAD: Black

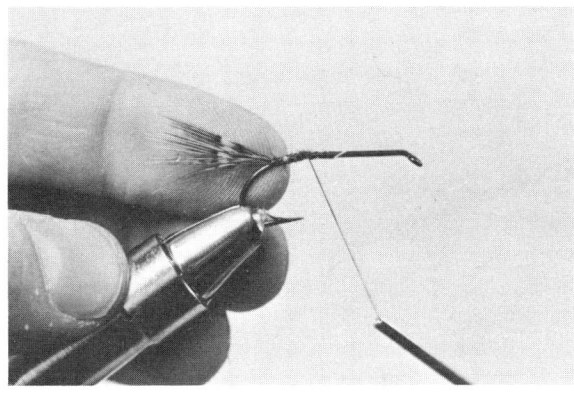

1. Tie in a piece of pheasant breast as shown above.

2. Tie in either black, green, brown, or any other suitable chennile color.

3. Wrap chennile forward and tie off.

4. Select the irridescent blue flank feather from a ring neck pheasant.

5. Tie in flank feather.

6. Wrap feather and use scissors point to unwrap any tied down hackle.

7. Wrap back with thread folding hackle back over body. Form head, whip finish and laquer.

Finished Fly

WESTERN COACHMAN

A creation from the vise of the late famous Wayne "Buz" Buszek from Visalia, California, it can be tied either wet or dry. I am illustrating the wet fly version, a California favorite. Buz Buszek was a man of exceptional fly tying talent. He developed and improved upon many great flies that are in use today.

I learned this pattern from my father who once owned a tackle shop in Jackson Hole, Wyoming during the late 40's. In those days it was customary for a tackle shop owner to hire local talent to tie his flies, but Buz's flies were so well tied that my father decided to have this California tyer produce all the flies for his customers. It was the close scrutiny of Buz's fine work that helped me develop some of my own fly tying methods and I will be eternally grateful to him for this.

The Western Coachman can be fished successfuly either wet or dry. For those who want to fish it dry I suggest tying the fly with stiffer hackles than the wet fly version. Tied down-wing style, it works well when Caddis hatches are occuring. California fishermen feel that it is an excellent match for the many caddis hatches which emerge on the Sierra streams. I have had excellent luck with this pattern in Idaho, Wyoming, and Montana. From what other fishermen tell me this fly succeeds all over the U.S., including the East. I suggest that you tie up several for your box and give them a try when nothing else works, just to see what happens.

MATERIALS: Western Coachman

THREAD: Black monocord.

HOOK: Mustad 7957B or 3906B or 3906.

SIZES: 8 through 14.

TAIL Golden pheasant tippets.

BODY: Wrapped peacock herl.

RIBBING: None

WING: White calftail.

HACKLE: Brown neck hackle — stiff for dry flies, soft and tied back for wet flies.

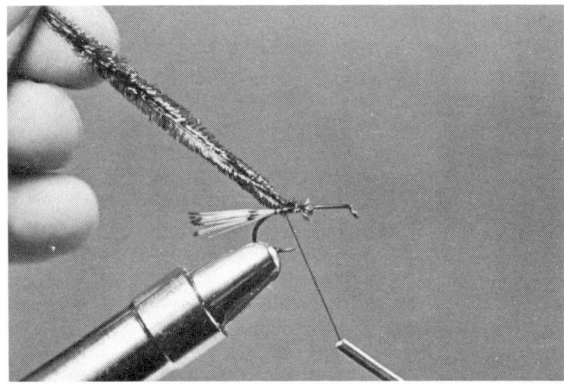
1. Tie on several fibers of golden pheasant tippets and also three to four strands of peacock herl.

2. Wrap peacock herl forward forming body approximately ½ way down hook.

3. Tie on streamer style white calftail or white deer hair making sure tips are even. Make sure that wing does not exceed length of tail. Note picture. Tie down wing securely, trim butt.

4. Tie on either furnace or medium brown saddle or neck hackle depending on side of hook. Wrap forward dry-style with glossy side facing you or in simpler terms, dull side facing eye of hook after hackle has been wrapped for dry version. For wet fly version or all purpose version, wrap hackle with dull side facing back and shiny side facing eye. Whip finish, laquer.

Finished Fly

WESTERN FLY PATTERN DICTIONARY

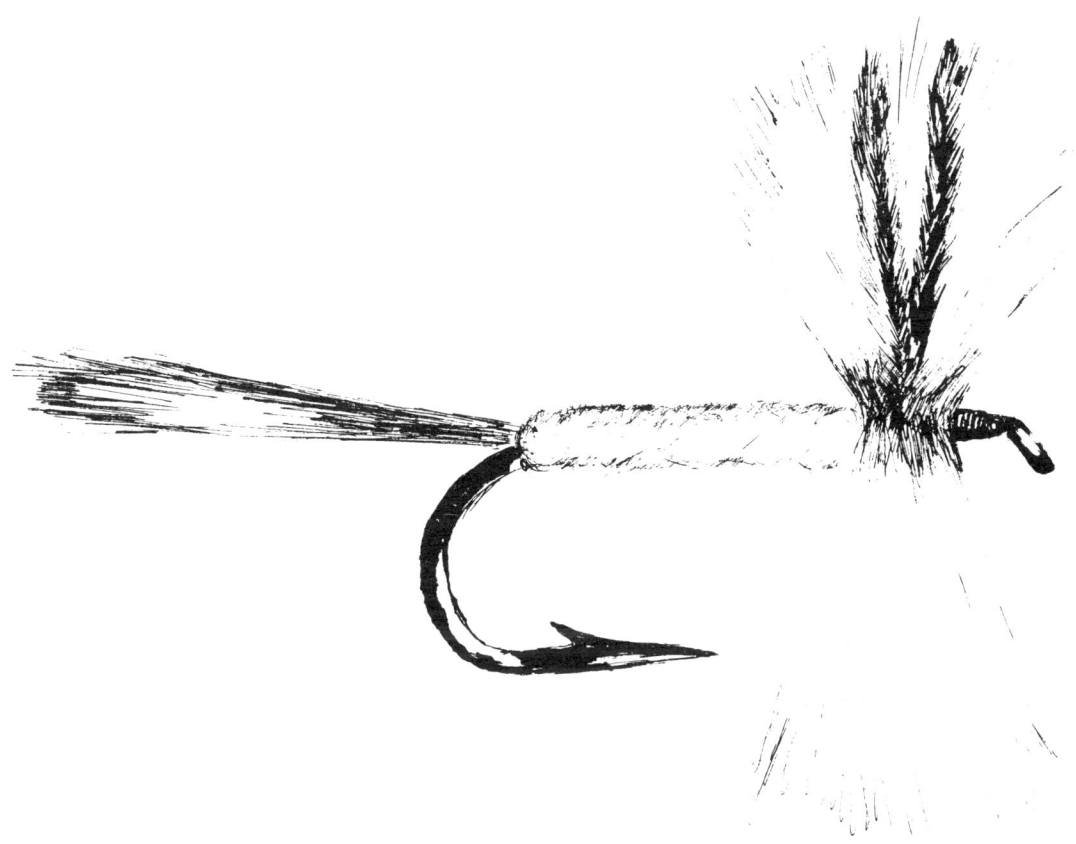

This is a selection of some of the more popular fly patterns which have not been covered by the step-by-step instructions in the manual. This by no means is a complete dictionary of western patterns, but it is a good representative list.

In the dictionary, the column entitled "Manual Reference" will direct you to the page in the manual which will depict some of the general steps and procedures in tying the pattern. I hope that you will find this feature helpful as you tie the flies listed in the dictionary.

Dry Flies

NAME	HOOK	TAIL	BODY	RIBBING	WING	HACKLE	MANUAL REFERENCE
Adams Midge	94840 or 7957B Sizes 16 to 24	Dark moose hair fibers	Dubbed grey fur, muskrat, fur	None	None or grizzly hackle tips	Reddish-brown mixed with grizzly hackle	24
Adams Spentwing	94840 or 7957B Sizes 10 to 20	Dark moose hair fibers	Dubbed grey fur, muskrat, fur	None	Wide grizzly hackle tips tied spent		24
Adams Yellow	94840 or 7957B Sizes 10 to 20	Dark moose hair fibers	Yellow wool or dubbing	None	Grizzly hackle tips		24
Badger Bivisible	94840 or 7957B Sizes 10 to 20	Badger hackle fibers	4 Badger hackle tied very thickly Palmer style all the way to the eye	None	None	One wrap of white hackle	
Badger Variant	94840 Sizes 10 to 18	Badger neck hackle fibers	Stripped peacock quill	Small gold wire	Two wide badger neck hackles, divided	Oversized badger, either neck or saddle hackle	27
Bearpaw	94840 or 7957B Sizes 8 to 16	Red neck hackle fibers			Gray duck quill tied upright and divided	Medium brown neck hackle	36
Black Gnat	94840 or 7957B Sizes 8 to 16	Black hackle fibers or dark moose fibers	Three fibers of black ostrich herl or black floss or black wool or black chennile	None	Black neck hackle tips or medium gray duck quills	Black neck or saddle hackle	36
Black Quill	94840 or 7957B Sizes 8 to 18	Black hackle or dark moose fibers	Stripped peacock herl or one light and one dark moose mane	Light gold wire or laquer or quill body thoroughly	Black neck hackle tips or gray duck quills, divided	Black neck hackle or saddle	39
Bloody Butcher	94840 or 7957B Sizes 6 to 14	Red hackle fibers	Red floss	One yellow and one red Palmer-tied neck hackle	Tied down-wing style fox squirrel tail	Red and yellow mixed neck hackle	130
Blue Bottle	94840 or 7957B Sizes 10 to 22	Blue dun hackle fibers	Silver tinsel tip one wrap; a blue floss tapered body	None	Gray duck quill divided and tied upright	Dyed black neck hackle	36
Blue Quill	94840 or 7957B Sizes 10 to 22	Blue dun hackle fibers	One stripped peacock quill or one light and one dark moose mane	None	A dark gray duck quill divided and tied upright	A medium blue dun saddle or neck hackle	36
Brown Ant	94840 or 7957B Sizes 12 to 24	None	A segmented body dove brown fox fur	None	None	Brown neck hackle tied between segments of body	51
Brown Bivisible	94840 or 7957B Sizes 10 to 20	Brown neck hackle	Three or four brown neck or saddle hackles wrapped thickly forward	None	None	One wrap of light neck or saddle hackle just in front of brown	
Brown and Brown	94840 or 7957B Sizes 8 to 16	Golden pheasant tippet fibers;	strip three ginger quills, tie forward	None	Medium shade of deer hair tied divided and upright	None	36
Brown Drake	94840 or 7957B sizes 8 to 16	Brown hackle fibers; tail is 1½ times length of shank	Brown floss, tapered thin	None	Dark brown turkey tail fibers tied upright and divided	Grizzly or variegated fibers tied barred upright and hackle divided	140
Brown Hackle Peacock	94840 or 7957B Sizes 8 to 20	Dark brown moose hair	Four strands of full, thick peacock herl	None	None	Medium brown neck hackle or saddles	48
Brown Hackle Yellow	94840 or 7957B Sizes 8 to 20	Red neck hackle fibers or dark brown moose hair fibers	Yellow floss tapered	Medium flat gold tinsel	None	Medium brown neck hackle	48
Brown Quill Spinner	94840 or 7957B Sizes 8 through 16	Stiff brown hackle fibers	Three strands of peacock herl, medium thickness		Gray mallard flank fibers tied upright and divided	A medium to dark brown tied	36
Brown Sedge	94840 or 7957B Sizes 8 to 16	None	A gold tinsel tip, a dun gray dubbing tapered body		Gray duck quill tied upright and divided	Brown medium tied Palmer-style from tail to front of hook	36

NAME	HOOK	TAIL	BODY	RIBBING	WING	HACKLE	MANUAL REFERENCE
Brown Variant	94840 in sizes 10 to 22	Brown hackle fibers	Medium brown wool or dyed brown dubbed rabbit	One peacock eye stripped quill	None	One brown and one grizzly mixed either neck or saddles	27
Buckskin Bob	94840 or 7957B Sizes 8 to 16	Dark moose body hair fibers	Dark brown wool or floss tapered	Yellow floss single strands	Dark deer or elk hair upright and divided	A medium to reddish brown either neck or saddles	119
Buckskin Hare's Ear	94840 or 7957B Sizes 8 to 18	Ginger neck hackle fibers	Light cream dubbing, medium taper	either gold wire tinsel or gold flat tinsel	A bleached ginger duck quill or ginger neck hackle tips tied	A medium ginger neck or saddle	36
Buz Hackle	94840 or 7957B Size 8 to 16	Red neck hackles	Peacock herl, three or four strands	A gold- tipped at front of fly; a silver tip at tail of fly —		Grizzly hackle at back of fly tied over silver tinsel and brown hackle	42
Caddis	94840 Sizes 8 to 16	Several strands of dark moose hair	Dyed yellow dubbed rabbit fur or yellow wool; a medium taper	Yellow hackle tied Palmer- style	A medium brown elk divided and tied upright	Furnace saddle hackle or neck	119
Cahill Quill	94840 Sizes 10 to 16	Four strands of light elk hair, very stiff	One stripped peacock herl or a long ginger neck hackle vein stripped	None	A lemon barred wood duck side or a dyed wood duck color mallard side	A medium ginger neck or saddle hackle	45
California Coachman	94840 or 7967B Sizes 8 to 18	Several fibers of golden pheasant	Peacock herl butt then yellow floss and another peacock herl butt	None	White duck quills divided and tied upright	A pale yellow or orange necks dyed hackle or saddles on larger sizes	36
Coachman	94840 or 7957B Sizes 8 to 22	None	A tip of gold flat tinsel then three or four heavy, thick peacock herl	None	A dark, slate gray duck quill or teal quill wing,	A dark brown neck hackle or saddle,	36
Coffin Fly	94840 or 7957B Sizes 8 to 18	Fibers of ring- neck pheasant tail	Light beaver dubbing or dyed light tan rabbit fur	None	Barred teal flank fibers tied upright and divided	A rusty blue dun neck or saddle hackle	36
Colorado Caddis	94840 Sizes 10 to 16	2 Moose or javelina fibers, divided	Gray, olive or brown dubbed fur	Grizzly, olive or brown hackle, Palmer- style	Fine deer hair	None	130
Cowdung	94840 or 7957B Sizes 8 to 18	None	Tip made of gold tinsel, flat small size rest of body of light green wool	None	A medium gray duck quill tyed upright and divided	Medium brown neck or saddle hackle	36
Crazy Goof	94840 or 7957B Sizes 8 to 14		Deer body hair tied on and then pulled forward over body to form shell	A dark olive polypropelene yarn tied thickly	None	Light barred grizzly tied very thickly	79
Creme Variant	94840 Sizes 10 to 18	Four to five strands of stiff light elk	One stripped peacock herl quill or a long ginger hackle vein stripped fibers	None	None	A light ginger neck or saddle hackle tied variant style	27
Cutthroat	7957B Sizes 10 to 18	Two red duck quill strips tied forked style	A medium yellow polypropelene yarn	Silver or light gray floss one strand	White calftail tied upright and divided	Medium grizzly tied thick	109
Dun Variant	94840 or 7957B Sizes 10 to 18	Blue dun hackle fibers	Stripped peacock herl quill	None	A dark blue dun hackle tip, preferably from a hen very soft	A light rusty blue dun, neck or saddle hackle, depending on size	27
Elk Hair Humpy	7957B Sizes 8 to 20	Either dark brown moose hair or dark brown elk flank hair	Light elk body hair	None	body hair tied divided and upright	Cream, ginger or badger saddle hackle Neck hackle for small sizes	79
Female Adams	94840 or 7957B or 3906 Sizes 8 to 22	Several strands of dark moose or brown and grizzly neck hackle mixed	A tip of yellow wool then dyed gray muskrat fur or gray spun angora	None	Two barred neck hackle tips divided and tied upright	Brown and grizzly neck hackle mixed or saddles on larger sizes	24
Flying Black Ant	94840 or 7957B or 3906 Sizes 8 to 22	None	Thread or wool body	None	Black hackle tips divided and tied back	Black neck hackle	51
Floating Fool	94840 or 7957B or 3906 Sizes 8 to 22	White calf tail	Peacock herl	None	White calf tail tied upright parachute- style	Grizzly and brown mixed tied parachute- style	133

NAME	HOOK	TAIL	BODY	RIBBING	WING	HACKLE	MANUAL REFERENCE
Golden Badger	94840 or 7957B or 3906 Sizes 8 to 22	Divided badger hackle tips	Full badger hackle body 4 hackles tied Palmer-style	None	None	None	
Golden Stone	94840 or 7957B or 3906 Sizes 8 to 22	None	Yellow or golden yellow wool or floss	Light ginger hackle ribbed Palmer-style	Light elk hair fibers tied bucktail-style	Light ginger hackle	130
Goofus Bug	94840 or 7957B Sizes 8 to 22	Deer hair	Deer hair pulled over to form hump	None	Deer hair	Grizzly and brown saddle hackles or neck hackles mixed	79
Grannon	94840 or 7957B Sizes 8 to 20	None	A butt of peacock herl a body of tanned beaver or tannish gray otter dubbed lightly	None	A light brown mottled grouse breast or a dyed teal breast	A stiff brown medium shade	45
Green Drake	94840 or 7957B Sizes 8 to 20	Dyed deer hair tied paradrake style	A continuation of the tail	A dark green or black thread	Either white calftail or dyed green deer hair or elk hair tied parachute-style	Green dyed grizzly hackle tied parachute-style	36
Green Leaf Hopper	7957B or 9671 Sizes 8 to 20	None	A light green or yellowish green lower body	None	A medium green dyed turkey quill	Spun green medium shade deer hair tied on "Muddler Minnow"-style	150
Green Worm	9671 Sizes 10 to 16	None	A medium light green tied along shank from bend to eye	A medium green thread tied to hold deer hair to hook — tied "X"	None	None	
Grey Back	7957B or 94840 Sizes 8 to 16	Dark deer hair very stiff	A light deer hair pulled over a chennile body of yellow or light green	None	None	Grizzly neck or saddle hackle depending on size	79
Grey Drake	94840 or 7957B Sizes 8 to 20	Mallard flank fibers or dark moose hair 1½ times length of shank	White or creamish dubbed fur	One single strand of black floss	Mallard flank fibers tied upright and divided	A medium barbed grizzly neck hackle very stiff and tied oversized	46
Grey Fox	94840 Sizes 10 to 18	Blue dun hackle fibers	Dubbed muskrat fur	Yellow floss ribbed wide	Mallard flank side divided and tied upright	Rusty blue dun then one wrap cream hackle in front of blue dun	46
Grey Hackle Peacock	94840 or 7957B Sizes 10 to 20	Either red hackle fibers or dark moose hair	4 or 5 strands of heavy peacock	None	None	Medium barbed gray or grizzly neck hackle or saddles	48
Grey Hackle Red	94840 or 7957B Sizes 10 to 20	Either red hackle fibers or dark moose hair	Red floss	Gold tinsel	None	Medium barbed gray or grizzly neck hackle or saddles	48
Grey Hackle Yellow	94840 or 7957B Sizes 10 to 20	Either red hackle fibers or dark moose hair	Yellow floss	Flat gold tinsel	None	Medium barbed gray or grizzly neck hackle or saddles	48
Grey Variant	94840 Sizes 10 to 16	Dark moose hair fibers	Dubbed gray muskrat or rabbit fur	One strand yellow floss	Barred mallard breast fibers tied upright and divided	A medium rusty blue dun tied over side	27
Hendrickson	94840 or 7957B Sizes 10 to 18	Either dark moose hair fibers or light blue dun hackle fibers	Dubbed gray muskrat fur	None	Wood duck breast fibers or dyed mallard	A medium blue dun neck hackle	45
Horner's Deer Hair	3906 or 7957B Sizes 10 to 18	Short stiff deer hair preferably off a young fawn deer or a pacific coast mule deer	Deer hair pulled over the back the same as in humpy	Usually black or gray thread in "X" pattern	Deer hair	Very stiff medium barbed grizzly neck hackle or saddles in large sizes	79
Humpy 2	94840 or 7957B Sizes 8 to 22	Deer hair	Deer hair	None	Deer hair	Grizzly and brown hackle mixed — saddles or necks	79
Humpy 3	7957B Sizes 6 to 18	Dark moose hair	Light elk hair pulled over same as deer hair in previous instructions	None	Elk hair	Cream or badger	79
Humpy 4	7957B or 3906 Sizes 8 to 20	Dark deer hair	Dyed green deer hair dyed in similar fashion as previously mentioned	None	Green deer hair	A dyed green plymouth rock	79

NAME	HOOK	TAIL	BODY	RIBBING	WING	HACKLE	MANUAL REFERENCE
Black Humpy	7957B or 94840 or 3906 Sizes 8 to 20	Dyed black deer hair or dark moose hair fibers	Dyed black deer hair	None	Dyed black deer hair	Dyed black neck or saddle hackle	79
Iron Blue Dun	94840 or 7957B Sizes 10 to 20	Several strands of dark moose hair or a dark iron blue dun neck hackle fibers	A red floss tag with dubbed gray rabbit or muskrat fur	None	Either a medium light blue dun hackle tips or a slate gray duck quill wing	A rusty iron blue dun neck or saddle hackle	21
Irresistable Black	7957B or 94840 Sizes 6 to 22	Medium brown elk hair	Clipped caribou or deer hair	None	White calf tail divided and tied upright	Dyed black saddles or neck hackle	103
Irresistable Ginger	7967B or 94840 Sizes 6 to 22	Medium light elk hair	A cream or off-white deer hair	None	White calf tail or cream neck hackle tips	A medium ginger saddle or neck hackle	103
Irresistable Rat Faced McDougal	7967B or 94840 Sizes 6 to 22	Yellow calftail	Medium gray deer or caribou hair	None	Two grizzly hackle tips brown and divided and tied upright	Brown and grizzly hackle mixed neck or saddles	95
Irresistable Red	7967B or 94840 6 to 22	A dark moose or dark elk hair	Dyed body red deer hair	None	A cream neck hackle tips divided and tied upright	Medium brown neck or hackle or saddle	95
Irresistable White	7967B or 94840 6 to 22	Either several fibers of elk hair light, or cream or white hackle fibers	White deer hair clipped	None	White calf tail or creamish hackle tips or badger hackle tips	Badger neck or saddle hackles	95
Irresistable Yellow	7967B or 94840 Sizes 6 to 22	Medium brown elk hair	Clipped dyed yellow deer hair	None	Either white calf tail or a pale yellow hackle tip wings	Brown neck hackle or saddles	103
Jassid	94840 Sizes 16 to 24	None	Orange floss	One medium brown neck hackle tied Palmer-style	One jungle cock hide feather tied flat and back over body	None	68
Jennie Spinner	484 or 7957B Sizes 8 to 18	None Tip red floss tied thinly	Tapered white wool very thin	None	None	Very stiff white neck hackle	36
Leadwing Coachman	94840 or 7957B Sizes 8 to 18	None	Gold floss tip rest of body is wrapped three or four strands of peacock herl	None	Slate dark gray wood duck or teal quill wings divided and tied upright	Either a dark brown or furnace neck hackle	36
Lehort Hopper	9671 Sizes 10 to 14	None	Yellow wool	None	Mottled brown turkey quill tied "Muddler Minnow"-style	Clipped deer hair tied "muddler-style"	150
Light Caddis	94840 Sizes 10 to 18	Several strands of light elk hair	Light cream dubbing either fox or natural rabbit	Ginger hackle tied Palmer-style	Slate gray duck quills or a medium blue dun	A very pale light blue dun	45
Light Cahill	94840 or 7957B Sizes 8 to 24	Several strands of light elk hair	The under side belly fur of fox cream in color	None	Wood duck barred breast feather or dyed mallard breast feathers	A light ginger very stiff tied sparse for small springs heavier for larger rivers	45
Light Cahill Quill	94840 Sizes 8 to 24	Several strands of light elk hair	Stripped ginger hackle veins tied tapered and laquered	None	Wood duck barred breast feather or dyed mallard breast	A light ginger or creamish neck hackle	45
Light Hendrickson	94840 or 7957B Sizes 8 to 24	Several strands of light elk hair or — pale light blue dun hackle fibers	A creamish or a pale or dyed pale light blue dun rabbit fur	None	Wood duck barred breast feather dyed wood duck color	A light pale blue dun	45
March Brown	94840 or 7957B Sizes 8 to 22	Brown neck hackle	A grayish brown dubbed rabbit fur	One strand of gold floss	Either mottled brown turkey divided and tied upright or one wood duck breast	Either a medium brown blue dun or a fiery furnace neck or saddle hackle	36
McGinty	94840 or 7957B Sizes 8 to 16	Red neck hackle fibers	One black and one yellow chennile wrapped to give striped effect	None	The irridescent blue quill feather found on mallard duck wing,	A medium brown or furnace neck hackle	36
Meloche	7957B or 94840 Sizes 10 to 18	Several strands of light elk har	Chennile should be small/ a dark cream or beige dubbed rabbit fur tapered	None	Grizzly hackle tips tied divided and upright	A light ginger or off-white neck or saddle hackles	36

NAME	HOOK	TAIL	BODY	RIBBING	WING	HACKLE	MANUAL REFERENCE
Michigan Spider	9523 Size 10 to 22	Badger hackle fibers tied three times the length of the shank	Light silver tinsel	None	None	Badger saddle hackle tied spider-style	54
Midge, Badger	94840 or 7957B Sizes 16 to 24	Badger hackle fibers	A stripped badger hackle vein tied tapered	None	None	Badger neck hackle	48
Midge Blue Dun	94840 or 7957B Sizes 16 to 24	Blue dun hackle fibers	Dubbed muskrat fur	None	None	Medium blue dun neck hackle	48
Midge Brown	94840 or 7957B Sizes 16 to 24	Brown neck hackle fibers	Brown ostrich herl	None	None	Medium brown neck hackle	48
Midge Ginger	94840 or 7957B Sizes 16 to 24	Ginger hackle fibers	Ginger hackle veins	None	None	Light ginger or creamish neck hackle	48
Multi-Color Variant	94840 or 7957B Sizes 10 to 18	Either light elk hair fibers or several fibers of variegated neck hackle	A stripped ginger hackle quill or a light dubbed green body — rabbit or fox fur	None	Light gray duck quill divided and tied upright or creamish neck hackle tips	Variegated ginger or a reddish brown tied variant-style	27
Olive Dun Dark	94840 Sizes 10 to 24	Several strands of dark moose hair	A dyed olive with a yellow tinge; a dark olive	None	A dark gray or slate gray duck quills divided and tied upright	dyed olive neck with a dark dun tinge	21
Olive Dun Light	94840 Sizes 10 to 24	Several strands of light elk hair or several fibers of pale olive dun	Light cream with a slight olive tinge some	None	A pale blue dun neck hackle	A light blue dun with olive tinge to it	21
Olive Quill Dark	9480 Sizes 8 to 24	Several strands of dark moose hair	Either a stripped peacock herl quill or an olive neck hackle stripped	None	A medium gray duck quill wing or a dark blue dun neck hackle tip	A dark olive either neck or saddle hackle	39
Olive Quill Light	94840 Sizes 8 to 24	Several strands of light elk hair or several fibers of a light olive neck	Either a light moose mane strand or a stripped cream or white hackle vein	None	A pale blue dun hackle tip	A very pale or light olive with tinge of yellow	39
Olive Variant	94840 or 7957B Sizes 8 to 24	1½ times the shank size of a dyed olive badger hackle	A creamish dubbed rabbit fur with olive tinge	One small strand of pale green floss	Wide neck hackle tips	Olive dyed ginger variant hackle tied variant-style	27
Orange Asher	94840 Sizes 10 to 16	None	An orange floss body tapered thin	None	None	Tied Palmer-style heavy wrap at rear of hook and sparse toward front	36
Orange Sedge	94840 Sizes 8 to 16	None	Orange floss ribbing with a duck brown neck hackle tied Palmer-	None	A dark divided wing of deer hair	Dark brown saddles or neck	36
Pale Evening Dun	94840 or 7957B Sizes 8 to 24	Several fibers of light blue dun neck hackle	A medium gray dubbed either rabbit or muskrat fur tied very thin	None	Cream neck hackle tip	A pale blue dun with a yellowish tinge	21
Pale Evening Spinner	94840 Sizes 10 to 18	A whitish badger hackle fibers	Light cream dubbing	None	White hackle tips tied upright and divided	A blue dun dyed badger neck hackle (light blue dun tinge)	21
Pale Watery Dun	94840 or 7957B Sizes 8 to 22	A dyed blue dun with yellowish tinge neck hackle fibers	Dubbed light blue dun either muskrat or rabbit fur tapered very thin	None	Medium gray duck quills divided and tied upright	A light yellow with a slight tinge of gray — neck hackles or saddles	21
Parachute Adams	94840 or 7957B Sizes 6 to 18	Several strands of dark moose hair	Dubbed gray muskrat fur	None	White calf tail tied parachute style	Brown and grizzly mixed — either neck or saddles	137
Parachute Black Gnat	94840 or 7957B Sizes 6 to 18	Several strands of black neck hackle	3 or 4 strands of black ostrich herl	None	One white calftail tied parachute style	Black neck hackles or saddles tied parachute style	137
Parachute Blonde	94840 or 7957B Sizes 6 to 18	Several strands of white elk hair	Cream dubbing, either fox or rabbit	None	Light elk hair tied parachute style	Ginger or light cream neck or saddle hackle	137

NAME	HOOK	TAIL	BODY	RIBBING	WING	HACKLE	MANUAL REFERENCE
Parachute Blue Dun	94840 or 7957B Sizes 6 to 18	Light blue dun neck hackle fibers	Medium gray muskrat or rabbit fur	None	White calftail tied parachute-style	A medium blue dun neck or saddle hackle	137
Parachute Red	94840 or 7957B Sizes 6 to 18	Several strands of dark moose hair	Red floss	None	White calftail	Medium brown either neck hackle or saddles	137
Parachute Geronomo	94840 or 7957B Sizes 8 to 22	Several strands of dark moose hair	Dyed green body deer hair	None	White calftail	Brown either neck or saddle hackles	90
Parachute White	94840 or 7957B Sizes 8 to 22	Several strands of white neck hackle	A white or light cream dubbed fur	None	White calftail	Badger neck hackle or saddles	137
Parachute Yellow	94840 or 7957B Sizes 8 to 22	Several strands of dark moose hair	Yellow floss	None	White calftail	Brown neck or saddle hackles	137
Parachute Irresistable Black	94840 or 7957B Sizes 4 to 20	Several strands of dark moose hair or fibers of dyed black neck hackle	Dyed black clipped deer hair	None	White calftail tied parachute style	Dyed black neck hackle or saddles	106
Parachute Irresistable Blue Dun	94840 or 7957B Sizes 4 to 20	Medium brown elk hair	Clipped gray deer or caribou hair	None	Medium brown elk hair	Blue dun light to medium shade	106
Parachute Irresistable Red	94840 or 7957B Sizes 4 to 20	Several strands of dark moose hair	Clipped dyed red deer hair	None	White calf tail tied parachute style	Medium brown saddles or neck hackles	106
Parachute Irresistable White	94840 or 7957B Sizes 4 to 20	Several strands of badger neck hackle	Clipped white deer hair	None	White calf tail tied parachute style	Badger neck or saddle hackle	106
Parachute Irresistable	94840 or 7957B Sizes 4 to 20	Several strands of dark moose hair	Clipped yellow deer hair	None	White calf tail tied parachute-style	Brown neck or saddle hackle	106
Paradrake Green Drake	94840 or 7957B Sizes 8 to 18	Dyed green tied as per instructions on page 140	Deer hair paradrake	Green thread or black thread	White calftail	Dyed olive or green grizzly hackle	140
Pink Lady	94840 or 7957B Sizes 8 to 18	Brown hackle	Pink floss	Small gold tinsel	Medium gray duck quill	Brown neck hackle	36
Professor	94840 or 7957B Sizes 8 to 18	Red hackle neck fibers	Yellow floss	Gold medium small tinsel	Mallard brown flank feathers divided and tied upright	Brown hackle	45
Quill Gordon	7957B or 94840 Sizes 8 to 22	Several strands of light elk hair	one light or one dark moose mane fibers tied tapered	None	Wood duck sided feather or dyed wood duck mallard breast	A medium blue dun or a rusty blue dun	45
Red Ant	7957B or 94840 Sizes 8 to 22	None	First gold tinsel tip then butt of a peacock herl and segment of red floss	None	A slate gray duck quill divided and tied upright	Medium brown neck or saddle hackle	36
Red Quill	94840 or 7957B Sizes 8 to 22	Several strands of brown neck hackle	One stripped brown neck hackle vein or a dyed red stripped peacock herl quill	None	A medium gray duck quill or a light blue dun hackle tips	A reddish-brown neck hackle or saddle hackle	45
Red Spinner	7957B or 94840 Sizes 8 to 18	Several strands of mallard breast fibers	Red floss or dyed reddish dubbed rabbit fur	Gold single strand floss	Medium gray duck quills divided and tied upright	A dark brown neck hackle or saddles	36
Double Renegade	9671 or 9672 Sizes 8 to 18	None	A gold floss tipped with three segments between hackles of peacock herl	None	First hackle of brown medium hackle ½ way down shank	a whitish cream and third hackle brown	42
Reverand Lange	94840 or 7957B Sizes 8 to 12	White calftail fibers	Black chennile or black polypropolene yarn	None	White calftail divided and tied upright	Brown saddle hackle	116

NAME	HOOK	TAIL	BODY	RIBBING	WING	HACKLE	MANUAL REFERENCE
Royal Coachman	94840 or 7957B Sizes 8 to 22	Moose hair fiber or red hackle fibers or gold pheasant fibers	Peacock herl butt then red floss then peacock herl tuff	None	White duck quill divided and tied upright or white hackle tip	brown saddles	116
Snow Fly	94840 or 7957B Sizes 18 to 22	Black hackle fibers	Black floss	None	White neck hackle tips	Jet black neck hackles	48
Spider Black	9253 Sizes 10 to 22	Black hackle fibers	Stripped brown hackle vane	None	None	Black hackle oversize 3 gaps or more	48
Spider Blue Dun	9253 Sizes 10 to 22	Blue dun hackle fibers	Stripped cream hackle vane	None	None	Blue dun medium shade oversize 3 gaps or more	48
Spider Brown	9253 Sizes 10 to 24	Brown hackle fibers	Stripped brown hackle vane	None	None	Brown oversized 3 gaps or more	48
Spider Furnace	9253 Sizes 10 to 24	Furnace hackle fibers	Stripped badger hackle vane	None	None	Furnace oversized 3 gaps or more	48
Spider Ginger	9253 Sizes 10 to 24	Ginger hackle fibers	Stripped ginger hackle vane	None	None	Ginger oversized 3 gaps or more	48
Trude Coachman	9671 or 7957B Sizes 8 to 16	Red hackle fibers	Peacock herl butt then red floss then peacock herl butt again		White calftail tied down wing style	Brown hackle	243
Tups Indispensable	94840 Sizes 8 to 18	Light ginger hackle fibers	Yellow wool then orange dubbed fur tuff	None	None	Light ginger hackle with one wrap of white or cream in front of ginger	30
Western Bee	7957B or 94840 Sizes 8 to 16	Red hackle fibers	Black chennile then yellow chennile then black chennile		Grey duck quill divided and tied upright	Brown hackle	36
Whitecraft	94840 or 7957B Sizes 8 to 16	Brown hackle fibers	Dyed yellow stripped peacock herl	None	Grizzly hackle tips divided	Brown and grizzly mixed	39
White Miller	94840 or 7957B Sizes 8 to 20	White hackle fibers	White floss	Silver flat tinsel	White duck quill divided and tied upright	White saddles or neck	36
White Wing Coachman	94840 or 7957B Sizes 8 to 20	Brown or red hackle fibers	Peacock herl fibers	None	White duck quill divided and tied upright	Brown hackle	36
Wulff Grizzly	94840 or 7957B Sizes 4 to 20	Medium brown elk hair fibers	Yellow floss tapered	None	Medium brown elk hair divided and tied upright	Grizzly and brown hackle mixed	119
Wulff White	94840 or 7957B Sizes 4 to 20	White calf tail fibers	White dubbing	None	White calf tail	Badger neck or saddles	119
Wulff Black	94840 or 7957B Sizes 4 to 20	Dark moose hair fibers	Pink wool or floss	None	Dark moose hair fibers divided and tied upright	Furnace neck hackle or saddles	119
Wulff Blonde	94840 or 7957B Sizes 4 to 20	Light elk hair fibers	Cream dubbed fur fox or coyote	None	Light elk divided and tied upright	Light ginger saddles	119
Wulff Brown	94840 or 7957B Sizes 4 to 20	Medium brown elk hair fibers	Dubbed brown fur: beaver, rabbit, other	None	Medium brown elk hair divided and tied upright	Brown neck or saddles	119
Wulff Bumble	94840 or 7957B Sizes 4 to 20	Medium brown elk hair fibers	Clipped dyed deer hair black then yellow then black then yellow	None	Medium brown elk hair divided and tied upright	Brown neck or saddles	103

Wet Flies and Streamers

NAME	HOOK	TAIL	BODY	RIBBING	HACKLE	WING	MANUAL REFERENCE
Alexandria	3906 or 7597BX Sizes 8 to 14	Peacock sword fibers	Silver flat tinsel	Ribbed oval silver tinsel	Black hackle	Peacock sword fibers	237
American Coachman	9671, 3906 or 3906B Sizes 8 to 16	Red calftail	Yellow Wool	None	Soft brown	White calftail	218
Black Buck	9671, 3906 or 3906B Sizes 8 to 16	Red hackle fibers	Black wool	Gold tinsel	None	Black bucktail or calftail	218
Black Gnat Bucktail	3665A, 9761 or 9762 Sizes 2 to 10	Red hackle fibers	Black chennille	None	Black hackle	White calftail fiber or white bucktail	218
Black Nose Dace	3665A, 9761 or 9762 Sizes 2 to 10	Red hackle fibers	Silver flat tinsel	Ribbed oval tinsel	Brown hackle	White bucktail, brown bucktail, black bucktail in that order equal amounts	220
Bloody Butcher	3906B or 3906 Sizes 8 to 12	Red hackle fibers	None	Mixed red and yellow hackle tied Palmer-style	Red yellow mixed hackle	Fox squirrel tail	232
Brown Bomber	9671, 7957B or 3906B Sizes 4 to 12	Black chennille	None or silver tinsel	Soft brown hackle tied Palmer-style	None	None	232
Brown Squirrel Tail	9671, 7957B or 3906B Sizes 4 to 12	Red hackle fibers	Red floss	Gold flat embossed tinsel	Brown hackle	Red fox squirrel tail	235
Bucktail Streamer	79580, 9671, 9672 or 3665A Sizes 2 to 12	Red hackle fibers	Silver or gold flat tinsel (embossed) can be used	None	Brown hackle	Brown well marked bucktail	218
Burlap	3906B, 9671 or 9672 Sizes 2 to 12	Deer hair fibers	Brown burlap from burlap bag cut in strips wrapped like floss	None	Grizzly soft hackle	None	218
Captain	3906 or 3906B Sizes 6 to 14	Gold pheasant tippet fibers	Black ostrich fibers	None	Brown hackle	White duck quills fibers or white calftail fibers	237
Carey Muddler	9672, 79580 or 9671 Sizes 2 to 12	Peacock sword fibers	Peacock herl	Oval silver tinsel	Pheasant hackle then caribou or deer hair head	None / Bead chain eyes	146
Cowdung	3906 or 7957B Sizes 8 to 12	None	Gold flat tinsel tip green floss or wool	None	Brown hackle	Slate grey duck quill wings	237
Dark Hendrickson	3906 or 7957B Sizes 8 to 14	Blue dun hackle fibers	Dark brown horse or moose mane tapered	None	Blue dun hackle	Grey mallard duck quills	237
Devastator	9672 or 79580 Sizes 8 to 12	None	Hot orange seal fur dubbed thick	None	Silver tipped grizzly hair with tips trimmed	Silver tip grizzly bear hair	
Duck Lake Special	9672 or 79580 Sizes 2 to 10	Red hackle	Brown chennille lead weighted	None or Silver oval tinsel	Soft furnace saddle	None	232
Dusty Miller	3906 or 7957B Sizes 8 to 14	Mallard breast fibers	Grey dubbing rabbit or muskrat	None	Grizzly hackle fiber	Grey turkey quill	235
Fish Hawk	3906 or 7957B Sizes 8 to 14	Brown mottled turkey quill	Gold tinsel	Dark brown single strand floss	Dark brown	Brown turkey quill	237
Fuzzy Worm	9672 or 9671 Sizes 8 to 14	None	Brown chennille	None	Olive soft tied Palmer-style	None	232

NAME	HOOK	TAIL	BODY	RIBBING	HACKLE	WING	MANUAL REFERENCE
Girdle Bug	3906, 7957B or 3906B Sizes	None	Black chennille	None	Rubber tied in three to four places straight out from body	None	232
Golden Pheasant	9671 or 9672 Sizes 4 to 12	None	Orange floss	Gold flat tinsel	Brown hackle	Ring neck pheasant neck feathers on edge over body	240
Gold Ribbed Hare's Ear	3906 or 7957B Sizes 8 to 12	English hare's ear guard hairs	Dubbed hare's ear fur with guard hair included	Gold wire	None or brown beard hackle	Brown turkey quill	237
Grizzly King	3906, 7957B or 9671 Sizes 6 to 12	Red hackle fibers	Green floss or green wool	Silver flat tinsel	Grizzly hackle (soft)	Mallard side feather fibers	237
Grumpy	3906, 7957B or 9671 Sizes 8 to 12	None	White wool full body	Black thread 3 to 4 wraps	Badger hair tied like hackle	None	243
Half Back	9672 Sizes 6, 8, 10	None	Peacock herl	None	Brown ribbed on body where overwing is tied	Overwing or overbody of pheasant tail fibers half way down shank	243
Kemp Bug	3906 or 3906B Sizes 4 to 12	3 Fibers peacock eye	Peacock herl	None	Furnace hackle	2 Grizzly hackle tips divided and tied back	182
King of the Waters	3906, 3906B or 7957B Sizes 8 to 12	Mallard flank fibers	Red floss	Gold tinsel	Brown hackle	Mallard flank fibers tied like bucktail	243
Leadwing Coachman	3906, 3906B or 7957B Sizes 8 to 12	None	Gold tinsel tip or tag peacock herl thick and juicy	None	Brown	Dark grey duck quill divided and tied back.	243
Leibs Bug	3906, 3906B or 7957B Sizes 8 to 12	Dark brown or black goose fibers tied in "V" fashion	Peacock herl	None	Brown hackle	Dark brown or black goose divided and tied back	167
Light Cahill	3906, 3906B or 7957B Sizes 8 to 12	Light ginger hackle fibers	Dubbed cream fur	None	Light ginger	Wood duck breast or imitation wood duck fibers tied like bucktail	243
Lucky Tiger	9672, 9671 or 79580 Sizes 2 to 12	Pheasant tail fibers	Built up yellow wool or floss (taper)	Black tying thread	Reddish brown	Long fibers of brown hackle 40 or more fibers tied like bucktail	220
Maribou Streamer #2	9672, 9671, 3665A or 79580 Sizes 1/0 to 12	Red thread	Silver mylar tubing	None	None	Brown and white maribou feathers	215
Maribou Streamer #3	9672, 9671, 3665A or 79580 Sizes 1/0 to 1¼	Red thread	Gold mylar tubing	None	None	Brown and yellow maribou feather	215
Maribou Streamer #4	9672, 9671, 3665A or 79580 Sizes 1/0 to 12		Gold mylar tubing	None	None	Brown, olive, yellow with imitation jungle cock eyes.	215
Maribou Streamer #5	9672, 9671, 79580 or 3665A Sizes 1/0 to 12	Red hackle fibers	Silver tinsel (flat)	Silver oval tinsel	None	Red and yellow maribou feathers	215
McCoy	9671 or 3906B Sizes 6, 8, 10	Red hackle fibers	Butt — peacock herl then yellow floss	None	Brown hackle	Deer hair bucktail style	218
Mackie Special	9672, 9671 or 3906B Sizes 8 to 12	Brown hackle fibers	Brown horse mane	None	Brown hackle tied Palmer from tail to head	Brown horse hair tied like bucktail	218
Mallard Spider	9672, 9671 or 3906B Sizes 8 to 12	Red hackle fibers	Yellow floss	Gold tinsel	Mallard flank feather tied as hackle	None	212

NAME	HOOK	TAIL	BODY	RIBBING	HACKLE	WING	MANUAL REFERENCE
Maribou Muddler #2	9672, 9671, 3665A or 79580 Sizes 1/0 to 12	Red hackle	Sparkle chennile silver	None	Grey deer clipped as per Muddler's instruction	Yellow, white, olive or black maribou feather peacock topping	159
Maribou Muddler #3	9672, 9671, 3665A or 79580 Sizes 1/10 to 12	Red hackle	Sparkle gold	None	Grey deer clipped as per Muddler's instruction	Brown and olive maribou feathers	159
Maribou Muddler #4	9672, 9671, 3665A or 79580 Sizes 1/0 to 12	Turkey quill tied tip down	Yellow floss	Gold flat tinsel ribbed tight	Grey deer clipped as per Muddler's instruction	White or black maribou feathers	159
Maribou Muddler #5	9672, 9671, 3665A or 79580 Sizes 1/0 to 12	Turkey quill tied tip down	Yellow floss	Gold flat tinsel ribbed tight	Grey deer clipped as per Muddler's instruction	Yellow and red maribou feathers	159
McGinty	3906B, 9671 or 3906 Sizes 8 to 14	Red hackle fibers and mallard flank fibers	Black, yellow, black chennile	None	Brown hackle	Mallard secondary white tip — divided and tied back	243
McGinty Bucktail	3906B, 9671 or 3906 Sizes 8 to 14	Red hackle fibers and mallard flank fibers	Black, yellow, black chennile	None	Brown hackle	Brown bucktail	220
Meloche	3906 or 7957B	Light ginger fibers	Dubbed medium cream wool	None	Light ginger	Light elk hair tied bucktail-style	243
Mickey Finn	9672, 79580 or 3665A Sizes 1/0 to 12	Red hackle fiber or none	Silver embossed flat tinsel	Silver oval tinsel	None	Yellow, red, then yellow dyed bucktail	212
Montana Bucktail	9671, 9672 or 79580 Sizes 4 to 12	Yellow hackle fibers	Rear 1/3 yellow floss front 2/3 red floss	None	Grizzly soft neck hackle	White bucktail	220
Mormon Girl Squirrel Tail	9671, 9672 or 79580 Sizes 4 to 12	Mallard flank fibers	Back 1/2 floss red, front 1/2 yellow chennile	Gold medium embossed tinsel over back 1/2	Grizzly soft neck hackle	Grey squirrel tail	220
Muddler Minnow #2	3665A, 9671, 9672 or 79580 Sizes 1/0 to 14	Turkey quill fiber curve up	Gold tinsel	None	Clipped deer hair bottom painted red laquer	Underwing brown bear hair upperwing brown mottled turkey	146
Muddler Minnow Gapen Style	9672 Sizes 1/0 to 12	Turkey quill fiber curve up	Gold tinsel flat	None	Clipped deer hair	Underwing polar bear upperwing brown mottled turkey	146
Muddler Minnow Mylar Style	3665A, 9671, 9672 or 79580 Sizes 1/0 to 14	Red thread	Silver or gold mylar tubing	None	Clipped deer hair	Underwing fox squirrel, upperwing brown mottled turkey	212
Mylar Body Bucktail	9671, 9672 or 79580 Size 1/0 to 12	Red thread	Mylar tubing silver or gold	None	Brown	Brown and white bucktail	212
Nez Perce	3906, 3906B or 7957B Sizes 8 to 12	None	Rear 1/2 black floss, front 1/2 white chennile	None	Medium Brown	Brown turkey quill place together tied on edge	237
Orange Asher	3906, 3906B or 7957B Sizes 8 to 12	Tip: gold tinsel	Orange floss tapered	None	Grizzly tied Palmer-style rear to front	None	237
Orange Coachman	3906, 3906B or 7957B Sizes 8 to 12	None	Tip: gold tinsel; butt: peacock herl; body: orange floss tapered		Orange (light) hackle	White duck quill tied divided and back	237
Orange Sedge	3906, 3906B or 7957B Sizes 8 to 12	None	Half stripped dark brown hackle wrapped tight Palmer-style	None	Dark brown	Dark grey deer hair tied down	237
Pale Evening Dun	3906, 3906B or 7957B Sizes 8 to 12	Tag yellow floss	Medium blue floss	Gold embossed tinsel	Blue dun mixed with yellow	White duck quill tied divided and back	237

NAME	HOOK	TAIL	BODY	RIBBING	HACKLE	WING	MANUAL REFERENCE
Parachenie Bell	3906, 3906B or 7957B Sizes 8 to 12	Red and white hackle fibers	Yellow dubbed fur	Silver tinsel	White tied Palmer-style	White duck quill tied divided and back	237
Picket Pinn	9671 Sizes 6 to 12	Golden pheasant tippet fibers	Peacock herl	Brown Palmer-style saddle hackle	Brown	Fox or grey squirrel tail peacock herl head	243
Platte River Special	9672 Sizes 4 to 10	None	None	None	Brown and yellow mixed	2 yellow and 2 brown saddles of wide neck hackle; hackles mixed and tied divided	209
Professor Bucktail	3906 or 7957B Sizes 8 to 12	Red hackle fiber	Yellow wool or floss	Gold tinsel	Brown (soft)	Brown bucktail	223
Rock Hopper	3906 or 3906B Sizes 6 to 12	None	Bluish grey wool or dubbing	None	Dyed blue dun grizzly	Dyed blue dun grey turkey quill divided	237
Rogue River Silver	Double hook Sizes 6 to 10	Red hackle fibers	Butt: black chennile; body: silver oval tinsel	None		White bucktail tied semi-spentwing	223
Royal Coachman Streamer #1	9672, 9671, 79580 or 3665A Sizes 4 to 12	Red hackle fibers	Butt: peacock herl; body: red floss; butt: peacock herl	None	Brown	White bucktail	218
Royal Coachman Streamer #2	9672, 9671, 79580 or 3665A Sizes 4 to 12	Golden peasant tippet fiber	Butt: peacock herl; body: red floss; butt: peacock herl	Ribb gold embossed tinsel on red floss	Brown	White bucktail imitation jungle cock eyes	218
Royal Coachman #3	9672, 9671, 79580 or 3665A Sizes 4 to 12	Yellow hackle fibers	Butt: peacock herl; body: red floss; butt: peacock herl	Ribb gold embossed tinsel on red floss	Brown	White calf topping yellow calftail	218
Rueben King	3906, 3906B or 7957B Sizes 8 to 12	Red hackle fibers	Peacock herl fibers	Ginger very stiff	Brown soft	White calftail fibers	237
Search's Muddler	9672, 9671, 79580 or 3665A Sizes 2 to 10	Pintail flank fibers	Grey dubbed fur	Gold oval tinsel	First white calftail then black bear hair then pintail flank feather on each side	Deer hair put on Muddler-style	146
Silver Darter	9672, 79580, 9671 or 3665A Sizes 2 to 12	Peacock sword fibers	White flat floss	Silver embossed tinsel	Badger hackle	Well marked badger saddles tied divided	209
Squirrel Tail Streamer (Grey)	9672 or 9671 Sizes: 4 to 12	Red floss clipped	Green or red wool	Silver tinsel	Grey hackle	Grey squirrel tail	235
Squirrel Tail Streamer (Brown)	9672 or 9671 Sizes 4 to 14	Red floss clipped	Yellow or red wool	Gold tinsel	Brown hackle	Brown squirrel tail	235
Teal and Orange	9672 or 9671 Sizes 4 to 14	Golden pheasant tippet	Orange wool	Gold tinsel	Brown hackle	Teal flank feathers	237
Tiger Bug		Dark grizzly hackle fibers	Light grey dubbing	Heavy black thread or gold tinsel	Partridge hackle	None	240
Western Bee	3906 or 3906B Sizes 8 to 12	Red hackle fibers	Black chennile then yellow then black then yellow		Brown soft	Dark grey duck quills	235
Yellow Grub	3906 or 3906B Sizes 8 to 12	Red hackle fibers	Medium yellow chennile	None	Clipped grey hackle Palmer-style	None	232
Zulu	3906 or 3906B Sizes 8 to 12	Red wool	Peacock herl	Black hackle Palmer-style	None	None	220

Nymphs

NAME	HOOK	TAIL	BODY RIBBING	THORAX	CASE	HACKLE	MANUAL REFERENCE
Amber	3906, 3906B or 7957B Sizes 10 to 14	None	Beige floss	Dubbed seals fur brown in color	Grey duck quill fiber	Beard hackle ginger hackle fibers	176
Atherton Light	3906, 3906B or 7957B Sizes 8 to 14	Natural or lemon side wood duck fibers	Cream dubbed fur ribbing gold oval tinsel		Jungle cock eyed feathers "V" formation length of shank	Brown partridge	176
Beaver	3906, 3906B or 7957B Sizes 4 to 14	Mallard sides feather fibers	Brownish grey dubbed fur	Brownish grey dubbed fur	None	Mallard breast fibers	191
Bird's Stone Fly	9671 or 9672 Sizes 4 to 10	Grey goose quill 2 fibers form "V"	Rear 2/3 muskrat fur front 1/3 peacock herl	Clear plastic strip		Blue dun or furnace Palmer-style	188
Black Nymph	3906, 3906B or 7957B Sizes 8 to 14	Guinea hackle fibers	Black dyed rabbit fur dubbed ribbing: silver tinsel		Black raffia	Black hackle fibers	179
Bread Crust	3906, 3906B or 7957B Sizes 8 to 14		Large brown hackle tied tip in and wrapped as chennile	then brown plastic ribbed with gold oval tinsel		Grizzly hackle	182
Brown Nymph	3906, 3906B or 7957B Sizes 8 to 14		Brown dubbed rabbit, tapered body		Brown fibers of cock pheasant tail	Brown hackle	179
Caddis	3906, 3906B or 7957B Sizes 10 to 14	Black nylon, 2 fibers form "V"	Rear ½ dark quill body, front ½ small black chennile			Black hackle	202
Caddis Larvae	3906, 3906B or 7957B Sizes 10 to 14	Tip: gold flat tinsel	Orange wool				191
Carot	3906, 3906B or 7957B Sizes 10 to 14	Tip: gold flat tinsel	Orange wool			Grey partridge hackle	194
Cream Nymph	3906, 3906B or 7957B Sizes 10 to 14	Brown hackle fibers	Cream wool	Cream wool full and thick	Brown floss	Brown hackle	176
Damsel	3906, 3906B or 7957B Sizes 10 to 14	2 Brown hackle tips length of body	Yellow floss ribbed with gold oval tinsel	Dark olive chennile	Brown grouse	Brown grouse fibers tied on each side	167
Dark Olive Nymph	3906, 3906B or 7957B Sizes 10 to 14	Olive hackle fibers	Dark olive dubbing ribbed with gold oval tinsel	Dark olive	Claret wool	Dark olive hackle fibers	179
Devil Nymph	3906, 3906B or 7957B Sizes 10 to 14	Brown hackle fibers	Yellow wool ribbed with peacock herl		Turkey quill fibers over body	Brown hackle	188
Gary Howell	3906, 3906B or 7957B Sizes 10 to 14	Grizzly hackle fibers	Tapered quill moose mane			Grizzly wrapped and trimmed top and bottom	191
Ginger Nymph	3906, 3906B or 7957B Sizes 10 to 14	Ginger hackle fibers	Light grey wool thin tapered body, ribbing: silver tinsel			Ginger tied Palmer- style	176
Golden Quill	3906, 3906B or 7957B Sizes 10 to 14	2 Fibers goose or duck quill tied as "V"	Yellow floss ribbed with gold wire			Ginger	182
Green Caddis	3906, 3906B or 7957B Sizes 10 to 14	None	Dyed green (light in color) dubbed fur		None	Badger or cream hackle, tips tied on side. Head: peacock herl	202
Grey Caddis	3906, 3906B or 7957B Sizes 10 to 14	Grey wool	Black hackle tips each on side of body. Head: peacock herl				202

NAME	HOOK	TAIL	BODY RIBBING	THORAX	CASE	HACKLE	MANUAL REFERENCE
Grey Nymph	3906, 3906B or 7957B Sizes 8 to 16	Grey squirrel tail fibers	Grey chennile			Grizzly hackle	194
Helgramite	9671 or 9672 Sizes 6 to 10	2 Grey duck fibers tied as "V"	Black wool (black ostrich herl ribbing)			Black hackle	170
Lead Wing Coachman	3906, 3906B or 7957B Sizes 6 to 14	Brown hackle fibers	Fuzzy peacock herl		Duck quill fiber	Brown	179
Light Cahill	3906, 3906B or 7957B Sizes 8 to 16	Natural or imitation wood duck fibers	Red fox cream dubbing	Red fox cream under fur dubbed thick			176
Light Olive Nymph	3906, 3906B or 7957B Sizes 10 to 16	Light olive hackle fibers	Medium olive rabbit dubbing. Ribbing: gold oval tinsel			Beard hackle olive hackle fibers	176
Little Jack Horner	3906, 3906B or 7957B Sizes 10 to 16	Sedge green flat floss	Shell back of body deer hair (grey)	Deer body hair spun at head clipped leaving ⅛" top			185
Martinez	3906, 3906B or 7957B Sizes 10 to 16	Mallard breast fibers	Spun black angora fur	Spun black angora fur	Green raffia	Black or mallard breast or guinea hackle	176
Midge Nymph	3906, 3906B or 7957B Sizes 20 to 24	None	Peacock stripped quill tapered	Peacock herl	Turkey quill	Grizzly hackle fibers	191
Montana Nymph #2	3906, 3906B or 7957B Sizes 4 to 14	Two brown hackle tips divided and tied as "V"	Black chennile	Light orange chennile	Black chennile	Brown tied over thorax Palmer-style	167
Olive Nymph	3906, 3906B or 7957B Sizes 10 to 16	Light olive hackle fibers	Dyed olive stripped peacock quill	Peacock herl	Duck quill fiber	Light olive hackle	176
Otter Nymph	3906, 3906B or 7957B Sizes 8 to 14	Mallard breast	Dark otter belly fur	Dark otter belly fur	Mallard breast feathers	Light blue dun or none	191
Pale Watery Dun	3906, 3906B or 7957B Sizes 10 to 16	Pale blue dun dyed mixed with olive hackle fibers	Pale ginger seal dubbed fur	Same as body	None	Pale blue dun mixed with olive	176
Willow	3906, 3906B or 957B Sizes 6 to 14	None	Light grey rabbit fur dubbed	None Ribbing gold oval tinsel	None	None	176
Yellow May Nymph	3906, 3906B or 7957B Sizes 10 to 16	Partridge hackle fibers	2/3 body of yellow wool or dubbing	Olive chennile	Grey goose quill fibers	Grizzly beard hackle	176